THE

RETURN

JOURNEY

Praise for *The Return Journey*

'*The Return Journey* is a lyrical and deeply moving meditation on the infinite capacity of the human heart to give, to risk, to love, and, ultimately, to live. Explorer Steve Bull has ridden through the valley of the shadow of death and refused to yield. Instead, he has written a love story that explores not the far ends of the Earth but the dark places of our grief, and demonstrates, as the apostle Paul wrote, that love bears all things, believes all things, hopes all things, endures all things; that love never ends.'

Ben Johncock, author of *The Last Pilot*

THE RETURN JOURNEY

An Expedition of Love and Loss

STEVE BULL

Red Door

Published by RedDoor

www.reddoorpress.co.uk

ISBN 978-1-910453-75-9

A CIP catalogue record for this book is available from the British Library

Cover design: Rawshock Design

Typesetting: Westchester Publishing Services

Printed and bound in Denmark by Nørhaven

For my wife, Kathryn

'I heard my country calling, away across the sea,
Across the waste of waters,
She calls and calls to me.'

'Urbs Dei' or 'The Two Fatherlands,' *Sir Cecil Spring Rice*

FOREWORD
by Sir Ranulph Fiennes

I have had the pleasure to have been Patron to several of Steve's expeditions; including the Polar Challenge in 2004. This particular expedition was ground breaking as it saw the first college students reach the South Pole. Having undertaken many pioneering expeditions myself to Antarctica I know what an unforgiving and harsh environment it is. All of us that have ventured into these white and wild lands have done so with loved ones in our heart. With the hope we will do them proud and return safely home.

This is part of what this book is about; of the venturing into such places, to carry out a journey of note with the love of those that make it happen. Whilst on my expeditions my late wife, Ginny, would look after Aberdeen Angus cattle. In a similar vein Steve's wife looked after horses and cared for them when he was away.

These pages tell of Kathryn's and Steve's story, from early beginnings to the horsewoman she became, and of the expeditions Steve led. Of riding horses of all types, working in all weathers and helping others. Her commitment to the local equine community and beyond. It's also about the smile so many knew her for.

Kathryn's love of horses and dedication to them is obvious, as is her support of Steve on his expeditions. Together they made a life; each supporting the other through thick and thin. From the South Pole to the fields of home, the bond between them smiles through and shines. Then when tragedy strikes and all is lost the bond gets stronger.

Here is the heart of what *The Return Journey* is about, the faith to carry on in the face of the deepest loss. Following Kathryn's death Steve decided to carry on his wife's work, looking after her horses and her livery yard. His decision to do so is a reflection of his love for Kathryn and the faith she gave him on his expeditions.

My wife Louise has a wonderful way with her horses and my father was Commanding Officer of The Royal Scots Greys. Albeit at a time when tanks took the place of the horse, the lineage is there. A link through time when horses were used in battle and also on expeditions such as Captain Scott's.

Carrying those with us that have departed is something we can all relate to; *The Return Journey* is not just Steve's and Kathryn's journey. It is the journey we all take at some point in our lives.

Sir Ranulph Fiennes

PROLOGUE

The large grey horse she arrived on caused quite a stir,
And was quickly dispatched back across to earth,
For heaven is a sideways step, not upwards.

In a field of Elysium dreams where grass grows deep in spring, and shadows lie long in summer. Where winter drifts in after autumn like an afterthought of nature, and a grey horse lives in perpetual peace. There under the weather of a destiny day and the stopping of clocks, Kathryn and the horse became one. She exploded into all the horses she had ever ridden, owned and loved. For on the 29 April 2016 at approximately 12.30 in the afternoon, the last horsewoman was killed by a horse. As the silent trees swayed in the meadow of wind and life the grey horse looked on. He watched as blue lights descended around the field, flashing in sorrow. He watched as the figures carried her away from the field, for ever. It was the ending of all things, except love.

In the beginning fourteen years earlier, we had a simple wedding; old-fashioned vows said in love. I remember the sound of hooves trotting on tarmac as Kathryn arrived at the church. There were only two of us in church, Kathryn and I, no one else existed. It was just her eyes and mine, holding each other's, as the horse and carriage waited on the road outside. The horses had brought us together, formed the beginning. It was fitting a horse carried us into the future of our lives. Into the unknown lands of our shared expedition. A time before the field, a time when the ghosts of the grass lay quiet and peaceful. Before the ending in the wind of the trees and a horse looking on. A time before the last expedition.

I am haunted by horses from the past. Horses she rode, horses I rode. Hooves echo on sandy paths in a dull ringing of lives in the past. They speak across the years of events we did together. Of times on gallops, laughing and crying with the wind in our hair. Of chases through pine trees on lazy Friday afternoons. The smell of cones and dust in the air. That damp straw smell that lies heavy in stables being mucked out. Early mornings when the sun hasn't woken and the moon hangs on. It was a long time ago, but only if you measure time in years. In reality it was a moment ago.

Their names bring back memories of a life: TC, Tommy, Nora, Peter, Gordon, Scarlet, Dan, Chancer, George. Their names aren't written down in any book, they were horses, destined to live out a life in work and leisure. To carry us on rides in forests and over fields. They did nothing important, but then that depends on what you count as important. They gave joy and laughter, meaning to a day and a weekend, a reason bigger than ourselves.

They had a touch, the coarse rough feel of equine hair, each one felt different. Like different people's hands. Each with its own stamp, a callous here or a scar there; a character and personality, just like us. They asked for nothing and gave their all.

I am haunted by horses in the present. The ones that live on without Kathryn. The ones I see alone and ride alone; look after without her. I like to think she looks after me whilst I try to do what she did so brilliantly and naturally. She was born to it; I was born to wander mountains. That's what's natural to me, wild places. Yet she gave me her love of horses, over the years she taught me. I feel like I now work with a great big grey shadow of a horse so strong not even she could ride. He rides that high ground on the distant horizon, in the fading light that is neither dawn nor dusk.

Times I spent without her on expeditions, in Africa and South America, in the Arctic and Antarctic were still times with her, because she talked to me over the oceans and guided my hand and leg when I felt unsure. She rode with me. She walked and skied with me.

Expeditions don't haunt me. There is a missing there I suppose. She doesn't write notes for me anymore and leave them in a passport or a Gerald Seymour novel for me to find on the plane. It's a paradox, because I don't want to go away anymore as there is no one to come back to. I already exist in an empty place. But if I go away the horses are left behind and the dogs too. So, the animals will still haunt me.

Mountains though, mirror the horses' moods and personalities. Some daunting in their height exhibiting a foreboding quality of dread. In the mist on a steep rocky ridge with rock wet from dew and rain, in the early morning. A hint of wind on the sky, whispers of being on a horse with a will stronger than yours. Stiffness in the back, a rising of withers and the tense body of the grey hunter give me that feeling of dread, of an unknown about to happen. It's a haunting in the wilderness. A feeling of a ghost, of the last grey horse and the last girl that rode it.

As a nation we are founded on the nobility and honesty of the horse, something many people have forgotten. Our horses made England, long before oak-made ships sailed forth across the high seas and made the world an English empire. The horse ploughed our fields and fed the people, led the charges in brother against brother, forcing change in how we govern this land.

We are also a nation founded on expeditions and exploration, an island race that set out to explore the world with only the arrogance and dash an Englishman could carry off. The ships became the charger carrying man and provisions to far-flung corners of the world. The horse was left behind in the fields and furrows of England, something to be dreamt of, ridden across hedges and walls to the bugle call on return. The horse has a unique place in our countryside and culture.

We name things like life and death, a human trait; in reality there is only nature and the rolling worlds of beautiful nothingness. Our life is so short though, as a species we try to find meaning in something else, some higher purpose. I used to find the answer on a mountain top, or on a glacier far, far away. Then it was about going home to Kathryn, to our dogs and the horses. Kathryn found her answer on a horse, riding in Sherwood, either on her own or with friends, or competing. Home was the two of us riding deep into the woods of the hearth. Now, it's all about trying to find a peace within, to survive the walk forward without the hand to hold at night. To find life again, to find the map that shows the way.

Well it's nearly 11 p.m., I haven't finished the wine. Missing you, love you loads, come back safe so I can look after you. You're my reason for living, you give me purpose and direction, something I lack – I seem to drift from one thing to the next, enjoying what I do, but never does anything feel permanent, only you. I keep wanting to text you, but you're not there anymore.

I was in Greenland. She was in my chair at home, with our dogs Otto on his and Jack upside down on the sofa. I feel the same as Kathryn now, wanting to text her, but there's no one there. The shortness of our lives is only heightened by the inability of modern technology to reach into the afterlife.

Our worlds, the way of the horse and the way of the ice collided and fused together over time; becoming one valley of

Thor. We would face our Ragnarök in the end, yet in the years before that we would write the essay, the tapestry of our life together. Adding it to the pages of all those that have lived and have died.

Yet even death has the power to bring new life. Each breath becomes a wonder; each sky is more open, bigger. Every leaf is beauty and we see through clear eyes for the first time. Everything is new again, we can see through our child's eye once more. This is death's gift to us if we have the courage to stare at new life. One I find hard every single day as I lie in bed summoning up the heart to move; it's there in glimpses. Just glimpses, but it is there, through the haunting of horses.

Ollie though, Kathryn's big grey horse, he haunts me the most. On the last expedition, the return journey to a new living. The right path though is the hardest one to follow; the map is so scarred and battered it's difficult to read in the darkness. But with her love in my heart and quiet whispering guidance, I pray the ride will be easier. On the long return journey back to Kathryn, to the everlasting smile; wherever that may be.

With just a seat of thought and hint of leg
They advance headlong through shorn
Stubble as clods fly and dance on dew
With thunder of earth through hooves
Beating in unison, a strain of bit
And strength of leather combine in one;
Holding the line as drums beat down
Through drenching rain, and steam
Rises from shining grey flanks pounding
Upwards through and out of pine dense
Forest, watching in memory of past charges.

PART ONE

The Outward Journey

'The future is in the lap of the gods; I can think of
nothing left undone to deserve success.'

Captain Robert Falcon Scott
Tuesday 31 October 1911
Cape Evans, Antarctica

'And I looked, and behold a pale horse;
And his name that sat on him was death.'

Revelation 6.8

You will be reading this on your way to Norway, whilst I am going about my normal routine. I hope that it gives you comfort, to know that whilst you are away I am still here. Everything keeps on going, waiting for you to come home.

KATHRYN BULL

CHAPTER ONE

The Ending and The Beginning

So, little do we know, of the belonging that drives us,
Of time's creep along the spine of mortality;
but the march matters little.
For it is the here and now of our love that counts . . .

I know one certain thing; I would give everything for five seconds in the field, a nondescript corner of an English field, to say goodbye. To say I love her, I've got her and I'll see her later. Or better still, to have five seconds to say hello. With the faith of that certainty, and her love in my hands I watched unfamiliar fields race by the train window. A silver spur entwined with a rose lay waiting, six thousand four hundred and eighty horses of power drew us towards it. The locomotive was our charger; we rode south to destiny, away from the forests of home and the grey horse.

She was three weeks at the hospital, yet it wasn't her. I knew that. But I sat with her in the chapel, said hello. Told her that her dogs, her horses and her yard would be all right. I would look after them for her. I promised her that as she lay in her favourite dress and best shoes. Lost phone calls drifted through me, memories descended. The snow was a long way off, the tent lay cold and the horses were hazy figures in a goodbye land.

I'd dreamed of being a great explorer, wandering the expanses of snow that lay at the far reaches of the world. Horses were far from my mind, so was love and marriage. I was engaged like most of us; in ambition for personal gain. Icecaps and geographical poles captivated my selfish desire, to the South Pole and back I dreamed of. Yet, I would survive, be praised and congratulated for completing the return journey that failed Scott. Little did I know then that the greatest expedition I would undertake would be to find a smile once more. That the smile would lie in the fields of home and a grey horse. And the congratulations would be for a girl I met deep in the heart of Sherwood.

Noise drifted across the great hall, the sounds collided with the blue lights in my mind. Dreams of a field in late April and a promise made in a white darkness room. Of the grey horse that had said goodbye across a dying in the meadow. A dream of saying hello. The noise of the present brought me back. As I opened my eyes the images drifted across the screen; images of Kathryn. Photographs of her on Strip Cartoon; with Ollie, her grey horse; smiling on our honeymoon. In the Saddlers' Hall, footsteps away from St Paul's Cathedral, Louise and I watched the past unfold. There in that building dating back to the fourteenth century, Kathryn was being awarded the prestigious Helen Barton-Smith Silver Stirrup Award, posthumously. It was recognition by The British Horse Society for her lifetime's work helping young riders. As the ancient ghosts of the worshipful company of saddlers looked on, I rose, taking nervous steps to collect the award on behalf of Kathryn.

As I walked through a red carpet lined with history, threaded a way to the front. The people looking on became the trees of the past; I was taken back in time to the beginning. Applause drifted into the sound of hooves thundering through dense pine. Of tents on wide-ranging ice fields, to a girl at home on a sofa waiting for a phone call. All the faces merged into one. One face with a great big beaming smile as we turned and headed up the pond path. Our horses sensed the joy in the life of the moment and we ascended into the dawn.

Sunlight drifted into the low glare of the room, the hooves faded away and the low clapping returned. I hid back tears of pride, emotion and longing. Wishing she was here in person. That the congratulations and shaking of hands were to Kathryn. And the one person I wanted to hug and hold and congratulate was the image in my heart. I wanted to call her, like I used to from a tent in the wilderness.

8 p.m. Had to stop writing to answer the phone, but that's OK 'cos it was Steve, calling to let me know he's in Antarctica. Best news I could have heard. Fingers crossed for a good trip.

On the expeditions I led, to remote drifting empty lands, usually once or twice a year, the highlight of the day would be to open the satellite phone case and power up the Iridium satellite phone, wait for the little signal that the phone had found reception and then hear the distant ring of Kathryn's phone. 'Kathryn's not here at the present, yet please leave a message and she'll call you back later', that was the usual response as most of the time she would be out of signal down the fields or riding. Yet, when she did answer it would be brief and lovely, matter-of-fact talk, normal talk, are the dogs OK? What's the weather like? A brief goodbye and then turn the satellite phone off; looking forward to the next night as the snow drifted round the fabric tent and the distance between us lay solid just like the ice.

The train clattered its way north, out of London. Kathryn's trophy lay on the table in front of me. Clad in its protective black box I rested my hand on the straps, held on and closed my eyes. The straps became reins and the train a huge horse, in the safety of this dream I remembered. I galloped back to the end of the

1990s, halting in a hoof-screeching skid at a college on the edge of Sherwood Forest.

I worked as a lecturer teaching sports science; by day I sat in a classroom, by night I dreamed and planned the 'last expedition'. My quest to reach the South Pole and back. Fate had other ideas though, destiny inspired my then manager to decide I should run the horse care course the college ran. This came as a surprise to me, I had never been near a horse, never mind knowing anything about them. I refused, but to no avail, the Gods had decided my fate. A week later I was driven into the heart of Sherwood to a trekking centre, trees reached to the skies and fields ran away into the distance. Bloomsgorse was home to over thirty horses that focused on taking people on rides through the forest from the nearby Center Parcs. Rides for the complete novice through to the experienced rider were catered for. The surrounding were idyllic, quiet; and a far contrast to the lecture rooms and closed-in corridors of a suburban college.

Zoë Grant was the owner; she viewed me with a certain amount of scepticism when she also discovered that I knew nothing about the equine industry; or indeed had no desire to learn. What I wanted to do was walk to the South Pole, the coldest place on earth, where the sun is continuously visible for six months and is then absent for the next six months. Not to ride ponies in the forests of home.

'If he's going to co-ordinate the course, then I want him here every Tuesday for the next six weeks.' It was a statement from Zoë to my superior, no argument. A week later I drove myself down the long track through the woods pulling up outside the stables. Girls were there, in jodhpurs and there were lots of them it seemed. There were no other males. To a single man this was an appealing prospect. I was also in the countryside and not in a classroom; again, another plus, maybe not as attractive as the first; but still good. Maybe the Gods had smiled on me after all.

That first day was a turning point in my life; a major one. Zoë decided to take the bull by the horns; she introduced me to Tommy, a huge horse. I later learned that he was over seventeen hands high and a Clydesdale. To me on that first day he was a huge charger, built for battle and knights of old. She didn't ask if I had ridden, she knew already. But we went straight out for a ride into the forest, her on Chancer, her own horse, with me behind on Tommy.

Walk, a nice slow pace, which requires on the face of it little skill (how little I knew then). Trot, a slightly faster pace that seemed to endanger any future romantic liaisons. Then canter, faster still, with the intention of removing any prospect of romance. Gallop; a better pace because you can stand up, giving the nether regions some respite.

We did them all. All four gaits of the horse's movement, each an increase in speed and flight on that first ride. It was, looking back with the knowledge I have now, a miracle I did not fall off. All I remember now is that I was hooked; this was the most exciting thing I had ever done. Period. The next day I paid a price, for my whole body ached as if I'd been run over by a steam train. But the thrill and the smile remained.

So began six weeks at Bloomsgorse, experiences and life merged into one as I was immersed into a totally new culture. The way of the horse, the history of tradition, true horsepower. Kathryn was there, but in the background; I was too engaged in the freedom of the open forest. In my head I had the tunes of cavalry and the romance of life on the open range, in essence being a cowboy was better than teaching. It was the gift of the horse. And that gift included Kathryn; later in the day I saw her for the first time, spoke the first words. She was bringing a horse out of a stable, her long hair tangled and she smiled awkwardly.

'Hello,' I said. 'My name's Steve.'

'I know,' she said. 'Mine's Kathryn.'

Then she and the horse moved down on to the yard and I looked back at her as they went. Unbeknown to me, the last expedition had begun. As the slow sun walked down into the fields at the end of a destiny day.

Co-ordinating the horse care course actually needed very little knowledge of horses; it was an administration exercise. Something, sadly, I am not very adept at. Yet, I was willing, keen and desperate to learn to ride by now. One single ride had transformed my life in such a way it was more akin to a religious experience. Teaching basic maths at the college in a dusty lifeless classroom was an appalling prospect compared with the trees and open range that were now my Tuesdays.

Kathryn was assistant head girl, which in effect meant she was in charge of the younger girls and weekend helpers. She would supervise the grooming and mucking out and lead the rides out into the forest; she was twenty-four years old. After that first haunting hello we didn't see each other much, Kathryn was shy and I was too interested in the riding. She was just there, working away and being Kathryn. Helping and getting stuck into the job she did, keeping herself to herself.

It was not long before I started going at weekends as well. Pushing barrows of horse poo to the muck heap, in return for a riding lesson and going out on the two weekend trotting rides. Expeditions and my dream to walk to the South Pole retreated to the back of my mind. I was up first thing and driving into the forest as the sun rose over the pines. Leaving as the sun said goodbye to me on the dirt track home. The smell of leather tack, oats and sugar beet filled the car. Horses' smells replaced the odour of rucksacks and boots, of damp maps and gritstone heather.

Following the first hello we met regularly in fleeting passes as I pushed my barrows. I don't remember being immediately physically attracted to her, and I think that was a good sign in retrospect; for it meant that our relationship would be based on personality and strength of character. Yet, it was a hidden love at first sight, a searing of memory and deep unsaid bonding.

After her death, Zoë told me that Kathryn chose me as the one person in this life she would love and take care of. 'She picked you, out of all the people in the world to look after.' Zoë's words echoed through my fragile heart as we ambled through the fields at Cross Lane. Back then I was still referring to her death as 'when Kathryn went'. In some ways her words, on a dirt track, far away from the world of false importance, are the most important I have ever heard.

The journey to the point of mutual love was to prove quite long and traumatic, and demonstrate the unique singular determination Kathryn had. And I do what I do now because she picked me out, she chose me. I owe her for that, and I have sought to repay her faith in me.

Back in the forests of the beginning, I rode. I was taught by Kathryn's immediate boss, Jayne. Having never ridden before, I had the suppleness of a brick. The first ride out on Tommy was the honeymoon; actually, learning to ride would prove a lot more difficult than I first anticipated. Kathryn had learned to ride as a young girl, and over the years her muscles, brain, body position and confidence had developed to the point of second nature. She was the same as all people who learn to ride as a youngster, they grow up in the saddle, they don't think about engaging effective movement of the horse, it just happens. In effect they are one with the horse, as Kathryn was.

It became the yard entertainment as I tried to train unsupple muscles to co-ordinate with the horse. Jayne taught me in a style more similar to the military school of thought; a style I responded to. We rode in all weathers, all seasons. Week after week I tried to gain what those who watched me had spent a lifetime doing.

I began to read about the Scots Greys at Waterloo, 'The Charge of the Light Brigade' and the best light cavalry in the world, the Native American. I wasn't that interested in mucking out, or grooming if I'm totally honest; I wanted to be able to ride like the 7th Cavalry did, charging across the plains to the sound of a bugle and a pennant flying. But I had a long way to go. For the immediate future I was the best barrow pusher in Sherwood Forest, the art of trotting was beyond me. By now, the initial six weeks had long passed and I was now becoming part of the fabric of the yard and the forest that surrounded it. And so the weekends moved by in a slow steady rhythm, I made new friends and my life began to revolve around horses, those that rode them and the places they rode them in.

There was an established friend set at Bloomsgorse that led an active social life outside of yard life. Working with horses is not glamorous; it involves long hours in all weathers, for little monetary reward. A good party or get-together is a welcome respite. It was the yard get-togethers that slowly pushed Kathryn and I together.

It was a late afternoon and the stables were framed by the dying sun; Jayne and I stood chatting about the coming meet-up later that night. 'Kathryn's picking me up from the pub,' I told her.

'You two will end up together,' she commented matter-of-factly.

I looked at her, squinting in the blaze of afternoon sunlight. I laughed. 'No way,' I said.

'Yes, you will,' Jayne replied, 'mark my words.'

I have no idea why I was so opposed to the idea; maybe I didn't like the idea that my future was somehow set for me. I even went so far as to see someone else first, but fate is hard to argue with. Some things in our lives feel as if they are set down before we know them, and the harder we try to avoid them the more strongly they happen. I'm not sure I would call this destiny, but I certainly think things happen to us that are difficult to explain on a rational and purely scientific level. I am convinced beyond any doubt that I was meant to meet Kathryn, love her and marry her; and that this would last a lifetime. Not 'till death do us part', but 'death will not part us.'

Would I have married her knowing she would be killed by a horse? Of course I would have done. I would have married her if I had known that she was going to die on the day of the wedding.

Yet, our culture today shies away from death, we have begun to think that death is something to avoid, probably because we are living so much longer than our recent ancestors. Most of us now do jobs that don't really involve a great deal of risk to our personal safety. We work in offices; are cocooned from injury and risk. Death is only on the news and Sunday night police dramas.

Riding and working with horses is a pleasure business, predominately; but it's a dangerous pleasure, so those that do it face risk in the same way a mountaineer does. They do it because it is there, as Mallory (the mountaineer who disappeared on Everest in 1924) so eloquently put it.

During the early stages of the inquiry into Kathryn's death, one of the witnesses interviewed at the stables said she had ridden out that same morning. 'I was glad to get back safe,' she said, as it was windy that day. Golfers don't go out for a round of golf and feel relieved they return in one piece.

Maria Coffey wrote about the subject in depth when her partner mountaineer Joe Tasker died on Everest in 1982. It's an expedition I am fascinated by: Peter Boardman and Joe Tasker head onto the North-East Ridge of Everest and are never seen again. Coffey struggles with the loss of her lover, yet finds a sense of peace when she travels to the mountain. Kathryn did not attempt an unclimbed ridge, nor step into the icy wastes as

Captain Oates did; who gave up his life to try and save his fellow explorers. She just went down the field to get two horses in, and never came back. However, they were all doing something they loved, whether climbing mountains, exploring or working with horses. And it stands true despite all risks; if we truly love someone we have to let them have the freedom, as Kathryn did with my expeditions. For all swans need to fly into the sunset of the distant horizon, to land on the waters they love and be allowed to take off again.

So, in the beginning we were separate and connections with unclimbed ridges and fields in April were just fantastic dreams in the future. I was immersed in learning to ride properly, while still harbouring my long-held ambition to walk to the South Pole. I would spend every weekend at the trekking centre, pushing barrows to the muck heap, picking up customers from Center Parcs, all in return for a lesson a week and tagging along on the trotting rides. I was made part-time co-ordinator of the horse care course on a permanent basis; and couldn't have been happier. It seems a lifetime away now, and all the days have blurred into one long memory. Of secluded hideaway stables deep in ancient forests. Long hot days in summer with a Springsteen sweat-soaked shirt to the end of the day; feeling cold days in winter, when barrow wheels dug down into frozen muck heaps, our breath mixing with the horses' breath in the frosty air.

Lit beacons fire in my mind now, events that stood out; rights of equine passage. Falling off for the first time, a complete somersault over the front of George. His Shire presence laughing at me as I lay on the hard track of the forest. Of a Friday in the arena, of lessons attempting to canter for the first time on TC.

'Sit deep and take the contact up on the reins, Steve!' shouted Jayne.

Sit deep . . . ?

'Now put your outside leg back and keep sitting,' she continued.

Then in a magical moment, TC moved forward into canter. For a couple of brief seconds, I was in control, and then I wasn't.

'Sit up, sit up!' shouted Jayne.

It was too late, I lost my balance and hit the sand, landing in a heap and winding myself. Looking up I saw TC's steel-clad hooves gracefully miss my head. Laughter echoed through the trees as the yard girls voiced their appraisal. The might of Rome roared. Distant cheers of remembrance, of the hard work Jayne and I put into getting an inflexible body to learn to ride. And I remember Kathryn being there.

On Fridays at Bloomsgorse no rides were taken out, it was a day to rest the horses and catch up on jobs that needed doing. So, it began. Kathryn and I would start to ride out together in the afternoon. She would get all her jobs done, I would tell college that I needed to do some horse care work; and we would skive off into the woods.

'Hey?' came her voice from the stable. 'What are you doing this afternoon?'

'Nothing,' I replied, 'just enjoying being here and not at college.'

'Want to go for a ride? You could take Tommy and I'll take Strip; just a walk if you want?'

'OK, that would be great; won't you get in trouble?'

'Zoë won't know!' she smiled.

Light shined down on us as we rode out for the first time into the forest. It welcomed the two of us, a new partnership borne out of English oak.

Although Claire, the other groom, was sworn to secrecy, Kathryn did get in trouble with Zoë, for leaving just Claire to do the work. She tended to get away with it, as I think Zoë quietly approved of our friendship, but as the boss she had to say something. She called Kathryn into the office one afternoon and reprimanded her for leaving Claire alone on the yard, yet it didn't stop us. By then, I was starting to get the hang of the horse-riding game, I was at least able to get on a horse and safely go out for a ride; staying in control for the majority of the time. Kathryn of course was an expert; yet back then she also had a lot to learn. For as in any job we are always learning. The day we think we have nothing to learn, life will trip us up. Even so, as a horsewoman Kathryn was hard to beat.

Meanwhile, I was still trying to get a South Pole expedition planned. The dreams of heading south stayed with me in the forest. Not in full daylight but the twilight hours; a slow kindling of desire. Steadily over the years I had built up experience; enough for me to contemplate the idea of a great geographic quest. Long school holidays working in education had enabled me to acquire a reasonable expedition CV; just as Kathryn was building up her equine portfolio. Everyone at Bloomsgorse and the people I met in the horse world all thought how mad I was to go on expeditions, how dangerous it was to be crossing glaciers, travelling around crevasses; braving frostbite and snowy wastes. In reality though, it was all pretty safe. Yet, riding horses, everyone at Bloomsgorse; seven-year-old girls upwards didn't bat an eyelid about getting on a live animal with a mind of its own.

This was a world where Kathryn lived and worked from the beginning and until the end. I was learning this world. The smell of straw damp with urine, cold dew taste of grass on the bit, tack creaking and hoof clodding. A far cry from the crease of a map, the weight of a rucksack and the swirling wind on a misty mountain.

And dogs; Kathryn had her fawn-coloured greyhound, Jack. She had rescued him from the vets when he was six months old. He had been found by the roadside with a broken hip, was due to be put down. Yet Kathryn stepped in and saved him. It was a big ask, as he needed hydrotherapy three times a week to help his rehabilitation, but it was a habit of hers, to save the helpless and forlorn, to bring back life to those about to lose it. For weeks, after long days at the yard, she would go the extra mile and take him to swimming lessons to rebuild his muscle. I on the other hand fell in love with Jayne's German Shorthaired Pointers. One thing led to another and I ended up with Too Much Talk – Otto for short; a little bundle of fluff, my own and very first dog. Too Much Talk was to be an important and lasting companion in my life; a pivotal link to stables, horses and also life itself.

When she wasn't busy with Jack, Kathryn would often drive to the pub I went to, walk in unannounced and sit down at the end of the bar. I also found out she would take the long way home and drive past my house, quite a big detour. No one had ever done that for me. Not before and not since. At the time I don't think I appreciated it, didn't think anything of it. I do now.

Time passed and we saw each other mainly as friends, with an anticipation that there might be more, yet nothing really happened. I was still resisting the hand of fate, that first dance of summer. I was offered a post leading an expedition to Mexico; it was a month away. Leading a group of students climbing volcanoes and trekking through jungles and mountains, it was a last-minute opportunity and the money was hard to turn down. When I left the stables my attachment to the horses felt stronger than I could ever have imagined and I cried in private as I drove down the track, not knowing why. At that time, I was seeing another girl; she drove me to the expedition departure point and I remember clearly Kathryn calling on our way down; the phone distant in the car. She wished me well and a good trip. I can't remember what I said to her. Distance surrounded us. I flew to Mexico with my group of sixth formers; to try and climb volcanoes, wander through Inca jungles and conduct project work in remote communities and generally have a great time. At the end of the trip I rode; galloped across sunburned sand, swam in the sea and felt the horsepower on waves. I never thought of Kathryn, and she in turn thought I was gone from her life. It was the furthest we have ever been apart. It was the twilight time, the time before the real sun rose into the sky.

The expedition ended and we flew back to the UK; I returned home to a girl I wasn't meant to be with and my dog; to the stables and to my job at the college. And then into a period of life that was to be dark for a long time, for clouds were gathering in the recesses of my sensitive mind. It was the start of the light also; it would be Kathryn's time. The light in the darkness. The light in the forest and the forging of the map. The light needed to be strong, for it needed to shine after her death to show me the way home. Her map was written in the forest and the sun of home.

I remember little things of those times now; sitting in the pub waiting for Kathryn. We would be going to a Bloomsgorse party. I would then go outside and wait for her car; I would say to myself, it will be the tenth car that comes up the road. If it's the tenth car, then we are meant to be together. Sometimes it was the tenth car; sometimes it wasn't. I always wanted it to be the tenth car. The little blue Citroën. I can picture it now, coming up the road. Indicator on and the turn of the wheels into the pub car park. She would always have her best black coat on and a smile. But still I held back, I was scared of the truth; so, we stayed as friends.

The three-beat rhythm of rolling stock on rail came to an end at Newark. I relaxed my grip on the trophy box and breathed a sigh of relief. The silver spur and its companion the rose were safely laid in the back of Kathryn's Defender; both Louise and I breathed a sigh of relief. Our expedition to the south of the Kingdom had gone well. The fields of home beckoned us back. Beginnings and endings all rolled into one long memory; a freezing of the clock. The hands stuck at the start of the story, a secondhand clicking on the finale. The dates in between are a tale of two lives. On past expeditions I used to joke that I missed my dog first, then my horse and then Kathryn, in that order. But that wasn't the truth; the truth was in the wind, in the smile she had and all the times she wore her best coat for me.

CHAPTER TWO

An Angel Descends

Breaching blue grey chasing oceans,
She appears,
Running down the heaven's wind . . .

I imagine sometimes a classroom of horses; all standing there waiting for the lecturer to impart great wisdom on them. To tell them the correct diet they should eat and how to exercise properly, or maybe the right way to dress appropriately for their chosen sport. Then I wake up and realise that could never work; and how mad to even dream of such a surreal world. And then I remember that I never fitted into the college I worked at; I was just like the horse, ill-suited to the classroom. Over time I was bullied, like the outcast pony in a large herd. Not in an overt way, but it seemed I was always told I was doing things wrong, yet my results in the classroom spoke for themselves. All the students who wanted to get into university did so. I have always believed in myself, yet people kept seeding doubts and the walls echoed to silent mocking. Depression in my experience doesn't just happen; it's a slow process as the mind's reserve to take the hits steadily becomes depleted. In the end there are no shields left and the mind caves in. Like a horse cast out into the wilderness, severed from the herd and left to die in the damp soil.

Depression hit me like a cavalry charge, but in slow-motion, soil-hitting thuds. A seeping of earth into the bones. I went off work, the doctor told me to take long walks with the dog. Instead I slept in late, took Otto for a quick walk, and then went to the video shop. Rented three films on their film deal, watched one in the afternoon, went to the pub and watched the other two with wine. The bosses came out to see me after about two weeks, they told me to take as long as I needed to get better. On full pay. I think I must have looked rough. I was off work for a year, and in that year, I went to the bottom and a little bit further. Depression is a dark illness; it can turn your soul into a black hole from which no light shines. It can also take down the people who care for you.

A dog and a human saved me: Otto and Kathryn.

Otto was with me twenty-four hours a day, for the full time. We developed a bond. One night I dreamed we were walking up the track into the woods, when horses galloped up the field by the track, Otto was ahead of me. The horses jumped onto the track, landing on Otto and killing him. That was the dream. The next day we were walking up the track. Horses galloped up the field. I called Otto to me. He came as the horses jumped into the spot where he had stood. Goose bumps became lost mountain ranges down my back as we both stood there on the sandy path.

Kathryn had now left Bloomsgorse, after a short spell at a local racing yard. She took a position as head girl, a role with considerable responsibility, at the Blankney Hunt in Lincolnshire. It was a long, hard drive from her house in Mansfield, early starts and late finishes. She had the afternoon off most days, but it made more sense to stay at the yard rather than drive back. Wednesday afternoons were spent riding Strip Cartoon.

By this point she would drive to my house at least five times a week at the end of the working day, to see if I was OK. I was in a dark place; by the time Kathryn came to the back door and knocked, I was probably half drunk. Not wanting to see anyone. I ignored her knocks, they went silent and I thought she had gone. But they always started again; eventually I would let her in. She just came in and sat there, sometimes we shared a cigarette. Looking back now she was the closest to a living angel that anyone could ever have. She asked nothing and expected nothing in return. It was friendship of the purest and most noble kind, a friendship I had never experienced before, and doubt I will ever see again. I just remember the devotion of one person to help another.

Her persistence paid off in slow time, gradually a bond began to form. One bad night I remember her taking me to see Oliver, the horse that I had bought and that was kept at Bloomsgorse; she thought seeing him would help.

'Come on! You need to see Oliver, feel him, touch him . . .' It was a command. Kathryn grabbed the car keys and out the door I was shoved.

'Zoë will go mad! What are you thinking?' I protested as I sat down in the passenger seat.

'She won't know, will she?' Kathryn commented.

The pines drew in around the glow of the headlights, she drove too fast and the gravel spat into the hedge. We headed into the tunnel of light thrown out by her car, deep into the forest. There in quiet darkness she guided my hand onto Oliver's head and neck. The stroking of my horse worked. I couldn't see her face as we sneaked back out through the trees, but I knew she was smiling, as was I. She had been right. Zoë wasn't impressed though as I remember her giving us both a right earful. She was the bad cop to Kathryn's good cop.

I got slowly better, or so I thought. For, depression can lay in wait, hide itself and then pounce. On one Boxing Day a horse became available at the hunt; the owner had come off and broken his leg the week before. Kathryn suggested I join her; it was her plan to give me something to live for. So, I found myself sat on Boy, a seventeen hand Irish Hunter in Newark Town Square. I was weak from not eating enough and with little physical activity I had gone down to a 32-inch waist. What followed was one of the best days of my life, going up stubble fields with forty horses flat out, to a sound of thunder hooves on the air. That single gallop in one mêlée of horses with Kathryn is the single most exciting thing I have ever done. I was weak with depression, hurt with living. We were a cavalry of life, flat out in a line. I think I fell off my horse at the end of the day but I didn't mind at all. I felt spent, but in that good way when you've worked hard in the fields or walked over the hills till sunset. Kathryn had put her wind beneath my wings and we had flown.

Two nights later I slit my wrist with a seven-inch hunting knife, having spent the prior evenings sharpening it.

This was a deliberate act, with the intention of ending my life. Yet, looking back now, I can see it was a deliberate call for help.

I called Kathryn, as instantly I realised, I wanted to live. I don't know why I didn't call for an ambulance. It was Kathryn I turned to. She was there in a few minutes. We put steri-strips on the cut and put the arm in the air, pressure applied to the artery. It took a long time to stop the bleeding, into the dark hours of night. But it stopped. The never-ending link that can't be broken was sealed in blood that dark night, and in that living room we forged the sword that would bind us for ever. The shield would come later.

I find it hard to drag up what was going through my head in those long distant days. My inner conflict led to the sharpening of the knife, and that sharpening was a statement that I had the right to hurt, and the right to ask for help. We all have that right.

I had that help, but many who suffer from mental illness fade into dark without a loving hand to hold them.

After I went back to work, I asked to be transferred to Learning Support; specifically, to help adult students who had suffered mental illness; it was a way of hitting my depression head on. I taught basic maths and English to troubled people. It was rewarding and uplifting, life-affirming in a day-to-day existence. Yet none of them seemed as troubled as I was, deep down. I was the only one with a deep scar on the wrist. The problem with depression is that it is invisible, and the soul it takes is the very weapon that can destroy it. Except love, for that trumps all cards in the deck.

It's hard to explain unless you've been in the darkness, but to me the mind is like a submarine. In normal life it operates fine moving up and down to the surface and to depths it can stand. Yet, when events stockpile upon the mind it gets damaged and can't self-right itself, then it can plummet to the depths. All submarines have rescue buoys; so that when the worst happens and they can't stop the descent they release it to the surface. The mind is the same, when it sinks like the submarine we release our rescue buoy, our cry for help. And just like the submarine that lies on the bottom of the ocean hoping for rescue, so do we. The mind is like a sinking submarine when depression torpedoes home. And strange things happen in the depths of the mind.

I sent the rescue recorder to the surface to kill or cure the depression. It cured it. For a time, years later it was to come back; but for the moment, it was gone. What I should have done though is bottom it out and seek professional help, for Kathryn and I would live with the invisible beast for many a year. It was also a turning point in our friendship. From that point on our path was set. The two individuals would become a partnership, born out of trial by blood, sweat and tears. The SOS of that night was always there.

A few years later we were sitting in the kitchen, reflecting that it was a hard time at work for both of us. The green kitchen tiles reflected the orange glow of the gas cooker as I stirred the chilli.

'It will never be as hard as it's been,' said Kathryn. 'We have been through what no one else has been through and we're still here; you're still here!'

I stopped stirring the chilli, turned to her and we hugged. She was right. Life would never seem as hard or tough again.

In the aftermath of the darkest time we finally we went on a date at a pub near Kathryn's house; she had been working hard at the stables all day. The Plough was busy that night and a friend was also in, joining us unexpectedly. Kathryn went to go to the toilet but was gone a long time. In fact, she had taken a wrong turn and walked into the kitchen, promptly fainting. The chef came out and informed me my girlfriend had collapsed on his floor. Kathryn needed to go home, so I called a taxi, I asked if she wanted me to go with her and see if she was OK.

'No need, I'm fine! I've been working all day and I've just not eaten enough.'

She was absolutely insistent that I didn't need to come with her. So, she left and I went back to the pub, thinking of what the chef had said; 'my girlfriend.' The thought felt good. I got a lot of flak from her friends for not taking her home myself. But it was the day I began to see her in a different light; it was the night of the beginning. It was like being welcomed back into the great herd that roams the high plains. A herd of big grey horses, free and unchained by the world of man; Kathryn's herd.

CHAPTER THREE

Seeds of Ambition

For this is our path, and this is our
Home, and all roads bring us back to
The slow silent pitter of drying rain
On soft fields . . .

Standing proud in its field or on the steppe under big skies I think the horse is unhindered by false ambition. The next meal is instinctively laid down in its core, as is the calling to be part of the herd. To mate and to be part of the ongoing process of wildlife. The horse is not constrained by the fickle dreams and hopes we as humans feel we are owed. Nor is it asked what it wants to be when it grows up.

When I was younger, if asked what I wanted to be when I grew up, the answer would have been an officer in a branch of the armed forces. It varied over the years from the Army to the Air Force and the Marines. So, with this romantic, perhaps clouded view, Richard Barrow and I cajoled our parents into taking us to the local air cadet squadron at the great age of fourteen. There we dressed in blue uniforms and paraded as little toy soldiers in the dusty halls and on concrete grounds. Other young future warriors joined our intake, Fergus Hunter Spokes and David Tait became part of the little band of tiny brothers.

Over the years in the cadets the adventurous life promised by a military career drew us in. The adventure that is war seduced our minds into thinking that our ambition was well placed. And the Queen's shilling gilded our pockets with the prospect of heroic deeds in foreign lands.

In hindsight, that wonderful gift of the future self, I should have realised that I was never cut out for military service if my air cadet career was anything to go by; I was too outspoken. I always opened my mouth at the wrong time, was always in trouble and in the end left as I entered; a cadet. A little boy in a larger blue uniform.

As my friends and I ran around the woods near home, acting out battles of Goose Green and the taking of Port Stanley, far removed from the real heart-breaking conflict that was going on for real on a far-flung island in the South Atlantic, Kathryn was glinting her own ambitions, not dressed in blue jumpers but child-sized jodhpurs. We would both play out our youthful games, unhindered by the real world in the playground that is Sherwood. The beginning of two worlds that one day would collide had begun amongst the deep-seated roots of the forest.

It was a glorious time looking back now with nostalgic binoculars. Sepia memories of roaming airfields, playing at flying; driven around the sky by real pilots. In turn all of us little Indians would run down to the Officer and Aircrew Selection Board at the hallowed Biggin Hill station. The what do we do when we grow up questions were fired at us now in seriousness. How do you feel about killing someone? A serious-looking officer would ask. I don't think any of us gave an honest answer. Would anyone?

Kathryn maybe would have done. With a definite 'What kind of ambition is that?' The horse has elevated itself above us in that respect; the grey charger doesn't ask of itself why it should kill. Nor dream up answers to defend such suggestions it might do.

But at the time I was consumed by the competition to succeed, to gain a coveted place in the ranks of the military.

And the one who was destined to be killed, who would have answered honestly and not been swayed by daring propaganda, stuck to her own self. To learn about the way of the horse, navigate the paths and tracks of home and the gardens of the woods. To fly in her own way. But flying wasn't for me; the moors and open lands of the wild land drew me in. So, I applied for the Royal Marines. I applied because it was hard, and not many were accepted. Over two years I ran through mud and more mud, went on courses and attended selection days. I failed the first test at the Commando Training Centre; but the word Commando spurred me on. I went back, fitter, tougher and grounded in the reality of my own limits. So, I refused to jump off the diving board in full kit and rifle, I swam twenty lengths breaststroke instead. Watching the lemmings jump in only to be rescued. Four of us passed, won through because we knew our own limits. And as potential officers that was deemed important. After more courses and interviews I was all set to buck the trend of the little gang of cadets. In the end I didn't join the Marines though; I was diagnosed with arthritis in my knees due to over-training. Now I wonder, do we ever grow up and become what was asked of us? Or do we just adapt to our own failings and others' false pressures?

I ended up working for a clothing manufacturer locally. A not-so-glorious profession in my eyes as my friends went into the Air Force to fly jets and be soldiers. After a brief dally with the 21st Special Air Service Regiment in Birmingham, which Dave thought we would be suited to, I joined the local Territorial Army to quell the longing of the uniform. I was the stubborn dog who could not give up the bone. The ambition engrained in me was hard to dispel. Just like the horse who needs the hay, he will do anything to get it. Due to my experience with the

Marines they made me an officer cadet which in reality meant I just had a white stripe on my shoulder. And for twice a week I paraded with the 3rd Worcestershire and Sherwood Foresters.

I learned about leadership for the first time; the soldiers in the platoon I belonged to were a hard, rough and to-the-point bunch. Yet, once I'd stood up to the sergeant major who asked why I'd taken the white stripes off my jacket ahead of a night exercise; my reply being I didn't think big white flashes on a combat jacket were suitable for a night attack, they accepted me.

Ambition is the doom of all youth though; the path we choose turns our lives into the rivers of the future. Once we set foot in the stream it's hard to swim back to the bridge. So, I listened to my friends in their blue uniforms and went back to the Royal Air Force.

With high expectation and excitement for the future I joined the RAF and attended Initial Officer Training at RAF Cranwell in the grand-sounding General Duties Branch: RAF Regiment. I'm still immensely proud that I was the youngest on our course to graduate, as Pilot Officer S M Bull. The commissioning course was hard mentally but not physically. I was commended on one occasion for the fastest appreciation of a leadership task ever seen by the training officer; of displaying 'unusual physical courage' on an endurance task. And on another not so glorious occasion I 'lost' the Queen's colours; the ceremonial flag presented by the Queen and blessed by the RAF Chaplain. I was duty officer of whom one's responsibility is to guard or rescue the colours in an emergency. It was a simulated fire exercise; I was out on a training run in the woods at the time of the simulated fire and nowhere near the officers' mess. The flag was deemed as burned, and the duty officer negligent. The subsequent report I had to write on the importance of the colours made a lasting impression on me.

The time we serenaded a young female officer cadet at the

Royal Naval College with 'Loving Feeling'; play-acting a scene from the film *Top Gun*, stands as a highlight of my military career though. Those of us deemed fit enough had been selected to run in the RAF cross-country team and at the end of a memorable losing weekend hosted by the Royal Navy we drunk too many beers and sung badly to the surprised lady.

My short but unsung military career was a great time though and one I'll never forget; my mum and granddad came to the graduation, as my dad was recovering from a heart attack. But the dream of forging out a career in the RAF was short-lived. At RAF Catterick on the Regiment Officers course the knees started playing up again, so with reluctance I pulled out and attempted to join another branch. I then spent several months carrying out general duties as I waited to be assigned another role. Postings at RAF Coltishall and Biggin Hill were fantastic. I was offered positions in Administration and Fighter Control, but neither of those careers interested me. With a heavy heart I left the RAF. Yet the RAF motto *Per ardua ad astra* (through adversity to the stars) has resonated with me in later years. It is testimony to those years in the blue uniform though that Fergus, Dave and Richard remain my closest friends.

But I wish now I had started out with the ambition of a horse, with no dreams to chase down in the western world of material and glory gains. Just to be content with running free on my own terms. Chasing the wind with the herd and sheltering down in the storms. Back to the wind and head into calm air, facing forward. Just that. No more or less. I think Kathryn began with those notions, riding a living animal, riding as a way of life and nothing more. The ambition of connecting with another living being, not dreaming of conquest and killing in the quest of a flag; however (falsely) noble that may be.

And I like to think that as a young girl curled up in the soft peace of bed, with the comforting sounds of home drifting on the landing, Kathryn dreamed ambitions of riding horses through endless woods. Falling asleep to the weight of her battered *Black Beauty* book laid across her duvet. For some ambitions are truly noble, they light the fire in our souls that can't be extinguished by man nor beast.

Yet the time spent in the various parts of the military paved the way for later life, on expeditions and especially for when Kathryn would go. It taught me to never give in, never give up hope and always to strive forwards in the face of impossible odds. My time at Cranwell taught me discipline and the ability to make a decision, any decision, because doubt and indecision are killers. Whether on a battlefield, or on an ice cap, or indeed riding a horse. Always ride forward, always act. Right or wrong, but make the decision.

I had learned the ability to make decisions based on little or no information; something that was to prove invaluable when I took over Cross Lane. I also held on to the lessons of my limitations, and the great gift of stubbornness; one of the greatest weapons against grief.

My first career was over. The one thing I had only ever wanted to do was cut short before it ever began. Now, looking back I'm glad; I'm not the type to conform and I think a service life would not have suited me, I like to do my own thing too much. That's why I rejected working at my grandfather's factory, the only family member not to. Two summers on the shop floor sweeping up oil and sand made me realise it wasn't for me, I chose my own path, just as he had done. When my brother went to work for a homeless charity, he virtually disowned him for two years, for what reason I have no idea; yet for some reason he respected my decision not to work at the factory. When his wife died on a cruise, he had the exact latitude and longitude co-ordinates where she passed away written on her headstone. Sometimes the hardest men are the softest underneath.

As I left the Air Force at twenty years old, Kathryn was only twelve, and learning to ride. She could have joined the Pony Club, which in effect is like the air cadets. It teaches young people to ride, care for the horse and all aspects surrounding horse care. She never joined, mainly because her family didn't own a four-by-four and a trailer. As Pony Club camps and events required you to get your horse there, the logistics made it impossible for Kathryn to join. I don't know if she regretted this or not; it certainly didn't hamper her career with horses in later years.

Kathryn let the dreams of working with horses flutter out for a while; she wanted to be an accountant. She was brilliant at maths, taking her maths GCSE a year earlier than normal. The exact opposite of myself. After school she went to Nottingham Trent University, close to the horses still though. It was easy for her in terms of transport also, for her brother Andrew worked in Nottingham and would give her a lift each day. She had been riding all her life, on the family ponies, learning her craft in the forests near home, on the edge of the old hunting grounds of Little John and Robin Hood. It wasn't long before she started going to Bloomsgorse to help out at weekends. It was inevitable in the end that she would choose this path instead of accountancy. The candle of ambition could not be extinguished for ever. Zoë would give Kathryn a lift to the trekking centre and home again, it was on a journey home that she asked Zoë if she could come and work for her. Zoë was adamant that she asked her mum first, after all she had only one year of her accountancy degree to finish. But Kathryn was positive; she wanted to work with horses. Her parents took it in their stride, so Kathryn gave up her degree and went to work full-time at the trekking centre in 1997.

She could have been anything in life, her intelligence and analytical mind would have complemented any career. I think she would have been the same as me in the military; she would have asked why too much, however, she became a great leader with the ability to solve problems and deal with people. Kathryn was the diplomat; she knew what to say and when to say it, the opposite of myself.

We make decisions in our life that over the years will have huge consequences for ourselves and those around us. Decisions made out of self-belief, stubbornness and dreams. I had decided not to go into my grandfather's factory and join the family firm; it would have been the easy way, the guaranteed future of prosperity and belonging. Kathryn could have chosen accountancy; yet, she chose horses. Out of love and because that was her dream. I chose the military first and later expeditions. Because that's what I wanted to do, that was my dream. It's a cliché born out of personal experience now, but life is really too short to do anything else. Without doubt Kathryn made the right decision, despite the outcome several years later that would end her life. For, she lived the life she wanted, and to quote Captain Scott; 'We took risks, we knew we took them, things have come out against us, and therefore have no cause for complaint, but bow to the will of providence.' For riding horses is risky, as is going on expeditions.

When I was young, I never wanted to get married. It was not an overriding ambition; maybe it wasn't Kathryn's either. At the time the Scots Greys charged into the French line at Waterloo a young lady of standing's ambition would have centred on marriage. How time moves on? Now I know that of all the past ambitions I had, the one I never thought of was the greatest. The reality ambition of being married to Kathryn, it was the singular greatest and proudest thing I have ever done. Asking her to marry me, all the callings in the world don't compare to such a glorious partnership.

CHAPTER FOUR

Our Place in the Field

Chase it down and ride,
Then sleep in the fold,
A cradling of beginning,
To belong to the big days.

Heavy cavalry was the tactical nuclear option on the medieval battlefield. Imagine over two thousand five hundred horses coming at you with only a musket in your hand, for that was the combined number of the English heavy brigade at Waterloo. The famous painting by Lady Butler of the Scots Greys' charge at Waterloo depicts the horses wildly thrashing their heads around; they were trained to bite the heads off infantry. The Scots Greys decimated the French infantry columns, only to perish as the charge rushed into French guns, the horses so steamed up the riders couldn't hold them. The Light Brigade at Balaclava in 1854 achieved their objective, they rode the valley of death to reach the Russian guns, yet once through the guns, the lack of a heavy brigade backing them up signed their fate. Most of the horses died in the aftermath, left on Russian soil to die in the cold and the mud. We have used horses throughout history, but very often we have neglected their welfare and care; at the substitute of glory. It's a sad tale of man's lack of love for the animal.

Dressage is all about military movements that were designed to kick and kill the foot soldier. Yet, today we marvel at the art of dressage. Saddles were invented to give stability and balance to the knight, stirrups to provide greater leverage for wielding the sword. Today, the horse is a recreational hobby animal, a sport and money earner. It wasn't always so, only those with large amounts of money could afford a horse, yet the opening up of grazing land and livery yards has enabled those who in the past could not afford the horse to achieve horse ownership. Yet, the horse's past and pedigree still remains one of military might. Not of recreation. This is something I think we have forgotten all too readily; they are not pets; but are treated so too much. Which only accentuates the risk associated with them.

They were also the burdens of man, ploughing the fields and feeding the nation. Towing the carts and the goods in them to market. From Shire horses to trotting horses; native breeds and warm bloods. Thoroughbreds that have entertained and enthralled man; little ponies down the mines bringing the minerals to the surface. The horse has been at the forefront of the climb of mankind to his position on the planet today.

In comparison exploration is very similar, the discovery of new lands and locations of great geographical importance was essentially driven by national pride. To gain land and dominance in the pursuit of an empire. Explorers did not venture into the Antarctic, the Amazon or the Himalayas for 'personal discovery' or to get away from it all. They went for glory, fame and fortune and endured great hardship, privation and sometimes death in order to plant a flag for queen and country.

Sir Ernest Shackleton saw the conquest of the South Pole, not as an ambition he had always dreamed of since a boy, but as fame and recognition. He would have got it any way he could, but fate led him to the south. And then, the risks linked with being the first to the pole were heavy. On his expedition to within a few miles of the pole in 1908, he and his team barely made it back alive. Scott and his companions that reached the pole in 1911 all perished on the return journey. Fawcett disappeared into the Amazon, searching for lost cities, Franklin and his men never returned from the North-West Passage; looking for the fabled shortcut from west to east. Scott, Oates, Wilson, Evans and Bowers were under no illusion that they might not get back, Shackleton faced the same in the Weddell Sea when his ship sank; no radio, no GPS, no nothing. And no one knew where he was. Mallory and Irvin pushed on to the summit of Everest in tweeds and Burberry as clouds swirled, never to be seen again. They knew. As do those that sit on a horse at the start line of the Grand National, they know that there is a large chance they or their horse might not make the finish. They gamble on their skill as a rider and the boldness of the horse under them.

Priority is everything, whether it is the first to the summit, the first across the line, the fastest time over a course of jumps. Exploration and horsemanship demands the same gamble of ability and nerve against a demanding mental and physical challenge. Kathryn accepted it and knew it, as I did when expeditions took hold of me in 1992. Just like *Black Beauty* had captivated Kathryn's mind; it was a book that also drew me into a life of romance and open lands.

The military life burned away in the hearth as I went to university to study a degree in sport. As the embers died down, I tried to focus on biomechanics and physiology whilst spending weekends climbing the sea cliffs of the south coast and crawling through the caves of the Mendips. Then one grey morning in the college library, lying unloved on the travel shelf, I found a book that was far more interesting. *In the Footsteps of Scott* by Robert Swan documented Swan's dream and realisation of walking to the South Pole; he had originally wanted to recreate Scott's journey and in the end did an unsupported walk from the coast to the pole. It was a major undertaking, being before Antarctica had opened up properly with guided logistic companies in place. The footsteps spoken of by Swan reached out of the pages and trampled over my heart. They left big boot prints over my soul; and I endeavoured to see where they would lead me.

The South Downs were a long way off from the poles at the ends of the earth, and my only snow and ice experience at that time was a few winter walks in Derbyshire with my dad. Not dissimilar to Kathryn's level of experience riding her mum's pony. We both it seemed were starting off from the same level. Yet both fired by a dream that seemed set out in the sky.

I went back to the library to find more books on the lands of ice and the explorers who went there. I read and I read, in the ruffling of the pages I felt the wind flow from the words. Eventually I did my dissertation on the exploration of Antarctica. I met many explorers, Sir Ranulph Fiennes and Colonel Andrew Croft most notably. It was Andrew Croft in the quiet of his London home who suggested I do my first trip to Iceland, to get on the icecaps and start 'cutting my teeth'; as he eloquently put it. My life had been geared to the military, yet here was a new ambition; I set out to learn the skills and gain enough experience to lead a team to the South Pole myself. In those days you could not pay someone to guide you as is the norm now. You had to lead the trips yourself, having spent several years gaining the experience. It was a long and expensive process; a bit like owning horses. However, I wanted to make my own footsteps out in the wild blue yonder of the frozen south.

Meanwhile Kathryn started riding at about the same age my dad took me out onto my first hill. In the beginning Kathryn's parents rented a field as her mum had always ridden, and there were three family horses for Kathryn to start to ride on. On a day with sun beating down Kathryn headed out into the old hunting grounds of Sherwood with her mum and sister. Deep in the glades, with the ghost of Little John looking on Penny took off with seven-year-old Kathryn; the little pony had decided it wanted to go home. The trot down the forest track turned into the desire to head for the stables and tea, and Kathryn had no choice but to go with her. Through the heart of the forest they careered out of control and with no brakes. Eventually coming to a sweaty and heart-thumping stop outside the stable yard.

Only the prospect of a new riding hat from her mum persuaded her to carry on with this strange hobby of sitting atop a seemingly untamed beast. With a new hat proudly positioned on her head she began lessons at a nearby riding school. At Woodside Stables she was introduced to Billy; a little Welsh pony with a totally different character to that of Penny. For a start he didn't disappear flat out home for tea with her; this animal seemed well behaved she thought. They started riding out in the woods under control, and slowly the fear went away, to be replaced by the dawning love when you find something you think no one else ever has. Just like the sunset from the top of a lost mountain range; it's yours and no one else's. Kathryn without knowing it at the time had found her place in the field.

I hadn't been galloped off with through the woods; instead every Sunday my dad would march us over hill and dale in nearby Derbyshire. The hills were mountains far bigger than Everest and we forded rivers wider than the Pacific; so it seemed to my nine-year-old legs. The wilderness daunted me, scared me and overwhelmed me. It wasn't until I was a little older and began heading into the same places with friends, that the true nature of the hills whispered their song. That quiet tune that invites you to play along, to walk a little further, climb a little higher and stay just another day more.

The staying a little more engrained itself in Kathryn's psyche, she began helping out with her sister Emma at the local Riding for the Disabled Centre, sowing the seeds of her unspoken ambition to help others. It grew inside her, started to take hold, she dreamed of doing more with the horses that began calling to her. In the dreams of her nights and most dangerous of all, in the dreams of the daylight hours.

Her brother chose chartered surveying, her elder sister accountancy and her younger sister physiotherapy. Her dad had been a builder with his own business. But Kathryn turned her back on conformity and went into the forest to work with the animals; and I think her dad could not have been prouder. Pride with my own father would come later, for I'd turned away from the family walks in my stubbornness.

It took me a long time to find my love of the outdoors; it was a creeping of mutual acceptance. Of finding my place on the rocks and moors, of knowing the empty places accepted me too. The wind in the heather didn't ask me if I liked it, didn't question me or argue. The waving heather on the lonely moors accepted me for who I was. Dave and I had slogged our way up the Pennine Way in seven days, a walk that haunts my feet to this day. But for a whole week the solitude of the big sky seeped into me.

The friendships shared in the adventure of an expedition, be it a one-day mad dash up a hill or rock face or a longer trip, cemented the bond with the nature on our doorsteps. Big days under big skies, I had found them. Just like Kathryn had found them. Each of us had wandered our path hesitantly at first, unsure of the right direction, afraid to trust the compasses in our hearts. We knew the map was there, we just weren't quite sure how to read it. The map that lies in our hearts and holds the key to our place in the field.

For the 'field' is where we belong, we all search for it. Question what we should do with our lives and why. Wonder why we are here and what purpose we should achieve whilst our hearts tick away the minutes of our existence. And if we find it then life is special and there is no doubt in our soul. But it doesn't come easy, handed down in a lottery card of blinding light. We struggle and fight, as I did with the burdens of youth, as Kathryn did with soul-searching debates; a secure future in accountancy or follow the ride into the forests.

Dave would find it too, high up in the Himalaya on the roof of Dhaulagiri. And he would carve a name on a prayer flag, he would write in his own hand a singular testament. For he valued the place of the field and the striving to reach it. The white pennant he wrote on would come back to the forests and the fields of home. Yet he could have never realised all those years ago, when as small boys we ran around the woods, the name he would write.

CHAPTER FIVE

The Cavalry of Ice

As the light moves into dark,
And rain combines with sun to perfect
Shining hope written in cloudless skies.

The white pennant lay in the future. It was to the lower ice fields I headed; at twenty-one I went to the Alps to learn how to cross glaciers, taught by a French guide I had met at university. Then in the summer of '93 a friend and I travelled to Iceland for a six-week exploration of the North-West Peninsula. We travelled by ferry out of Aberdeen, braving the northern seas arriving on the east coast of Iceland two days later. For six weeks we would shoulder unbearable loads of food and fuel in our little quest on the land of fire and ice. Andrew Croft's seed had finally taken root and we sharpened our teeth in the far north.

Our aim was to carry out a study on lichens for the University of York, or to be accurate, that was Sue's aim. However, the Drangajökull icecap was shrouded in bad weather, the mist and rain drove into our faces forcing us into a humble retreat. We changed tack and headed to Vatnajökull, the largest icecap in Europe, hoping to find calmer weather. It was a time of learning, a lesson in the basics of expedition leadership and life. We felt like explorers, and in a way, we were; for we were carrying out geographical research for the furthering of knowledge. In essence what expeditions have been historically about. It felt as if we were part of that long line of tradition extending back to Cook. And it was the first step on the ladder to the South Pole.

After Iceland I needed another expedition; a relationship had gone wrong which I thought was significant at the time. I now know it didn't work out so Kathryn could come into my life. It sounds strange, but it's true that some people move out of our lives to make way for others. Some flowers never take hold, and stronger buds flourish.

Situated on the fringe of the Jostedalsbreen glacier in the heart of Norway, the Flatbrehytta hut overlooks a majestic view of fjords and mountains. A friend and I based ourselves in the cosy wooden shack and explored the glaciers and mountains of the highest icecap in Europe. I learned more about travelling in heavily crevassed terrain and started to gain a feel for the snow-clad landscape. After a week we had run out of food and therefore headed down to the valley, the ferry down the fjord and home by sea.

The seeds were sown for my next trip, an expedition to the same area to cross the icecap with a team including people with disabilities. I wanted to do expeditions that involved 'firsts', and in the early 1990s true expedition firsts were hard to find. Planning began therefore for the 'Integrated Norway Expedition', but in the meantime I needed to earn a living in a more traditional sense.

Following my degree, I'd undertaken a teaching course, but I didn't fit into the traditional mould of a PE teacher. After a spell of supply-teaching I strangely ended up as an auxiliary bank nurse at the local hospital. It was a life-affirming period that had transpired from knowing a medical student who believed that everyone should spend some time nursing. The forest of home always called, so I ran there regularly, despite the sore knees. I ran into the woods and the pines into the safety of the greenery. It was out running one day I stumbled on Fountaindale School; a specialist school for children with special needs. After an interview which involved a morning in the swimming pool helping get the students ready, I was offered a post at the school teaching physical education. At Fountaindale I found a place I could believe in.

For two years I worked there; I was terrible at first as the job was demanding. Yet I had my own tutor group of eight children, whose disabilities ranged from muscular dystrophy to cerebral palsy. Looking back now it was the best job I've ever had. I'm still in touch with some of the students from my tutor group. Funding issues were responsible for my departure, but my experiences at the school cemented my desire to plan expeditions involving people with disabilities. The Integrated Norway Expedition began to take shape, the plan being to cross Jostedalsbreen, Europe's highest icecap, with a mixed team. Our team comprised one registered blind person and one with disabilities due to breathing difficulties; plus able-bodied members. With these dynamics we set sail for Norway.

We were on the cusp of a new age in expeditions. Our generation was probably the last to go into wild places without a satellite phone, or an emergency beacon. If you got into trouble on an icecap, you had to sort it out yourself. My friends and I would travel in the mountains without mobile phones. It was the days of keeping 10p in your pocket and knowing where the nearest red phone box was.

Modern technology has changed the face of exploration with satellite phones and computer software allowing the exploring to blog direct to social media from the middle of nowhere, and emergency beacons that can summon help when all things go south. Yet, explorers still need to navigate and be able to negotiate crevassed terrain, overcome seracs and steep mountain faces, negotiate wild rivers and deep jungles. And when it all goes wrong technology can't save you, as in the tragic case of Henry Worsley in Antarctica, who died at the end of a solo crossing of Antarctica. Our expeditions never reached that level of danger, yet we were one of the last generations to venture out without the aid of satellite phones and the backup that adventurers are used to today.

In today's modern world of expeditions, mapping tools have taken away the art of exploring. Young people sit in front of computers and plot their Duke of Edinburgh expedition using fancy software packages. Distance and height gain are printed out for them, yet they don't get the feel of the country. They don't count contours and realise how steep the hill is. Something has been lost, a missing in the art of the old ways; yet the young need to have adventures like we did. To find the limits on their own, to know when to back off; to know how to face hardship without a safety net. For life doesn't have a safety net in the real world.

The same sometimes applies to riding and looking after the horse. I see people now just wanting to jump higher and higher and they lose sight of the bond that is required between horse and rider on the ground. Few people feed their horses barley anymore, or put black tar on the hooves and wipe down in the wet with straw, all good practices that Kathryn followed. Old ways that have stood the test of time.

Whilst I was planning Norway, Kathryn was still in school. The conversation with Zoë in the car was a way off still; it was her unplanned expedition. Yet, whilst at school she began at Bloomsgorse. Days helping out turned to weekends and in turn to holidays. She rode her horse through the forest, a stone's throw from the school I would work at. In the same woods I had played at soldiers as an air cadet, often sleeping out in the woods without tents or sleeping bags. It seems now that we were both bound by the forest, from our youth and into adulthood. We both were drawn to the deep quiet of the trees, a landscape that hasn't changed since King Richard came back from the Crusades. It's a perpetual landscape, old deciduous trees still stand that saw the crusaders return. I feel like my life is entwined with the trees. As they grow, I grow. They die and then take spread once more, from new seeds. So, the forest becomes the circle of life.

The cavalry that was her life began to trot unknowingly towards the ice I was melting into. I, in turn, was taking a steady walk into the future; the forest had shaped me and driven me into wanting more of the open spaces. The mistress of fate plotted her story and sent out the troop of grey horses to lie in wait for the unsuspecting foot soldier.

CHAPTER SIX

Over a Distant Horizon

Silence moves through our rooms,
Your presence calls to me,
Images on print weather time,
Outside a world moves.

Kathryn would get up very early to write a note and hide it in either the passport or the first page of the book I had with me. I would find it at the airport. These notes sent me away knowing I was wanted and that I could go away without fear or dread, for she was waiting. She would always wait. I was not alone wherever I went in the world. And after a while I looked forward to finding the note more than going away. And I couldn't wait to get back. I think I went on expeditions to read her note.

As I sit here now listening to the opening music of *Stand by Me*, my favourite film, I know how much better it was to receive a handwritten note rather than a text, or an email or voice message. On my early expeditions we didn't have such communication technology, the expeditions when Kathryn was here, we did; yet still she wrote by hand, with pen and paper.

Dear Steve,

I hope that all goes well and that you enjoy yourself. I'm already looking forward to you arriving home. You'll soon have been to every continent! Take care explorer! Lots of love, Kathryn xxx

Words mean so much more when the person has taken time to write in their own hand. It's like they have left a small imprint of their soul on the paper.

The horses Kathryn rode became a part of her. They imprinted on each other, like the notes on paper. She took Strip on when he came to Bloomsgorse because no one else would. He would turn in the stable when you went in to get him, threaten to kick you, and he was willing to run off on a ride. I think now he was the mountain to Kathryn and she was the young climber, determined to pit her skill and ability against his 'north face'. Problem horses would become her trademark; it was what she was good at. In a way just like the dogs she would own. Somehow, she was drawn to those that needed help, whether equine, canine or human. Her puppy greyhound Jack and Kathryn became inseparable. Alone in her house on Prospect Street she would play ball in the living room with him. He was mad as they come. They loved each other.

One evening when we were married years later, she walked into the kitchen later than usual. As I stood preparing tea the door swung shut, there was no fawn greyhound pounding in after her. Kathryn stood on the threshold ashen faced. 'Jack's dead.' Her words fell onto the kitchen carpet and stayed there. We held each for a long time. He'd chased her sister's horse up the field and got too close: one kick and he was dead in an instant. We buried him by hand in her parents' field. What Jack gave her was a love of greyhounds, and what she gave Jack was a life free and roaming.

Riding out in Harlow Woods on a Wednesday afternoon, her afternoon off; dog, horse, rider, all as one.

When she took Jack on, our future together was not yet written. It was the time when I went away on an expedition and there was no note in my passport. Norway was a success; a three-week trip travelling by ferry from the UK and driving to the icecaps in a Land Rover. It wasn't a long crossing of the ice, but it was a novice team and tested everyone to their limits. We then headed to the Folgefonna icecap where John Brimble, who had one lung, successfully climbed to the summit. It was the major achievement of his life, he later told me. I was starting to learn the business of expeditions; we had gained sponsorship and been lent clothing and equipment. All the processes that make an expedition happen I was learning to put together. It was also the start of Ran Fiennes' patronage of our expeditions; I had written to him asking humbly if he would like to add support to the trip. He readily agreed, and this was to become a long-lasting association.

On the back of the Norway expedition I was invited by the Hong Kong branch of the Royal Geographical Society to speak to their members about the trip. With them paying the flights I couldn't turn it down, it was to be an experience in exploration politics. On arriving in Hong Kong, I was met by the host who asked if I'd led for Raleigh International.

'Oh no,' I replied. 'They're all ex-Sandhurst toffs . . .' The reply: 'I'm an ex-Sandhurst toff and I led for Raleigh.'

The silence that followed was heard long after the Empire left Hong Kong. He led me to the lecture hall and explained how much it cost per hour; it was more than I earned in a month as a teacher. The atmosphere remained awkward as he explained also that the first lecture was by Commander John Young on his space shuttle missions. I couldn't help but think my slides of a few mates on a Norwegian glacier wouldn't cut it. Yet, several glasses of wine helped and the lecture went down well, after which I met a lovely couple who liked my down-to-earth approach. So much so they invited me to stay on their yacht moored at the Royal Hong Kong Yacht Club. He had retired from the army having served with Ran Fiennes in Oman; they had built a boat and were sailing round the world. I spent a magical short time on their little yacht, a hurricane hit but we never noticed it as the bar stayed open all night.

Two years later, I set out to cross the Greenland icecap, which covers eighty per cent of the country, with an integrated team. It was an ambitious plan, hardly possible, for no one had ever attempted such a trip. Yet, it was a challenge that I needed, it felt like we were setting out to be explorers. At the time, integrated expeditions (those involving people with disabilities and those without) were popular with the Royal Geographical Society (RGS) and in those days I was a frequent visitor to the society's headquarters in Kensington. I became involved in the first RGS conferences on integrated teams, as well as spending hours poring over maps and expedition reports. Sitting in the rooms of history where all the great explorers had started out, their expressive faces seemed to stare down at me in silent judgement.

It was in an age before the Internet, so I wrote letters to gain sponsorship for the next trip; one of whom was The Paul Vander Molen Foundation. My handwriting was so bad they called me to ask what I wanted, and to my surprise helped sponsor the expedition. It was the days when we sent pre-written postcards to all the sponsors written on the ferry and posted when we docked. It was the changing time between the old ways of expeditions and the modern world, for we had a state-of-the-art Global Positioning System for navigating on the ice.

Kathryn however had no need of a GPS or even a satellite phone, for Sherwood didn't call for one. In fact, mobile phones were not accessible when Kathryn started work at Bloomsgorse. Now we complain if we don't have 4G in the forests. Back then if you had a problem in the woods you had to sort it out by yourself. As we had to do on the Greenland expedition.

It was an ambitious project, a person with no sight and one with impaired vision, with me and one other would cross Greenland. The plan was simple; cross the icecap from east to west, a distance of approximately 370 miles. I received a Winston Churchill Fellowship, a grant from the Winston Churchill Memorial Trust, for the expedition, having sat through an interview in London with Winston Churchill's grandson, Nicholas Soames MP, Sir Roger Bannister and the Commandant General of the Royal Marines. The first question I was asked threw me though: 'Either you're very brave or very stupid, which is it?' They were referring to my plan to free-fall parachute onto the icecap with the RAF Falcons, a plan I had previously discounted as mad having done a trial jump at RAF Weston on the Green with Nigel Rogof, chief instructor of the RAF Falcons. It was an awesome experience, but I didn't think it was wise, plus it reinforced how scared of heights I was. I think they were pleased with my answer, which outlined the risks involved, as a full grant was sanctioned. (Nigel would later die from parachuting; crashing onto the roof of a football stadium after the wind blew him onto the pitch, breaking his legs. He never recovered, dying a few years later. The best in any sport or vocation go young sometimes.)

It was a learning curve in fundraising; the expedition wasn't that expensive in modern terms, yet we still needed sponsorship. We featured on TV and the day before we left, were driven into London to the BBC for a radio broadcast. Media and expeditions go hand in hand, companies like their products in the public eye; the media does that. Greenland was sponsored by a whole host of local companies and grants from various sources. It's all part of the expedition trade, Scott did it and so did Shackleton. Modern expeditions do so also, for the amounts of money needed to go to the Polar Regions are beyond the normal person's budget.

Sir Ranulph Fiennes became Patron again as he had done on the Norway expedition. With full hope we sailed south down the coast from Ammassalik in south-eastern Greenland to our drop-off point on the east coast. The last instructions Hans Christian, the local doctor in Ammassalik had said, was, 'Don't use the emergency beacon, unless it's real life and death.'

Giant icebergs and tumbling glaciers dwarfed our little boat. Heading up a fjord to a little sandy beach we landed safely. There in the Tolkien-inspired quietness we unloaded and carried the pulks (sledges used to carry equipment) a few metres and set up camp on the glacier itself. Ahead of us lay over 370 miles of ice and snow. The scale of our challenge dripped into our hearts as the boat chugged away to that which was lost to us for now, civilisation.

It took several days to move the pulks up the glacier, yet the crevasses were snow-free and therefore our passage was easier. Crossing each icy hole took care and time, for half our team couldn't see anything. Each footfall was earned threefold that of an able-bodied team.

Like a horse crashing into the first fence of the Grand National though, so too did our expedition. One team member twisted his ankle jumping a crevasse. A dawning realisation descended on us, our antlike figures just tiny drops on the ice. We were insignificant in this world of cold. We rested and waited in the tents for two days, yet it was apparent to me that we were not going to cross with a wounded man, when already the odds were against us. The weight of responsibility lay heavy on me in the tent, the fabric walls closing in; demanding a decision. With a heavy heart I faced reality; to head back to the east coast and try and find the nearest village marked on our map. Yet, the map wasn't the most detailed. It was woefully sparse in its detail. We headed back east, into the rising sun and the landscape played with us. Enticing us one way and then another through a maze of dead-end crevasses and false trails.

Six days later we saw the coast again from the top of a mountain. We moved half our kit down the mountain, then returned to the summit with the view to moving the rest down in the morning. We pitched our tents, rock-anchored down by stones we found lying around. I went down to the coast on seeing a local hunter in his boat. We communicated across languages; me in English, the hunter in Inuit but to no avail. In the end I moved my watch hands to six o'clock. He put his thumb up and left. On returning to camp I related our exchange, we assumed he would be coming back at six the next evening. In the morning we headed down the mountain to retrieve our kit, four pulks fully loaded with skis and all the team's kit. Yet, it had all gone. I remember at the time we actually thought someone had stolen it. We were stressed and therefore confused and could think of no reason why all the kit was missing from a mountain in the middle of nowhere.

The two of us who were able-bodied set off for a village shown on our map. We took food for one day, yet our rescue was cut short by a glacial river; try as we might we could not wade through it. It was too cold and too deep, Beeches Brook to our tiny metaphorical pony. So, defeated and humbled we headed back to the others. We reconsidered the hunter; maybe he was coming at 6 p.m. after all? We decided to wait till six, and if he didn't come then we would have no choice but to press the button on the little gadget that would send a distress signal.

Bang on 6 p.m. the little boat chugged up to the sandy beach, and inside it were four pulks and sets of skis. Shame is a lonely feeling, and we all felt it. We found out the hunter had been baffled by meeting a strange blond man who mumbled in a strange language and talked through the hands of a clock. He'd seen our kit on the mountain though and decided to help; carrying it down on his own. We climbed aboard and he took us to the village, which happened to be about half a mile off the coast on a little island, so we would never have made it anyway. The map hadn't shown the gulf of sea that blocked our route. If the hunter hadn't come, we would have had no option but to activate the rescue beacon.

In the seven-day wait for the next resupply boat to the village, the goodwill in our team began to fracture. Two members thought we should have carried on, yet at the time I sensed it was the right decision to turn back. There is a time to push on and there is a time to back off, if we accept what nature is telling us.

Just as Kathryn found from riding.

Jumped Strip today – stopped twice, first time was my fault, stopped again in opposite direction, but my fault again.

The failed Greenland trip was a huge learning curve in terms of leadership, of fundraising and of course planning trips. Indeed, if you look at most famous explorers' expeditions, they don't always achieve their goals. Sometimes when we strive to go that little bit further, push a little harder, we dare to fail. And when success does come it is so much the sweeter.

There is one obvious difference between horses and expeditions however. The horse is a living animal with a mind of its own, it's exceptionally intelligent, and reacts to different people in different ways. A horse can detect fear and nerves in someone, either on the ground or on their back. Mountains and icecaps don't care one way or the other, they remain oblivious to the actions of people on them.

We move slowly forwards in life, in our chosen field. Taking the knocks and learning, falling down and getting up. Each day is an expedition, sometimes we make good progress over the glacier, others days we don't and we have to try a different route. Or sometimes we have to lie up in the tent and wait for the storm to pass. Such is life and all the journeys we each must travel.

After the Greenland expedition, I moved on, took the beating and began planning another trip. I'd met a friend, Ian Forsdike via one of the sponsors. He wanted to get involved in expeditions, polar expeditions specifically, and be the first person with a disability to reach the South Pole. Our mutual ambition suited us both. Ian was born with arm deformities due to the drug thalidomide, yet it doesn't stop him doing what we all try to do; to get through life as best we can with the cards dealt to us.

Along with Punch Wilson who had been to the South Pole (whom I met through a mutual colleague), and a local friend, Mick Barnes, we headed to Norway the year after my first Greenland expedition, to explore the length of the Jostedalsbreen glacier.

We started at the northern side and spent several days crossing the expanse of whiteness. It was an enjoyable trip; discreet in its challenges but large in the friendships we shared. It also got Ian thinking about the very real possibility of the South Pole. For several years we would get close to pulling off a South Pole trip together yet the lack of funding always let us down.

Back home in truly wet miserable weather I completed my mountain leader course enabling me to lead groups in the mountains of home, at the same time Kathryn embarked on her NVQ Level 2 in Horse Care. Instead of going down the British Horse Society qualification route Kathryn followed the NVQ path, whilst working at Bloomsgorse. She started to learn formally how to groom and plait up horses, how to exercise horses on the lunge line, a technique for working with horses without riding them, and how to ride schooled horses on the flat and over jumps. Schooled horses being those that have been trained to be ridden, other than those that have never had a rider on them. An obvious difference in risk and danger. Managing horses in the fields and in the stable all constituted part of the course. With her logical mind and her work ethic she completed the course with ease.

She suffered a setback though when she crashed her car on the lane heading out of the forest; this was to be a humorous trait of Kathryn's, to the amusement of her family and friends, maybe not Kathryn herself though. One evening heading home she thought she was Colin McCrea and drove her little Citroën too fast up the dirt track, losing control and landing in a tree. She got off lightly with a broken shoulder and too much mickey-taking from everyone at the yard. She would go on to write off several cars in her career. On one trip I was away she crashed or banged all three of our cars in succession. She had a unique knack to the art of bumping, scraping or crashing a car.

I remember all the cars she crashed, just like the names of all the students in my class at Fountaindale, just the same way Kathryn knew all the horses names at Bloomsgorse. I can still recall the looks on their faces when they received letters from famous explorers in aid of their geography project. Sir Vivian Fuchs, Robert Swan, Sir Ranulph Fiennes, Doug Scott and Sir Chris Bonnington all wrote to Year 9. It was a special time for the little school in the woods. I recall faces and personalities from my first group at the college I taught, their stamp of a smile and the way they talked. Full of hope or indecision as to the future. The horizon loomed large for the students at the college; those faces at Fountaindale did not have the same view. The horizon wasn't as distant. Unlike mine, for some of us the time and tide of our lives takes hold and we are propelled forwards into the future. The events rule us, for a meeting was coming.

Meeting Kathryn was not a single event; the meetings happened slowly. Pushing a barrow for her. Seeing her at the front of the ride on the lead horse. Her voice shouting down instructions from the back of the ride. Seeing her walk across the yard with her grooming kit, or sat shyly in the kitchen with the other girls. Prospect Street, lifts in her car and South Forest leisure centre. The meetings trickled in and seeped down, becoming immovable. Set and comfy, secure and laid down for the journey ahead.

Kathryn had concentrated on her horses, she lived a frugal life. She couldn't afford to go out much as all her money had gone on her house on Prospect Street and looking after Jack. I on the other hand had rented a room with two other girls in a local village, moved out and rented a room nearer college; eventually buying a little house near my parents. I wasn't frugal and went out most nights.

On her way home from Bloomsgorse she would give Claire, a groom at the stables, a lift home, as she lived down the road from Kathryn. My house was not on the route. Kathryn would drive past my house when she was driving. And when Claire was driving, she would ask her if she would drive by my house. They would stop for a second then move on. Claire told me this later after Kathryn left. I can't put a price on that. Who could? Sometimes they would turn up in the pub; as I sat at the bar the two of them would walk in. Kathryn always looked pleased to see me. Our end-of-the-bar talks buzz round my head like bees hunting fresh pollen now, a constant in my mind. They are too thick to waft away; and why would I? They are the horses of the air; they carry priceless memories; deposits of gold for the rest of my life.

CHAPTER SEVEN

A Light in the Forest

I walk the sandy lane with ghosts around me,
Down through the early bird song kingdom,
I follow hallowed footsteps from past times . . .

We walked up the road from the pub on a gorgeous lazy summer night. The junction signalled the route uphill to my house, and down to hers. She wore a thin white cotton blouse.

'Do you want to come back for a coffee for a bit?' She smiled and there was a shy nervous tension in the air.

'Thank you; I think I'll head back home.' I wasn't sure and was nervous.

'OK, that's fine. See you soon.'

'Yes, take care, it's been a lovely evening. I enjoyed being with you.'

'Me too.'

She turned and walked down the hill to her house, I walked up the hill, constantly looking back. Watching as she walked home, wishing I'd said yes. Even now I can picture that blouse. And each time I drive past the end of her old street, I picture the girl in the white blouse. Wish it was all those years ago and I had said yes.

Bloomsgorse was a trekking centre set in the heart of Sherwood Pines, the largest public forest in the East Midlands, and part of the ancient forest of Sherwood. And riding through the pines and woods old and new, it was easy to imagine a time long before. For, on a horse nothing has changed, the skills needed now are the same as in the Middle Ages and the time of the crusades.

There were horses of all shapes and sizes, from Mr T and Toby, the two little ponies, up to TC, Tommy and George, a 17.3 shire cross. At 9.30 each morning the novice riders from the nearby Center Parcs would arrive. As I could drive a minibus my job soon became to drive into the park and pick the ride up. Then they would be briefed on safety and allocated a horse or pony for the hour's ride through the forest. It was all hands to the deck as everyone fetched horses and put their riders on board.

In time I was given my own list of horses to groom and tack up for the rides. Everyone had about five or six horses to get ready. I learned later on that I was always given the dirtiest, muck- and pee-stained ones, singled out because I was the only male there at the time.

Alex, a medium-sized cob would lead the ride out of the yard, the larger horses behind with the ponies at the rear. A total of about ten horses and riders, in one long line. Out the back gate into the forest, up to the pylon road, then down to Catchman's Hollow and a right back up the hill to the yard. Most of the time the rides went without incident, apart from a pony diving off to eat the grass by the side of the track.

To start with I didn't go on these rides; I concentrated on my barrow-pushing. Yet after a while Zoë deemed me competent to ride Alex at the front, it was just a walk and Alex knew his job. At the same time as the first 'slow' ride, Zoë would take out the fast ride; consisting of four riders and horses for an hour's trot and canter and sometimes gallop. This was what I aspired to. To take my own fast ride. At the time it felt like trying to get to the South Pole.

The barrow-pushing and minibus-driving earned me a private lesson once a week, Jayne the head girl had this dubious pleasure. I was approaching thirty years old when I started learning to ride a horse. It's definitely best to start young as Kathryn had done. To be born in the saddle as they say, as the Norwegians are to the ski, as English we can't compete; it's the same with those that have been riding since a young child. You gain a feel for the horse that in reality you can never acquire when you learn as an adult.

Jayne realised that the syllabus the army use to teach novice aspiring cavalrymen was the way forward for me. As softer approaches didn't work, I was given no quarter and driven to succeed by her. With stirrups and without stirrups, sometimes using a mounting block, sometimes not. I rode without reins and with them. Sometimes the stirrups were tied to the girth, the strap that keeps the saddle in place. Rising trot without stirrups, rising trot with stirrups. As the lessons progressed I was put on the intermediate rides, these were the trotting rides, for those people who could ride a horse in trot. At this level riders had to fill in a form to say they could ride, and then demonstrate in the school they could actually trot. Most could not.

Over time my lessons progressed, I had stopped falling off as much – much to the disappointment of the yard watchers. I was now beginning to learn the feel of the horse, to be able to ride without thinking. Much like driving a car; after a while we change gear automatically; the actions are engrained in our brain and muscles. It's the same with riding; I could now move into the different gaits of the horse's movement without much thought. Turn and halt without having to think.

Weekends went by like leaves flowing in a wind, never ending and always flying into golden autumn. Riding horses was becoming a natural thing to do for me now, not the alien concept I felt it was months ago. Kathryn and I continued to sneak out on Fridays whenever we could, and Claire would continue to cover for us.

'Are you ok if we go for a ride?' Kathryn tentatively asked Claire.

'Yes, but don't be gone all afternoon!' was Claire's answer.

Kathryn beamed a smile back and shouted over the yard; 'Grab TC, Steve and I'll get Strip.'

We headed out onto the dirt tracks, lined with trees and the sound of summer humming on the wind. It felt like our special time, and somehow, we both knew it. That these days were great days, ones to be treasured.

The seasons moved by and eventually I found I could ride. I was never going to be as one with a horse or as effective as Kathryn, but I could hold my own at Bloomsgorse. And at the time that's all I wanted. I didn't really jump; it was all riding on the flat. Yet I graduated to taking out the intermediate rides and eventually the time came when I did lead my first fast ride. I knew the woods and how long it took to get back to the yard from any given point, to be on time for an hour's ride.

I would spend more and more time at the yard in the forest, Kathryn and I also spent time away from the yard together; at the college we ran team-building events for the students. We were always short of female staff and willingly Kathryn would step in on secondment from Bloomsgorse. She would come out on three-day expeditions at Edale, walking, camping and gorge walking with my students. I can still vividly remember her immersing herself under water and rocks at Padley Gorge; we were becoming entwined by the waters of life. A joining was being sealed in the heart of the earth and the rocks that lined it.

I'd wanted my own horse for a while, and Zoë recommended Oliver, a seventeen hand hunter, part Percheron and part Irish

Draught. He was big and he was fast. He came to Bloomsgorse and I began riding him, we got on. There was a connection between us. Some horses find us, just like Strip found Kathryn; I know Oliver was meant for me. So, Zoë sold him to me, at a cheap price as he was prone to napping; he would shy away and try and return home. However, my granddad actually bought him, and when he was ill in hospital once, the nursing staff said he was mumbling incoherently about his supposed horse. He's fine, I told her, he does own a horse!

The weekend I paid my money over I took Oliver into the indoor school. I intended doing some canter transitions without stirrups. Heading round the top corner he bucked me off. Back on I got. The next thing I was on the floor again with three cracked ribs. I lost total confidence in him and myself. It took six months to get it back. He still napped and the only way to cure it was to give a tap on the bum with a crop, yet you then got a big buck, as Kathryn found out when he launched her into the straw bales in the school. But the confidence came again. And after that we never looked back. I still own him and he is at the family field in Blidworth, happy in his retirement.

A horse has a mind of its own. In the mountains in winter the untrained person can get caught out by avalanches and many an experienced mountaineer has died abseiling, but it's human error in the main. A mountain is not going to suddenly move twelve feet to the left and rush off at 20mph in the opposite direction if a leaf is a different colour to the one next to it. Or when a helicopter flies over it's not going to bolt through the woods.

There were many incidents at Bloomsgorse, nothing serious in the grand scheme of things. I fell off several times, I went straight over George's head on a hack, got thrown off Oliver, broke my fingers leading a pony on a ride. Piled into a tree when Alex shot home around a corner, got taken off with Peter; one horse I never rode again. A Harrier Jump Jet came low over the woods one day as a ride came up the hill to home, scattering horses and riders in all directions, except Nora who just stood and ate the grass, something she always did.

Kathryn gave evidence once in court for a case where a woman had fallen off a horse. She claimed the tack hadn't been fitted properly at Bloomsgorse. It was Kathryn's cool and logical assessment that helped send the case out without a penny being given. She later on expressed that she would have liked to have been a lawyer; she would have been exceptionally good at it.

Our dogs rode out with us, hounds and horses running free across the land, but those rides were not without risk. Otto nearly died on one ride, out on one of the trotting rides he was running around in the heather then came straight out and under TC, the horse I was on. A ball of brown and blood exploded in front of me as Otto tried to run out under TC's front feet in trot. The Bloomsgorse minibus rescued him and after an emergency vet visit, he recovered in time. Remme, Zoë's dog, also came close to the happy hunting grounds in the sky after running out in front of us as we went full pelt up one of the forest tracks. I looked behind me as she was spun out from under the horse's feet; she shook herself off and ran after us. But on the whole the dogs and horses got on well together.

And there was the social side, swimming pool parties at South Forest, the local leisure centre, barbeques at people's houses, meals on Saturday nights. Kathryn held a birthday party at her house, but was completely drunk by the time anyone arrived, and I can't remember what happened at the party apart from a large order of Kentucky Fried Chicken arriving at the door. Practical jokes were played: Calum, Zoë's son, would drive by and ring the doorbell in the early hours. On New Year's Day we would do the horses early and go to Scarborough to walk the dogs and eat chips by the sea.

We would host meals at each other's houses. Kathryn was a notoriously fussy eater, and as a child her dinners were mainly fish fingers or something on toast. So, when I hosted a chilli night all she ate was the rice. In later years chilli became one of her favourite meals. Just like her car accidents, her food choices were a source of amusement for the rest of us.

Bloomsgorse was everything; it took over my life completely. I was fully in, all paid up, and my life had changed beyond all recognition. I was still working at the college, yet it felt like that was now the 'unreal' life; the forest and its folk of horses and people had consumed me.

Fridays though were the best, not only because it was the day Kathryn and I rode. Calum, Zoë's son, who was also the farrier, came on Fridays to shoe at least nine or ten horses and ponies. Sometimes I would help him take the shoes off; mostly just make the tea and talk. Just sitting there on the yard, lazy sunny days listening to the sound of steel on steel, the smell of burned hoof; hiss of shoe being put on. They were magical days, great days. It was the time of Kathryn.

Looking back now it was the purest time. For when dark times come it's not money that we remember, it's not materials or goods that comfort us in the dread of the late hour. It's the happiness that we have experienced, the belonging we have felt at some point. Each of us will face the shutting out of the light. For some of us it's early, hopefully for most it's late in life with a full deposit of happy memories. The days in that forest with the people I met and the horses we rode, the dogs that ran with the pack. They were ample enough days to last a lifetime.

There's a picture in the office at Cross Lane. It's faded down one side, yet her smile is shining through. Kathryn is sat on Oliver in the indoor school at Bloomsgorse. She's just got back on after being thrown off him. He's still got the dapple of youth and she looks so alive. The world is alight in her eyes and Oliver is standing proud. We all have similar photographs of our loved ones to remind us of what life is all about: the capture of a loving moment. The moment of a life.

CHAPTER EIGHT

They Always Met at Eleven

Over the horizon, through dew
Of a morning blue to dazzle and wonder,
A rumble of thunder, a quixotic white.
In their splendour and truth.

We all think that our security and safety will last, yet change is the only real certainty in life. At Bloomsgorse she felt that she wasn't really going anywhere with her career, so with a heavy heart she felt she had to move on. She worked for a short time at a local racing yard, there she exercised and worked with race horses in training. It was short-lived however; for she refused to get on a horse she felt wasn't safe. It was then though, that the job came up as head girl at the Blankney Hunt in Lincolnshire, just outside of Newark in the village of Brant Broughton.

The rambling old country house housed the local vets with stables situated behind. Behind the stables were fields that the horses were turned out in and fields for the hounds. The hunt was run by the 'master' Margaret, who was employed to manage and run the hunt meets. Two or three grooms worked on a part-time basis to help out. The head girl was employed to manage the day-to-day yard work which included exercising the horses and running the yard. It was to be a hard life, steeped in history and tradition, a sometimes-brutal world. I remember visiting one day to see the hounds scavenging on a dead horse's hind leg. At times the countryside and nature in general can be a cruel mistress.

Kathryn was settling in at her new job, riding, exercising, mucking out and grooming. She was in her element now and her ability to ride well and effectively took on a new level. Margaret insisted that when they hunted Kathryn would ride alongside her, would jump what she jumped, which included some big dykes, typical of the flat Lincolnshire countryside. They hunted on a Thursday and Saturday, meeting at eleven in the morning, and rode the day out into the dusk. On the wide ringing plains, where the fields stretch as far as the eye sees; Kathryn became the horsewoman she was meant to be.

It was the time before the Hunting Act of 2004. It was a job that courted controversy in all corners of the land. The arguments over the rights and wrongs are deep-seated, the rural community argues it's vital to the well-being of the countryside; it supports feed merchants through to farriers. But what benefit does hunting actually achieve? How does an old or injured fox actually pose a threat to livestock? By eating rabbits, foxes save the British crop farmer £7 million each year, one single fox can be worth up to £900 in its lifetime in revenue to farmers.

Hunting is seen by some as the quintessential image of the English countryside. The horses with riders in red coats atop, galloping through stubble and trotting through lazy smoky autumn villages. And to some it's the very essence of the raping of the land, mankind's cruel ability to disregard life and nature at its best. The very presence of hunting in our culture will always sit uncomfortably in our society. Like it or not though, hunting is a business that is pivotal to life in the countryside, and it's a link to the past, of tradition and heritage.

Kathryn did what she always did. She was paid to do a job and she did it to the best of her ability. She loved the land and nature, but was only too aware of the reputation hunting had. Publicly she would never get into a discussion about the rights and wrongs of hunting foxes with dogs, although privately she agreed with it. The hunt hardly ever caught a fox and when they did it was either old or injured; and death was fast and quick. Maybe though hunting is now out of time with modern society, the days of an English gentleman like Oates riding out to hounds sits awkwardly with current thinking.

Both of us took it for what it is – part of our history, of our country, our community. Captain Oates was a big rider and missed his horses and his hunting whilst in his tent deep in Antarctica. 'Oates took the lead in the conversation. He told us about his home and horses,' Lt Evans commented later. Sue Limb referred to the 'quintessentially English tradition . . . the hunting and the horses' in her book about Captain Oates.

The hunting I saw was that of bold riders, riders with more confidence than was sometimes prudent. It was not always about riding skill, it was about the ability to have pure bottle to go over very big fences or large dykes. There were those that obviously had huge amounts of money, spending every penny they had to ride out on the fenland, and those that had none. They rode for the love of their bond with an animal, whether horse or hound or for the nature in the fields.

She realised though that she would never spend her career in hunting:

Horses [are] my passion, my career – although not in present yard. I have an overwhelming desire to do things my way – so tired of other people's strange ideas and methods.

She was beginning to find her own feet in the equine world, she was confident on the outside but inside she was insecure and lacked belief in herself. It would be many years before she would develop the self-belief that she was known for in later years.

After we had started dating properly, I would drive out to meet her at Brant Broughton sometimes, just to say hello and sometimes to ride out with her. She worked long days, starting at about seven in the morning, with a break between noon and two. Then finishing about five in the afternoon, yet mostly later. Lunch times were spent watching *Neighbours* in the communal living room or shopping. On one particular lunch I picked her up and we drove into Newark, and it was on the way back that our life together nearly ended when I underestimated the speed at which a lorry was coming towards us on the A17. On overtaking one lorry I realised we had run out of space. The little Golf GTI was on the edge of the rev limiter, I looked at Kathryn and she had closed her eyes. I turned the wheel and in a wail of horns we escaped. Both of our hands were shaking when we stopped at the pub for a drink. It was the last time I would ever overtake again without being sure. More people die on the roads each year than they do climbing or riding.

Most times though my visits were less stressful. We enjoyed the early beginnings of our relationship; halcyon days in the flat lands of Lincolnshire. We would take Jack for a walk, or ride out down the flat deserted Lincolnshire country lanes. Even now, when I want to feel Kathryn closer to me, I will take the new Golf GTI (red, as the original one – which Kathryn wrote off in the end) over to Brant Broughton and drive the lanes we used to ride and walk.

The annual hunt ball was always a special night, it was a chance for people who spend their lives in mucking-out clothes and jodhpurs to get dressed up. Each year at the end of the hunting season a huge marquee would be put up in a farmer's field, from all around friends and supporters of the hunt would don their best dresses and black ties. Then as the sun dropped, they would gather to celebrate and enjoy the night until it rose again. Kathryn especially liked dressing up; she never got the chance to any other time. As is the same with all people who work with horses.

It was whilst at Brant Broughton she confessed to the most terrifying thing she ever did on horseback; ride flat out over a course of point-to-point jumps. Point to point is amateur racing for hunt horses over large fences. And the Blankney horses sometimes took part. On a cold winter day, I accompanied her in the yard lorry to the Northern Racing School; it was only a training session. Even so, it was hard to watch, never mind ride. On a fresh thoroughbred hunting horse Kathryn went flat out over jump after jump. Back in the lorry heading home she looked ashen-faced; 'Never again,' she whispered to me. I nodded my agreement.

She stuck to her word and didn't ride point to point again. They still needed exercising though; this she was happy doing. As was I, for sometimes I would join her as we rode headlong round the vast fields at full tilt. The eleven o'clock meets carried on in their finery; but it was to be Oliver that Kathryn said gave her best-ever day on a horse. After she had left the Blankney she carried on hunting occasionally, sometimes with the South Notts, sometimes with High Peak in Derbyshire.

Oliver was a horse that I like to think Oates would have liked. On a hunt he had to be ridden at the front; there was no holding back; no half measures. Oliver had no fear when moving fast over open country. He would hear the hounds and tremble with excitement, desperate to fly for the chase. He would jump anything and gave the impression he would ride into hell if you asked him to. He went over dykes like they didn't exist, the faster he was going the safer you felt. He would go around corners like he was on rails.

It was in the hills of the high peak that she and Oliver rode. One day in Derbyshire in an autumn glow they became as one. Oliver the horse he was meant to be, and Kathryn the rider to ride him. It was not without mishap, as with all great adventures; he jumped a five-bar gate from standstill as Kathryn was on the floor closing the gate, disappearing riderless after the hunt. That was a day of legends in the grassy sun and rolling stone walls, the kind of day Captain Oates would have liked to come home to. To ride like there is no tomorrow. Like there is no past. For sometimes when the wind is right, and the air sits on the ground like an English country smell of golden leaves burned in the autumn sun, there is a way to the day that is like no other.

CHAPTER NINE

With This Ring

It's not just love,
There is more.
More than being.

The sound of steel hooves on tarmac is the most distinct of sounds. It's a sound of the old ways meeting new ways. It's a rhythmic beat through history; it calls out the time before, the time now, and the time to come. It was the sound that heralded Kathryn's arrival at St Peter's Church for our wedding. The sound beats through me like a drum, each and every time I hear shoe-clad hooves stamping down; taking me back to that time.

Kathryn had moved in to my place bit by bit, time by time. She would stay after work, sometimes getting into bed with me until I fell asleep. She would go home, she sometimes stayed over. The staying became more frequent. Her friendship was always there, it was the friendship that stood the test of everything. It was Kathryn who came around on New Year's Eve for a fillet steak dinner on the old oak table, slow candles heralding a new year. It was Kathryn who picked me up from the pub on the way to a yard party.

We rode the lonely deep long lanes of Lincolnshire, deserted save the two of us. Our horses' breath rising in slow steam mixing with ours. We rode hunters born to the chase, tall rangy horses that would stay the length of the day. The wind never blew cold across the expanse of fenland, we were happy in our pair. Content in the warmth of the trot. Little did I know that years later I would drive down the same lanes, alone in a red car; remembering. They were carefree times, riding and talking.

Times of arguing, normally over the horses. Once on a pleasure ride in Derbyshire; Kathryn was so competent on a forward-going horse (one that needs no urging forward) and I wasn't. I'd get ill-tempered and lose my patience. Arguments out with the hunt, we'd left the ride and headed back; or at least I tried to, for Oliver was being a pain. Kathryn knew what to do; yet I wouldn't listen. The arguments were a normal part of being a couple; for they send you away from each other for a while only to bring the two of you back together again. I wish there had been another way to get to the coming back bit without the argument. Especially now.

The hand of fate finally played its cards on a normal nondescript day, the earth and the moon aligned and the sun nodded in agreement. I stood outside the large overbearing college building and pulled the phone out of my pocket.

'Hello!'

'Hi, what are you up to?' I said.

'Not a lot, just mucking out Boy's stable. You?'

'Just finished a class and nipped out to call you. What are you doing later?'

'We've got two to exercise this afternoon, then start the afternoon jobs. Why? What were you thinking?'

'I was wondering what you were planning on doing much later?' I said, and there was a long pause. 'Kind of rest of life later stuff?'

The phone had never felt so awkward . . .

'Well, I don't know! What do you have in mind? I'm open to suggestions . . .' she said.

'Let's ride Friday at Bloomsgorse and maybe chat about it . . .'

'OK,' she said, 'that would be great; see you there . . .'

In Sherwood Forest we rode out on a Friday afternoon once more. I took TC and Kathryn rode one of the trekking horses. There was an awkward tension in the trees, certainly for me. Kathryn just seemed to be smiling through her hands and her being. The forest relaxed me as I looked at her and saw the soft hands that showed no tension.

In the heart of the forest is a deer glade next to a small pond.

'Let's stop here,' I said.

By the little island of water, I got off my horse. Kathryn looked down at me with a quizzical but warm look.

'Fancy joining me?' I asked.

'Yes, I will,' she replied.

Hesitation is the doom of all prospective marriage proposals, so like every man who had done the same I opted for haste. I dropped to one knee, conscious of my horse peering down at me.

'Will you marry me?' I asked as I produced my grandmother's engagement ring, a band of gold lit with rubies.

There was a magical moment whilst she gave me her answer without saying a word.

'Yes, I will,' she said. And she dropped to her knees and we kissed as two horses looked on as witnesses and the leaves fluttered in the summer breeze.

I don't remember the ride back to the stables. It's lost in the ground of the day.

Her parents needed to approve it, though; well, her father Ian did. I had rarely met them, so I was nervous when I called at their house. Tea was on the table and the strip lighting laughed at my nerves. The TV was still on when I asked Ian permission to marry their daughter. He smiled and gave his consent with no reservation. Her mum never said a word, just smiled also.

I know now that 12 January 2002 was the best day of my life. I like to think it was Kathryn's also. It was the day the mountain joined with the horse. The day everything that there is aligned.

Canon Warburton, an old-fashioned fire and brimstone vicar, asked us to attend meetings before the wedding. He gave no quarter in his warnings and advice about staying together. You got married and you stayed married, end of. If you didn't you would have to answer to him and God, pretty much in that order. (I think that's why I still feel married.)

Kathryn and her sister planned most of the wedding. Her list was written on one sheet of notepaper:

Wedding
Book church
Sort hymns, flowers, vows

My role came down to the cars, and the secret horse and carriage that Kathryn knew nothing about until the day. Seeing the way weddings are planned now, it was relatively simple and very cheap. Kathryn's dress was stunning, white and elegant, from a second-hand store, only worn once. The cakes were bought from Tesco and then embellished by her mum and friends. Sometimes less is more.

We bought her ring together in Nottingham, a plain yellow 18 ct gold band for the princely sum of £108.

The whole wedding was low key, just like the cakes. The highlight was the horse and carriage that carried Kathryn and her father to the church; her mum was ill and couldn't attend. I find this sad beyond words; that she was too ill to be with Kathryn on her greatest day. She would make the funeral years later though.

I don't recall anyone in the church; I don't remember all of the hymns apart from 'Jerusalem' and 'I vow to thee my country.' It seemed that we were the only two people there.

We didn't hang around with the photos outside church, with it being January; just stood in the church doorway and kissed. Then walked out as a married couple to the horse and carriage which carried us to the local swimming pool's car park, where we transferred to cars and headed to South Forest leisure centre for the meal and reception.

As is traditional I gave my wedding speech after the meal, I thanked those that had come and those that had been there for both of us. The main theme of my speech was for Kathryn, for I hold firm to the belief that she was and still is my angel, sent to help me on a dark night. We cut the cake together.

In the upstairs suite we prepared for the first dance, the first as husband and wife. It was the one thing I'd overlooked in the wedding preparations; the DJ didn't have 'Thunder Road' by Bruce Springsteen, so I asked for 'Stand by Me' instead, and we awkwardly danced to it. I'm still dancing to it. She did stand by me.

Dave ended up dancing on a table with no top on; he's still single. Kathryn and I went home. It was the best day and the best night. It was enough to last a lifetime.

Our honeymoon was to be the longest holiday we ever had together, six nights at Armathwaite Hall in the Lake District. It's a cliché but it was the best time of my life, we lived in glorious splendour. There were only six other guests because it was low season. The dress code was strict and comfortingly old-fashioned; I don't think it's the same now. There's something sad in the passing of old ways into new, which aren't always for the better.

Although we had no intention of riding, after a few days away we were restless for horses. We looked through the brochures in the hotel and found a trekking centre near Blencathra. Kathryn had actually packed her riding chaps. We booked a two-hour trek that went out on the lanes and bridleways around Great Mell Fell. I don't think the instructor expected much of us; we both played down what we had done with horses, especially Kathryn. So, it was with some surprise to the instructor when she found out we could both ride. The ride was glorious; we rode further than was normal because we could ride our horses properly. It was riding that brought us together, so it was fitting that we rode on our honeymoon.

We wandered the deserted fells in the day. Every night there would be a different six-course menu; we would sit in the lounge by the big open fire and spend ages deciding what to have. There was a sorbet (Kathryn always had mine), a consommé, then the main course and dessert. Men had to wear a shirt, jacket and tie, women an evening dress. Kathryn's long red dress lit up her subtle lipstick in the glow of the hotel's fire. We rode, we wandered the towns and we began a life together. It was at Honister Pass that I took my favourite picture of Kathryn. She has the cheekiest smile in that photo, half covered by her hand. You can just see her rings on her finger. We had just been up on the fells above Buttermere. It's the most precious image in the world to me. The best of times.

We drove home stopping off at Bloomsgorse on the way, to see the forests and fields and friends that helped to bring us together. They were all there. Then back to our little mews house that was to be our home as a married couple.

Being part of a team can be hard work. For that's what marriage is, being a two-person army and facing what life throws at you. And, like all teams you fall out, argue, and have different agendas at times. Yet, and it's a big yet, you stand by each other. You never ever leave each other. Sometimes this is hard. But you defend the colours of your marriage. Kathryn and I had big ups and we had big downs, in the early days mainly due to my selfishness or lingering depression. Sometimes they were just standard couple tiffs. Sometimes chasms opened up between us, yet we crossed them as a couple. We argued over silly things, me putting her socks in the dryer or not putting the right rubbish in the bin. I would give anything to argue about shrinking her socks in the tumble dryer now, to see her frown in disapproval.

It wasn't perfect, but it was ours. We would go away twice a year for a short holiday. Kathryn's job meant she couldn't take a great deal of time off. My job too created time limitations. Over one two-year period I was overseas for several periods of weeks at a time leaving Kathryn to look after our home and life. So, we did the best we could. Mainly we went back to the Lakes.

> . . . dropped Steve off at Honister to run back over Dale Head, Hindscarth and Robinson. First solo lakes walk, not very high but fabulous day – more like September. Amazing colours, very still and sunny. Practised navigation and looking up features on the map. Good times.

One time whilst staying at Buttermere we planned to wild camp high on the fells; yet the prospect of tent life on holiday didn't appeal to me, and Kathryn preferred the warmth of the pub:

> We had planned to wild camp but due to dodgy weather and being a bit worn out we booked two more nights at The Bridge. The ascent to Bleaside Tarn was a little slippery and it started to rain making the final part up to Red Pike a little unpleasant. We sheltered on the north ridge and had lunch then walked head on into driving rain towards High Stile, but it stopped and we had fabulous views once the clouds cleared. Bit of a slippery descent down but we made it back to the hotel where we took over half the drying room!

We dreamed of going to Montana on a ranching holiday; we always talked about it over the years. The big skys of the beaches at Cromer had to suffice though; Kathryn's parents had a holiday chalet there. We would walk the dogs on the beach, eat fish and chips and get a Chinese from the takeaway. It was normal couple holiday dreams. But also magical in a sea-rolling-in, footsteps-in-the-sand way. Situated a short walk from the sea cliffs the sound of the sea sounded like a beacon calling us there to forget horses and expeditions.

A stone's throw from the chalet also lay the Royal Cromer golf course; we would wander its fringes on the cliff top, then one day Kathryn suggested I play it. The two of us wandered the fairways; she was caddy to the player in me. On top of the course the mist came down, near the lighthouse. A group of four asked us where the thirteenth hole was; the mist was so heavy they couldn't see it. Neither could we. But we will play it anyway, Kathryn said. Practical as ever, she announced she would find the green, and then when she was next to the hole, she would let me know. She walked off into the mist. Then she shouted: 'I'm standing by the hole holding the flag!'

It was my one and only authentic shot, the shot I was always meant to play. It was a shot that went home to Kathryn, the angel of the morning. Next, Kathryn shouted out through the mist, 'It's landed next to the hole!' The group of four cheered us.

Most of the shots we play in life land in a bunker or go wayward into the woods. Yet once in a while we make par, or even hit one under par. As we play the field, the field that is marriage, we take the rough with the smooth and aim to get around the eighteen holes in one piece, and then home to the club house.

Golf is a patient game, as is living with someone. Over years of wear and tear things break down, marriage is not immune to this. We now live in a throwaway society: if it breaks, buy a new one. So, people often give up on marriage and throw it away. Yet, stuff used to get mended if it broke; you worked at it, fixed it and made it good for a few more years. Then you fixed it again. But you have to believe that what you have is worth fixing. Worth mending; that's the key to marriage, the key to lasting happiness and true love. That was married life with Kathryn, we broke it sometimes then we fixed it, because the thing we had was priceless.

I wasn't the perfect husband, I was good at large gestures but not the simple everyday stuff. I thought problems could be solved by flowers or a note saying I was sorry. Sometimes I was a rock Kathryn threw her love at. A lot of the time I was tired from the depression and struggled with life, and this affected Kathryn. Something I was acutely aware of, yet Kathryn bore it with her outstanding grace and love.

Have a good trip, secure in the knowledge that all is OK at home. Remember what's important – that we need to take time to understand and care for each other. We are both so busy, it would be easy to not bother about the little things – the kind gesture, the hug, or the 'well done' or 'I'm proud of you', but these are the things that are important, and moments to be cherished. Sorry to have rambled on a bit!

All my love, Kathryn xxx

The years drifted by in what seems like long seconds now, a weekend in Warwick, three days on a canal boat and returning visits to Cumbria. Kathryn never complained about the rain and the uphill wanderings that seemed to occupy most of our holidays:

A long and tiring day with difficult exposed descent off Fleetwith Pike at the end but fabulous panoramic views of many mountains and a well-deserved ice cream at Sykes Farm Café.

Half-days here and there summed up our leisure time together. In truth though, we spent too little time together, away from our careers. I was either on an icecap or Kathryn was looking after horses. Even meals out were rare, dinners were reasons to celebrate a birthday or our anniversary.

I went away with friends on occasion and early on Kathryn did her own expedition to Iceland with all the friends from Bloomsgorse. Our two worlds crossed as she rode horses across the volcanic plains of the tundra.

Steve,

Thanks for the kit and expertise. Thanks for the time and patience. Thanks for the inspiration. Thanks for looking after Jack. Love you, miss you. Take care, Kathryn xxx.

Yet like most couples, 'together time' was mainly spent on the sofa after tea; *Ice Road Truckers* on in the background. It was normal married life.

At the end of each day, Kathryn always said it was the best part. Lights would be out and the curtains shut; we would be two spoons curled up in bed together.

'I've got you,' she would say.

'I've got you too,' I would reply.

Then she would squeeze my hand.

Our marriage worked, I think, because we both accepted who each other really was. Kathryn without horses would not have been Kathryn, and I wouldn't have been me without the expeditions. We each had our own life and passion; take that away or try and restrict it, and the life in the other person's eyes goes out. We never even talked about it. It was written into us before we met.

Pride of place among all the pictures on the walls of the house is a print of Ran Fiennes and Charlie Burton at the North Pole signed by all the members of the Transglobe Expedition. Not because of the image, but because of what's written by Ran in the bottom left-hand corner; 'Kathryn, best of luck with your engagement.' To me this is an acknowledgement of all the hard work that marriage takes; every day is an expedition, every day brings new challenges and new excitement. It's not easy, but the rewards at the end of the journey make everything worthwhile.

I like to park near to the swimming pool when I go into town; walking back to the car I make sure I have some loose change and hope the gate to the church is open. For if the gate's open, then so is the church. I light a candle and remember Kathryn. As well as the field it's the place I could stay in forever. I remember a time when just the two of us stood side by side in the church, and it felt as though no one else was there. Sometimes I just go to church and sit there in peace, and to see a day long ago, feel the peace of the memory that lingers in the walls. The picture that was captured by the seats and handmade cushions, the candles that remember in their flame a girl in a white dress. A man stood proud next to her in his best suit. And one ring that bound them both, as the horse stood on the road outside waiting.

CHAPTER TEN

The Polar Challenge

Give me that strength back that was given in the beginning,
When the smoke rose fresh over the mountains and all
Truth was just a step away.

There is always a delay as the signal goes into space and back down to earth. I would listen to the distinct Iridium dial tone and wait. She would be sat on the sofa, or have just rushed in from the yard. Or be at the field. The tea was in the oven, or just ready. Just like going to bed at night and holding each other, it was the best part of the day on an expedition; knowing the dogs and the horses were OK. Knowing she was OK. Just knowing she was there.

The expedition time with Kathryn had begun in earnest, the power of our two worlds generated the will and horsepower propelled us both to the frozen south. I would be at the forefront and she would be the support. The fires of home would melt the ice and distance that led to Antarctica.

It says in the ancient scriptures that God made Australia last; I politely disagree. I think Antarctica was made last. For there is nothing there; it's as if God had run out of paint; only had white left – hence the snow. And there are no animals in the interior;

he'd run out of them apart from a few penguins that he pencilled in round the coast.

Scott declared it an awful place, the point on the earth's surface where all lines of longitude and latitude converge. Ninety degrees south. A spot in the snow. Men have laboured and risked everything to get to the South Pole first, for fame, for fortune, for geographical discovery and for immortality. Scott and his men found it on their return journey from the pole having been beaten by Norwegian Roald Amundsen who arrived at the South Pole on 14 December 1911. Here is not the place for me to recount the full details of Scott's last expedition, yet like many boys having been told the tale I have been fascinated by the epic trip since hearing it. As Kathryn became passionate about horses, reading everything she could on them, I read everything I could find on Scott and polar exploration. Last letters written from a frozen tent, deeds of sacrifice haunted me; the humanity that expired in the frozen lands ghosted me in my dreams.

Otto wasn't dreaming of the South Pole as he chased a squirrel in the park, but I still was. I was thirty-three and felt like my expedition ambitions were drifting away; the news that morning announced the youngest person to reach the South Pole. In a few hours' time I was due to be working with my students on the outdoor course. The phone rang in my pocket; 'Someone's just become the youngest to walk to the South Pole . . .' Kathryn said.

'I know, just twenty-three years old.' Was my disconsolate reply.

'Well, why not beat it?' Came her reply.

'How am I at thirty-three supposed to become the youngest?!'

'Take your students . . . they will be the youngest; and also, no one has taken students to Antarctica; it'll be a double first. And don't shout at me!'

Otto never did catch his squirrel; yet we strode home with winged angels at our feet. With that feeling that something important has just happened, and if you don't chase it down it will vanish. Like ice it will melt away unless you can freeze the moment just long enough to act.

I walked into the principal's office at West Notts FE College and said I would like to walk a team of students from the Hercules Inlet on the west coast of Antarctica to the geographic South Pole. Di McEvoy-Robinson listened, and said, 'OK, put a proposal down on paper, and I'll think about it.' There began the Polar Challenge.

Proposals went in and they weren't blocked; Di gave permission to carry out a feasibility study to take two students, both under eighteen and two staff members to the pole. The accepted route was from Hercules Inlet, past the Theil Mountains and then across the plateau to the pole itself. The money was the biggest hurdle. To get the ball rolling I persuaded my mum to write a letter to the college saying that as a local business person she would pledge £28 000. She never intended to give the money, yet it did the trick and reassured the college that the money could be raised. We were looking at that amount per person. There is no fuel on the continent and everything has to be flown in – fuel, food and equipment – in a chartered Russian Ilyushin organised by Antarctic Logistics Expeditions.

Even so, the Polar Challenge felt as if it was over before it had begun as I sat on the Greenland icecap with Ian Forsdike in the spring of 2003. Kathryn's note had beamed hope and optimism.

Saturday 26 April 2003

Dear Steve, I hope everything's going well – you should be in Greenland by now. I wonder if you started crossing today or just camped and got organised . . .

I had set out to cross Greenland's ice sheet once more from east to west with Ian, who wanted to be the first person with a disability to do so, but after three days he was exhausted. His heart was willing but the whiteness in the cold beat his body. It was another failure to my mind, even though I knew it was the right decision. Why would the college back a 650-mile walk to the South Pole if I couldn't get one person 350 miles across Greenland?

I made a satellite call home to Kathryn as Ian was treated in the local hospital in Ammassalik.

Later Kathryn wrote:

I know you must be terribly disappointed, but you did the right thing, the only thing you could have done. I wish you had got across – maybe next year.

As I drove back home to Kathryn, I wondered how the college would view my latest disaster.

'It shows that you won't put personal ambition ahead of the students' safety,' Di announced, so in terms of the South Pole trip the Greenland failure had been a success. Life can astound us in the face of its quirks and shadows of fate. The echoes of chance, of knowing our place in time and that it's right.

I advertised for participants for the Polar Challenge, canvassing students on my Outdoor Education course; I needed two students plus a reserve. Since I had returned to college after my depression I now ran a course training students to be leaders in the outdoors. On a two-year course we trained young people to become leaders in climbing, walking, canoeing and caving. It was a fantastic course and the place from which to recruit potential explorers. Even so, we didn't get many applicants, only three, mainly because they had to raise £5000 as a contribution to the expedition. I approached Gary Dodds, a fellow lecturer, and asked if he'd like to join the team. Gary was an avid and experienced mountain leader. He jumped at the chance. Over tea each night Kathryn and I planned the selection process: a 24-hour endurance walk, team-building challenges, and an interview process with the Young Explorers' Trust. The final test was a meal at our house; for Kathryn thought it was good we got to know the candidates socially, as they would be sharing a tent with me for several weeks. In many aspects the most revealing part of the selection process was the meals, nothing contrived or hidden. The devil was in the detail with Kathryn.

After several weeks we had a team, including a student on the learning support section at college. Gary had recommended Robert. I was told that he couldn't read nor write, had been in trouble at school; I felt he needed a break. According to Robert, one of his teachers at school had said he would never amount to anything and he wanted to prove them wrong.

The plan was simple really. Train the team to be able to walk to the South Pole. Dan and I would walk the full distance from the coast. Gary and Robert would fly in to the Last Degree – a shorter duration trip and sixty nautical miles from the pole, yet still physically demanding. We would team up and walk the last section together. The two-year training plan was geared to going to Antarctica in the 2004/2005 season so we would be away for December and January: Scotland in winter was planned early on, then crossing the Greenland icecap, then consolidation in Norway during the summer. Also a risk assessment in Antarctica itself needed to be carried out, ideally before the Greenland trip. Then the expedition itself. How hard could it be?

It was hard, yet looking back now the challenge happened at the right time and in the right place. The fundraising was the biggest obstacle. With hard work and providence, we chipped away and the funds slowly came in. Lots of local companies gave money for the opportunity to be involved in something special. I spent the first year writing reports for the college and getting the ball rolling, and after time the college with the support of Di realised it might actually happen. Yet, the risk assessment of the trip presented a problem; we needed to do a site visit to satisfy the college, for all external visits needed an onsite check, Antarctica being no different. A local man who had been to the pole with his wife ran trips there, and was planning to walk the last two degrees in the 2002/2003 season. The last two degrees being a walk over the two degrees of latitude, from eighty-eight degrees south to ninety degrees south; where the South Pole lies. A total distance of 120 nautical miles. Taking the plunge, I used all my savings when he offered me a chance to be his assistant leader on the expedition. Kathryn and I agreed it was an excellent opportunity to do a risk assessment, plus I was also hedging my bets for if our trip didn't come off then I would at least get to the South Pole.

Funding for the Polar Challenge took flight when out of the blue a TV production company telephoned the office. Windfall Films were filming the Royal Institution Christmas Lecture; which happened to be about Antarctica. Professor Lloyd Peck from the British Antarctic Survey was giving the lecture. The film company wanted to involve an actual South Pole expedition, follow the training and actual expedition itself. It would go live on Channel 4 on Boxing Day 2004. They wanted to know if we could help. All sponsorship problems ceased to exist from this point on. As Napoleon apparently commented about his generals: 'I would rather have a general who was lucky than one who was good.' We were lucky. There was no other explanation. Or maybe there was?

Our expedition to the South Pole was now to be covered extensively by the education press and Ran Fiennes agreed to be Patron once more. We'd met not on an icecap but in the electrical department of a high-street store in Nottingham. I'd heard on the local radio he was appearing on a Saturday afternoon; Dyson had sponsored one of his expeditions. So, he was there in the store surrounded by Dysons.

Seeing there was no one with him I took the chance to introduce myself.

'Hello Ran, my name's Steve Bull,' I said nervously.

'Ah hello; not *the* Steve Bull the explorer?' Ran replied.

In one fell swoop my nerves vanished.

Those words felt like the greatest compliment I could have been given in my expedition career. We proceeded to spend the whole afternoon talking expeditions, watching the rugby on the department's TV screens. In a light-hearted moment I mentioned the Hoover display we were stood in, and Ran instantly said: 'Don't mention Hoover, Steve! I'm sponsored by Dyson! Not Hoover.'

I talked about Kathryn and her horses and he talked about his wife Ginny and her cattle. And he was totally encouraging of the Polar Challenge. Years later he would also support the Fuchs Foundation trips to Antarctica.

On a cold, frosty morning Kathryn dropped me off at the Thornewill's house in Nottinghamshire. It was a hard goodbye, especially for Kathryn. It was so cold that day that the Land Rover door froze; as I headed south she spent an age trying to shut the door.

The trip to the South Pole where I was assistant leader was a massive learning curve for me, and a personal disaster. The team was an interesting mix of people wanting a personal adventure including Ellen MacArthur's business partner; who during the trip taught me lots about fundraising and public relations. Invaluable lessons for the coming year. After landing at eighty-eight degrees south we moved off on the trek to the pole. We spent some time acclimatising, for even though the altitude is about 11 000 feet (3500 metres) above sea level, due to the latitude the effects can be greater. In layman's terms this is due to the spinning of the earth and the increased effect it has at the ends of the earth.

I was pushing myself hard, helping one of the other participants pull his sledge. After only three days in I became ill, eventually forcing a camp. Following phone calls to the base at Patriot Hills, then the only private seasonally occupied camp in Antarctica, it was decided that I was too ill to continue. If we could have waited for a few more days to acclimatise then maybe I could have continued. It was a gloriously short and pathetic attempt after all the years I had wanted to walk to the pole. In tears on a call from the middle of nowhere to Kathryn I also thought that our own polar challenge would be over. And I just wanted to be home with her, whilst the rest of the team carried on.

Where to start? Steve's not going to make it to the South Pole. He has to be flown back to Patriot Hills suffering from altitude sickness (I think although the statement issued states 'illness compounded by altitude and extreme cold'). I'm not worried about that so much as that he'll be devastated. So much love for him, I don't know where to put it all.

Kathryn had hit the nail on the head; it was devastation. When you want something so badly it feels as if all your happiness rests on the realisation of a particular goal. When in reality the source of our happiness in life rests solely with the ones we love; at times in those years wanting to achieve my expedition goals and personal dreams I sometimes forgot that and let my ambitions to reach the pole take priority. Even though she wanted me back home, she also wanted the same success I did, because she knew that if the restless spirit in me could be tamed then I would be a better person to live with.

Steve rang. Very upset. Didn't know what to say except he's done right and how much I love him. Rang off in tears. Wanted so much to hold him and make everything OK, but he's so far away. Even when he's back all I can do is be here, must concentrate on next time, Greenland and South Pole 2004/2005.

So much love. Hope message I sent is of some comfort in a small way. Much love.

I can't remember the message. But I do remember not feeling so alone with her in my life when I was waiting on the Polar Plateau. Even though it was a matter of weeks, I hated being away, I hated the ice and snow and just wanted to be on the plane heading home to Kathryn and all that was home.

The doctors both at Patriot Hills and in hospital at Punta checked me out. I was diagnosed with exhaustion and an infection; was reassured that the right decision had been made. That didn't make it any easier for Kathryn waiting for me back at home:

19th Jan 7 a.m. All I want to do is be with Steve. I don't want to be nice to clients and be responsible. I want to drop everything and go.

I flew back and within two weeks we headed to Armathwaite Hall; actually, going to Antarctica helped me put life in some sort of perspective, as I still suffered from depression. The white desert mirrored my mind it seemed, the open vastness helped equal out the darkness of my soul. But it was Kathryn who provided the anchor to keeping the depression at bay. Sometimes even her presence couldn't fight the illness, but for now the darkness was shut out by the light.

Life and death roll on together, whether in this country or another country, and our little movements across the ice and through the fields of home mean nothing compared to the love we feel and try to give.

On return to the college I was greatly reassured by Di's take on it. 'Well, at least we know now that the students can be rescued if there's a problem.' I was also put full-time on the planning of the expedition; my role was now to make it happen.

My risk assessment trip to Antarctica had made me re-evaluate the trip logistics and overall plan. Having been there and seen how fragile the weather windows were and the implications, I decided to drop the plan for two team members to walk all the way and meet the other two at the Last Degree: there were too many risks. Now all four would walk the last degree of latitude to the pole. The team changed also, as Dan pulled out due to not being able to raise the money he needed. Carl stepped up to take his place, and joined Robert for the student team. James was the reserve in case neither one could make the final trip.

Next, it was full steam ahead for the training trip to Greenland. Kathryn as usual wrote and left a note in my passport.

20 April 2004

Dear Steve,

I wanted you to know how proud I am of you, and how lucky I feel to have you. You have achieved so much and been through so much – your strength of mind is such that many could only wish for.

Remember that I'm thinking of you whilst you're out there in your tent. I'll be with you and I'll be here waiting when you come home. I'm sure that success is waiting for you – you deserve it.

Take care, All my love, Kathryn xxx

Her notes kept me going, they were a link to home and all that mattered; for there is no point going away if there's nothing or no one to come back to. She gave me the purpose to follow my ambition and dreams. So, with love and hope in my heart I headed to the ice once more.

Carl, James and I joined an existing group who had booked

with a private guiding company for the expedition. Before the trip Gary and I had decided that he and Robert would not attempt the icecap crossing; this was due mainly to not 'over-phasing' Robert and keep him enthused for the main trip itself. It was my third attempt, following my first expedition in 1996 and the one with Ian in 2002. Paul Rose was leading his team of clients, and I my team; it was logical for us to share a tent. Paul had worked for the British Antarctic Survey, was an accomplished polar veteran; by comparison I felt I had done very little. Yet we got on well in our small tent, sharing the jobs and looking after our own little teams. Yet again events didn't quite go to plan. Unseasonably warm weather meant the snow was damp, deep and impossible to pull pulks in for long distances, and it wasn't forecast to change. After several days inching westwards, both Paul and I concluded that it was unlikely we could cross without risking running out of food and fuel. Carl was distraught, he was adamant we could cross. Yet, my decision had to be final. (This would be a pivotal point in Carl's career; he would use his ambition as his driving force later, going on to cross Greenland several times.) Once again, the powers that be at the college backed the decision to turn around in Greenland; student welfare had to come first.

It was another call to Kathryn to say we had not achieved our aim and ambition. Kathryn was always outwardly positive. This was one of her outstanding qualities, that whatever negative thoughts she had, she very rarely expressed them. Although at times living with me, she had no choice but to say her piece. Whilst all these trips were going on, she kept calm and lived her life with horses. She supported me to the ends of the earth; I in turn supported her life with the horses and gave her freedom. Yet, it felt little compared to the support she gave.

Finally, in the summer the whole team moved to Norway for final training. We sailed from North Shields accompanied by the camera crew from Windfall, arriving in Bergen. Through tunnels made as if by the dwarves of Tolkien, and valleys carved by Thor himself we threaded our way north to the Jostedalsbreen icecap. The final ice team comprising of myself, Gary, Robert and Carl and we were also joined by two other lecturers. We spent a week on the icecap testing all the kit and systems we would use in Antarctica. It was a happy team who returned to England. The icing on the cake was the Young Explorers' Trust's approval following a two-hour interview in London that examined the trip's planning in minute detail. It was after this meeting that the college met the shortfall in funding. After two years we had raised £150 000, trained a novice team of two students from scratch and reached the point where we felt able to walk to the South Pole as a self-contained unit.

Our attempt to get to the South Pole was the culmination of two years of hard work, luck and faith. Looking back now, it was also the recognition that being in the right time and place is a gift. In the years to come I would speak to many schools and colleges that wanted to take a team of students to Antarctica and the South Pole, yet none has achieved it at the time of writing. The Polar Challenge at West Notts College happened because several key people bought into the dream: to show people that anything is possible. The college's motto was 'aspire and achieve' and putting two students at the end of the earth surely demonstrated that. They also backed a maverick card in me.

When I flew home from the risk assessment trip, Kathryn wrote in her diary that she couldn't wait to get in the car and drive to Heathrow. On a plane over the English Channel I couldn't wait to land at Heathrow. As she parked up her parents' estate car, I walked through arrivals. I'd not slept for two days; I was tired and grumpy, whilst she was anxious to know I was happy to see her. How could I not be?

'Hey you!' she said smiling, dressed in her usual jeans and T-shirt.

'Hey you too!' I replied, still in expedition kit.

'Missed me?'

'What do you think? Of course, I have; I love you!'

'I love you too! Let's go home . . .'

I wish now that I was still in that plane, and down on the ground somewhere was Kathryn waiting for me.

CHAPTER ELEVEN

Kathryn's Cross Lane

She arrived just after lunch time on a Friday,
Yet it was still called day five in heaven,
In honour of the Boss's epic seven-day universe built,
Scratch built, made by memory. And done well.

I would wait on the yard having groomed Oliver, half a mind on snow and ice, half on how badly I had brushed my grey horse. He wasn't so much as grey, more like the colour of dirty moraine ice. As always Kathryn was late and still down the fields. Impatient as ever I would walk through the outdoor school and onto the lane that leads down the side of the fields to see if she was on her way up yet. Most times she was not. Yet, sometimes she was a figure at the bottom of the lane, a barrow full of empty feed buckets in front of her and Ollie on lead rope behind her. This was Kathryn, on her beloved yard, in dark blue over trousers, red coat and grey woolly hat. And black woolly gloves with straw embedded in them.

She always used to get on board Ollie via her Land Rover, leading Ollie to the front of the defender she would stand on the bumper and get one foot in the stirrup. As Ollie walked off, she would climb up and settle into his saddle. It was effective and it was Kathryn. Then they would warm up in the collecting ring and get ready to compete. Dressage, show jumping or one-day eventing. She saved her money from clipping horses (shaving the hair of the horse's coat), doing other people's yards and odd jobs in order to compete. There is an album on the sofa still, of Kathryn and Ollie. Photos she collected and labelled. A keepsake that is priceless.

In 2003 as the Polar Challenge began Kathryn started her own dream; Cross Lane Equestrian. Initially she rented it off the owners; fourteen stables and approximately nine acres of grazing land. In the early days she would spend most of the time mucking out, as most people kept their horses in at night. So, it was feed, turn out the horses, muck out. Then bring them in again at night and feed. A hard life, a basic life; but one Kathryn loved. It was a start, the beginning of finding her true place.

If you drive south out of Mansfield past Harlow and Thieves Wood and head up the hill to Newstead Abbey there is a tree shaped like a table top. Take a left turn here and follow the little country lane with views of open fields with horses in, of deep forests, of ancient royal hunting grounds. Follow your nose and turn left down the little hill until you come to a low, long white building. Here is a little corner of the world far from the madness of life.

Cross Lane Equestrian stands on the top of a rise that descends down into the little valley of Fountaindale, where a little stream runs through. Little John fought Robin Hood for rite of passage across the stream in the legend that is the history of the woods. On a clear day from the outdoor school you see down the paddocks and into the little vale, then the eyes are drawn into the fields that rise on the other side; up to the old hunting house and low stables on the top of the hill. The scenery changes with the seasons, fields of crops standing still, weathered wind blowing through wheat. Tractors moving at the same pace they have always done.

Out of the outdoor sand school a little lane runs down the land, paddocks on the left and trees on the right. Down to the bottom fields where the bigger horses spend their time. Turn right into the fourteen-acre field and a walk to the top of the land brings a larger view; across to Harlow Wood. Here rider and horse head into the forest to forget the life that occupies the weekly treadmill.

Kathryn commented at the time that if there was one yard in the area she wanted for her own, then Cross Lane was the one. She's not an overly pretty yard in terms of her stables; they vary in size and form a sort of horseshoe around the yard. In the middle are old plastic huts where people store their feed and rugs. If she was to be likened to a ship, she'd be a little Corvette, built for a job in hand; tough, hardy and pretty indestructible. Her party piece is the land and grazing, and she never gets swamped in rain and mud. Her second biggest asset is the off-road hacking a little walk down the lane into the woods, where for as long as you want you can ride through the trees and paths and forget what century you're in.

It wasn't an easy road to Cross Lane for Kathryn, like all of us she was trying to find her true path in life.

What's important to me? Steve, family, dogs, horses – in no particular order, for different reasons and in different ways. Steve, the love of my life, my inspiration, my hero. I wish I could achieve even a fraction of what you have done. I'd love to share in your adventures but I lack experience and confidence and I think you might prefer to keep that part of your life separate.

Family – always there, always supportive – I just want to offer the same.

Dogs – devoted love and care for them – so utterly dependant on our care and so unashamedly adoring and affectionate, especially

Jack – always going to be special – because we only had each other. I could cry when I see your disappointed face when I leave you, imp, sorry.

Horses – my passion, my career. I know it's not an ideal world, but at least you can make the best of it. They deserve that much for their willingness to please (most of the time). I'd like to see the world, to achieve something for myself – a journey, not a holiday, like life itself. I need to prove to myself that I have the strength and the stamina to succeed, at the moment I am too unsure of myself to attempt anything.

So, what does the future hold? I have some aspects (hopefully) secure – the main being a happy home life – I am no longer searching for someone to share my life (although I would like to share it a little more!)

Words and thoughts Kathryn wrote are hard to read now, like any diary written by someone who has left us. Especially so when you didn't even know it existed. In expedition terms the most famous diaries are those left by Captain Scott. As he neared the end, freezing to death in a tent in Antarctica, he wrote his last diary entries and last letters: 'Should this be found I want these facts recorded . . . it was blowing a blizzard. He [Oates] said, "I am just going outside and may be some time."' The manner of Oates' death is haunting and Scott's words have fascinated me since I was a boy. But they don't fascinate me as much as Kathryn's words written down in a little pocket notebook, found in the living room foot stool. And it is the lines that the surviving expedition members engraved on a wooded cross, words from Tennyson's 'Ulysses'; and then placed on Observatory Hill overlooking the ice that seems to link Scott's famous diary and Kathryn's not so famous diary in my mind; 'To strive, to seek, to find and to yield.'

Scott's phrase '[we] bow to the will of Providence' links to Cross Lane. At the north-west corner is a farm, Providence Farm. It's an old building with land to the south that borders the stable fields. 'The protective care of God or of nature as a spiritual power' is how the Oxford Living Dictionary defines the word providence. Cross Lane was to be in Kathryn's protective care, as well as all the horses, dogs and people that would come there over the years. And, despite events that would unfold several years later, Cross Lane would look after Kathryn.

In summer, life at the yard was good; long hours of daylight to get the daily jobs done, no mud and little rain. Time to get the fields picked of poo and repair any broken fences. Kathryn's dad would undertake most if not all of the repair work on fences and rails. In winter though it's a different story, one of the current liveries – the people who keep their horses at the yard – said to me that her most abiding memory of Kathryn was of her pushing a barrow full of empty feed buckets, hard work through the sand up the yard lane, waterproofs on, looking tired.

Like all journeys it started with the first step. Steps move us forward, so Kathryn kept walking; developing and improving Cross Lane into the yard she had dreamed of and wanted all her life. Kathryn had been working with horses for many years by this point; yet when she took on Cross Lane she commented that it was a very steep learning curve.

. . . new liveries arrived today. One horse jumped out – great start – hopefully a one-off. Just need a few more.

But she climbed the curve and rode the wave, learning how to deal with people and their horses, how to manage the land and take care of the fields through the changing seasons. To care for a yard in the depths of winter, when all the pipes had frozen and the ground was harder than stone, or in the droughts of summer when rain couldn't find the way to dry land, or in the autumn and spring months when there was too much rain and the sand land fought hard to drain the water away.

She started helping other local people with their horses and yards, to build a reputation. In another world when I took over the yard I went around to Lara's, a field next door, as Kathryn had helped her out; it was a cold and dark day with weather of similar stamp.

'She didn't charge me much you know.'

'How much is not much?' I queried.

'A pound. She liked me to pay her at the end of the month; that way she said it seemed more.'

That was Kathryn and Kathryn's ethos, a castle of helping that became the walls and bridges of Cross Lane.

Cross Lane was also Kathryn's South Pole; it was the attainment of her life's goal. Kathryn never compromised in this quest. If she was doing something, then she was in it for keeps and she would endeavour to be the best she could. And if she didn't make much money, then so be it.

When the ex-race horses came, she brought them back into work and got them safe and ready for sale. She was in her element. Her effective and bold riding style honed at the hunt yard enabled her to pretty much get on any horse. Many times, she would be given a leg up as the horse walked round in circles and off she would go, down the lane and into the woods. Meanwhile Oliver and I would load up and head back to Sherwood Pines at weekends to ride with friends from the Bloomsgorse days. Oliver had stayed for a while at Bloomsgorse, yet eventually came to live at the family field on Rickett Lane.

As her diary had indicated she also wanted to have her own adventures. Iceland beckoned in the form of a British Horse Society challenge ride. The prospect of herding native Icelandic ponies across the interior of wild tundra was a challenge she couldn't resist. For the eight days she was away I had a taste of what it was like for her when I was gone – made worse because Kathryn had forgotten to take her phone.

Back in site [sic] of the icecap today, my second horse hated any contact on his mouth, managed to slow him with my weight after a while . . . couldn't get him to tolt much.

The Icelandic native ponies have a unique gait called a 'tolt', an exceptionally smooth four-beat gait where one hoof is always touching the ground, which was new to both of us.

Yet I was missing Kathryn;

Message from Steve to Zoë – 'I miss KB, made my day, miss him too.'

The hearts and minds of the people she looked after horses for were hers. Each Christmas the little tree would be snowed under with presents from the people who kept their horses at the yard. They ranged from socks, to riding clothing, photo calendars of her and Ollie; even a painting of the dogs at the yard.

But time spent with animals is not without heartache, as Zoë once said to me; 'If you have livestock, then you have dead stock.' One dark July day Kathryn found Gordon, the ex-racer she had brought on, with his leg broken in the field. In a matter-of-fact tone of voice, she called the vet stating her horse was poorly; they put him down where he lay. Losing Gordon hurt her more than she ever let on.

25/7/10
Gordon
Pretty Horse.

I took Ollie out today on our own. I think he's coping quite well – I guess you're taking care of him.

Her notes on Gordon lie in the drawer by the bed; they are intensely private and longing words. They call down a faith in the nature of life, of the angels that live in the waving air. Of the movement of the memories through our minds and the stamp of a life's soul, that carries on in the hinterland of the wild places.

CHAPTER TWELVE

An Angel at the South Pole

Sometime near the end of his road he sat down in the snow,
And there he stayed, cold in old clothes and a blue bag,
With nothing in it except an empty space, used once long ago,
And he wished to be on his mountain,
Or better still; that she was here.

Amundsen beat Scott to the Pole; he used nature in the form of fifty-two huskies to do so. The dogs were fed to dogs and men alike. All the men returned safely, along with eleven remaining dogs. It was an exercise in ambition carried out with ruthless expediency. Our expedition was to be a footnote in the footsteps of dogs; in no ways to be compared. We would be tourists of the ice.

Yet as Scott had commented that they bowed to the will of providence, it would seem the same hand of fate guided us into the secluded land. For us though it would be a willing, friendly hand that smoothed the wind and laid firm the snow. It would seem as if the angels of heroic past times would steer the compass.

As we tramped the heart of Heathrow though I was filled with trepidation; Gary noticed the tension in me and sat me down on a soulless airport couch. He pulled a black book out of his chest pocket and said, 'This is a copy of the bible, from my church in Langwith. [He had recently admitted that he was also a Methodist minister.] What's going to happen now is this; we will arrive safely in Punta Arenas, then we will arrive safely in Antarctica. From there we will walk to the South Pole. At the pole we will be asked in to the base; at the end of a small room there will be a book case. It will be full except one space for this bible. There I will leave it. We will then return home safely.'

'If that happens then when we get back I'll go straight down to St Peter's Church in Mansfield and offer a prayer of thanks,' I said.

Gary laughed. 'You'll be doing just that,' he said.

As he strode off to buy something to read, I searched my bag for my book. Opening the cover revealed Kathryn's note:

22 November 2004

Dear Steve,

You are the best person I know, I am so proud to be your wife. I wholeheartedly believe in you and your team, you have the experience, training and strength to fulfil your aims. Above all else, remember that you are loved and missed and that someone is back home waiting for you, whatever happens.

I know you will succeed. Strength and Honour, all my love,

Kathryn xxx

The couch didn't feel as soulless and the sky seemed to beacon us upwards; out of the gloom of an English winter's day and on to the clean snow that only lay on the last continent on earth.

We flew without mishap to Madrid and made the connection to Santiago in Chile. As we walked through the airport at Santiago the background music was Robin Williams singing 'Angels'. Released in 1997, the song wasn't even in the charts in

Chile at the time, yet the words echoed through the busy airport concourse. I thought nothing of it at the time. The four-hour connecting flight to Punta Arenas took us down the spine of the Andes, mountain after mountain glimmered and leapfrogged us south.

Punta, a fantastic homely town at the edge of the world, is the gateway to the last place on earth if you are heading south: Antarctica. Dusty streets blow hard in the face and welcoming smiles stand on each street corner. We reunited ourselves with our baggage on the doorstep of the Fitzroy Hostel; an outpost of friendliness overlooking the Magellan Straits. Misael the owner, who was busy hoovering up, smiled and welcomed us into his home. On the CD player, 'Angels' was playing.

We spent a couple of days packing and completing our food shopping. We talked and walked the streets of the dusty town, attended safety briefings by the logistics company. Then like Battle of Britain pilots we waited for the call to say the plane was ready to fly. The plane could only land on the ice if the wind was not too high; the only runway in the world where planes take off and land into a cross wind. Yet the wind at Patriot Hills also blew away accumulated snow which would make it impossible to land a plane; so, the right wind speed was crucial. I made a last call to Kathryn as we waited for a weather window to board the Ilyushin 76, the Russian bomber that would fly us into Patriot Hills. The weather gods were on our side and we didn't wait long for the four-hour flight over the Drake Passage and onto the Antarctic continent, the coldest, driest and highest land mass on earth.

The Russian bomber landed on the blue ice runway and we stepped off into the magical kingdom. For that's what Antarctica is, it has a special feel, like nowhere else. The air has that crisp polar smell and the horizons stretch as far the mind can see. We walked up to the little camp from the runway, a distance of about a kilometre and into the guest tent for a complimentary meal and drink.

Ronnie Fines, the camp chef at Patriot Hills, was busy cooking away as we sat down and listened to the music coming out of the battered CD player on the wooden table. There were only two CDs from which to choose; the song playing was 'Angels'.

There on the white ringing plains of the last kingdom we pitched our homes of modern fabric and lightweight poles. Dug them in and anchored them down and settled into the dream that was the ice and snow. There were no phone calls home as I had decided that it was best to run a no contact policy: we would only miss home and home would miss us, and if we made the pole then we would call from there. Everyone had agreed to this before we left the UK.

For two days we carried out training walks round the local area, but one of the pulks' (the small plastic sledges we were using to pull our kit) runners had been damaged. We needed some rivets and a rivet gun to mend it, and the camp didn't have any. Carl was pretty sure he could get some; from where I had no idea, as we were in a fairly isolated spot. Undeterred he went to the camp manager, and to cut a long story short he found out that a British Antarctic Survey plane was due. Using the gift of the gab, Carl had persuaded them to bring some rivets and a gun, and hey presto they dropped them off. It was a miracle of thinking outside the box and good fortune. But fortune does favour the brave.

I would constantly think of Kathryn and home, of Otto and Oliver. Wondering what she would be doing either at the yard, or at the field. She was a world away but also not. She was to walk every step of the trip, for we had shared the trials and heartache of getting to the point where we would step onto the Twin Otter and fly to the drop-off point.

The time came to fly to eighty-nine degrees south. It would

have been good to have done a 'full journey' from the coast, but that trip was not the one that was meant for me or the team. The 'full journey' involves a 650-mile trek which takes over fifty days and is in many ways the true test when walking to the South Pole. Carl and I have spoken a lot about this, and both agree that our little trip was right for us at that time, with the team we had and our motives for doing it. Carl has gone on to become one of the top polar guides in the world. But for all the trips carried out in the Polar Regions, I will take ours. Yes, it was to be only a last degree walk, a distance of sixty nautical miles, but it was ours. (Nautical miles are used for ease of navigation in the Polar Regions, and sixty of them equates to one degree of latitude. This is how the globe is divided up, along with measurements in longitude.) I had trained the team and I led them on the ice. It was the journey that was meant for us; and I believe that's why everything clicked into place. And most importantly of all; it was Kathryn's idea.

Sometimes we have to let an event find us through a process of pushing and finding, failing and learning; then if we can get out of the way and let the authentic experience find us, the truth will happen. I know that sounds all a bit mystical, but having been through a lot in my life so far, I honestly believe it is the case.

We had a goodwill send-off by Fran, one of the cooks, and Mike Sharp, one of the owners of the logistic company, as we climbed aboard the little Twin Otter at Patriot Hills. We took off into the sun and snow blanket below, landing a couple of hours later at the Thiel Mountains for refuelling. A fuel dump dug down in the snow marked by a bamboo cane serves as a lifeline for flying to the pole. After hand-pumping the fuel into the plane we took off on the last leg.

Eighty-nine degrees south on the Antarctic Plateau is a pretty remote spot. The nearest land is thousands of miles away in any direction. The nearest humans are at the Scott Amundsen South

Pole base; for the next two days we would rest, drink tea, eat and acclimatise: for after my experiences the previous year I was taking no chances. As the human body goes higher above sea level it finds it harder to get the oxygen it needs. I sat outside the tent and watched the horizon drift into the sky, thinking of home and all that meant. I watched the thermometer on the side of the tent drop to minus 39.5°C. I missed her, but there was a job to do for the both of us.

We steered a course to the South Pole across the wasteland, taking it in turns to lead the way, skiing for eight hours a day. On the front of our skis we had written words to inspire us. I had written Kathryn on mine and on the pulk. It wasn't polar exploration and we weren't polar explorers, we were travellers in a polar landscape. The pulks contained ten days' food and fuel for the walk, plus another seven days' emergency food and fuel as stipulated by Antarctic Logistics and Expeditions. So, the pulks were not light by any stretch of the imagination, and the weight combined with the altitude made the walk demanding. In contrast, those that have walked from the coast by the time they reach the last degree are fit, acclimatised and have lighter pulks. We crawled along, over wind-blown snow called sastrugi – wave-like ridges caused by winds on the surface of hard snow – and we inched south. Each night we would call in to Patriot Hills to update them, and we would also send a small blog post to the website via software installed on a Palm Pad. We did this instead of settling down the dogs as Amundsen had done, or Oates tending to his ponies on the lower barrier. 1912 was a gulf away across the ice, a different world.

After a few days Robert was skiing out front but he was weaving all over the place, I spoke to Gary and said that he would have to come off the front. The sastrugi were causing us headaches and making the going very hard. Gary said he would be fine for a bit; that we should give him more time. I did, and after an hour or so we walked straight onto a single bamboo cane placed in the snow. Next to the cane was a manmade track that a vehicle had made, cutting through the sastrugi to make a flat road in the snow. I got out the GPS and checked the position and where the tracks led. They pointed due south to the pole. We all stared at each other in wonder, and followed the white brick road to our own wizard.

On the horizon bright white lights headed towards us, out in the middle of nowhere. They turned out to be a Chilean Army survey group, two or three tracked vehicles. Stopping in front of us, a crew member jumped down from the middle vehicle, wearing sandals and smiling. He invited us in to the vehicle for coffee and cake; well, how could we refuse? We weren't undertaking an 'unsupported' trip; we were skiing the last degree.

Inside the cab the TV was on, showing a live broadcast of a concert back in the civilised world. We sat down to our hot drinks to watch. Robbie Williams was singing 'Angels' live in concert, from where we had no idea; yet it was being streamed straight to the Antarctic Plateau.

Our hosts had already been to the pole and were heading back to the coast. We bid them farewell and skied on, each in our own silent world. I imagined Otto running ahead of me, of Oliver carrying me over the snow; of Kathryn pushing me. Of the world of the horse and dog, of the forests and fields of home. The snow stretched out like a giant duvet, discarded in a dash to the shower. For the room was cold and the water was temptingly hot. Yet, the thoughts in my mind comforted and held me; I followed them over the ice.

Hour by hour and day by day we moved closer to the pole. Due to the clarity of the air and the endless horizon you can see objects from a great distance in Antarctica. A full day out from the pole we saw the Scott Amundsen base. The final day we skied relentlessly towards the base at the bottom of the world.

Once-in-a-lifetime days are few and far between, but that day as we passed the low frequency radio antenna that guards the route to the pole, was one of them. Strange scientific buildings loom out of the ice, runways criss-cross the snow and the imprint of activity lies all around. Scott only found Amundsen's black tent waiting for him. Now the area is transformed and built up as the Americans study the ice and meteorites on Antarctica and search for signs of extra-terrestrial life by firing neutrino waves (elementary particles) deep into the ice. All this fascinating *X-Files*-type information we found out by chatting to people in Antarctica.

Unbeknown to us at the time, a friend who had been to the South Pole had emailed the base commander of the Scott Amundsen research station. We had no inkling or expectation that we would be allowed into the base; just reaching the pole itself was enough for us. Operated and run by the US government agency the National Science Foundation, visits inside the station are strictly off limits; unless you are just visiting the shop. (Yes, there is a shop at the South Pole, which sells souvenirs such as hats and badges.) After we had walked round the various low-frequency antennas and carefully crossed the runway we followed the map that shows the way to the ceremonial pole. And the pole itself? Imagine a striped barber's pole; that's what it is, with a reflective ball on top. Just meters off to the side of it is another marker, set by the US Geological Society, which marks the exact spot of ninety degrees south.

The base commander was waiting for us at the pole. He held out a hand and congratulated us, welcomed us inside the base and gave us a tour of the old station (which was officially closed in 2003) as the new one was just being opened. The iconic silver dome was accessed via a snow ramp, as over the years the base had sunk down into the ice. Like a scene from *The Thing* the base is like a movie set at the end of the earth, especially when you consider that the station is located on a moving glacier. We were showed round the inner workings of the base, with photo after photo lining the walls documenting the history. We were truly privileged for hardly anyone outside the National Science Foundation gets such a look. After the tour the commander offered a place for us to have a drink and food. He directed us towards some stairs, mentioned he would join us in a while and left us to it.

We walked up a small spiral steel staircase. Two twists, and then we were into a small utilitarian room with polar images on the walls. At the far end of the room, three quarters of the way up the wall, was a bookcase.

'Steve, do you see what I see?' said Gary.

We looked.

'Yes, I do, and I see that there is just the one space left.'

'I don't want to say I told you so, but this was written from the start,' Gary replied.

'I see that now; I still can't quite believe it though . . .'

Gary took his bible out of his left breast pocket and strode over as if it was the most natural thing in the world to do. In the only empty space in the bookshelf he slid in the bible.

'It's time to go home now, our work here is done,' said Gary.

There wasn't a lot I could say to that; he just smiled. A knowing smile that someone gives when they know all is right with the world and our place in it. There are no explanations and none are needed. I realised then it was not the South Pole I was aiming for, even though I thought it was for many years. The reason I went to the South Pole, left Kathryn and all that was home; was to find that smile. It was the faith behind that smile. I had to travel to the ends of the earth to find it, but in that room, where all compass points head north, and home, I found it. It was Kathryn's smile; and now I just wanted to go home to her.

Akin to talking to an echo, it's easy to talk over each other's voices when using the satellite phone. Yet, we both had had plenty of experience at it. I can't remember what we spoke about when I called Kathryn from the South Pole. I don't think it matters now. But we spoke over the snow, the oceans and the continents. Two people connected by a satellite in space. But it was more than that. It always was and always will be.

It wasn't exploration, but after all the failed expeditions this one, the most important one, succeeded. Every trip had led up to it; every failure had been banked and learned from. And when it mattered, we succeeded. We had stood at the South Pole, walked in the footsteps of legends from the past. We flew our flag at the pole just like everyone else does, and felt as proud as only our mums could know.

Events coming home slotted into place just like the bible in the room, good weather intervened and we flew back to Patriot Hills in time for an evening meal and a beer, just as the Ilyushin flew in from Punta. We spent a couple of days in Punta, long enough to soak up the joy, but not too long to get homesick. Before we knew it, we were back home and the expedition was featured on national news programmes, Robert's face beamed out on the ITV news, Channel 4 News and the local news.

Robert walked out first into the arrivals lounge where journalists were waiting to interview us, and got the success he wanted; the media portrayed him as the youngest to walk to the South Pole. In a way he was, although we hadn't walked the distance from the coast. Yet he did walk into his old school and find the teacher who he claimed had told him he was no good; he gave the teacher a picture of himself stood at the South Pole. Robert went back to college, enrolled on English courses and learned how to read. Later he would get a full-time job and buy his own home. He had found the skills to make his own way in life. Carl went on to cross Greenland several times, east to west and also south to north. In 2014 he guided Lewis Clarke all the way to the pole, and at the time sixteen-year-old Lewis became the youngest person ever to ski the 650 miles from coast to pole.

Behind the reporters, behind the relatives of Carl and Robert, past Gary's family, there she was. Kathryn stood alone. She was smiling, wearing old blue jeans and a polo top. It was as though no one else existed, like being back in church. All the years of planning and hoping, the dread of failure, fell away with each step toward her.

'I'm so glad to see you, I love you,' I blurted out.

'I love you too, I'm so glad to see you too!'

She beamed. We hugged and held each other, neither of us wanting to let go.

'We did it, we finally made it,' I said.

'I know; and I'm so proud of you, so proud,' Kathryn said with a little tear.

We kissed and hugged once more. 'I've got you,' she whispered.

'I've got you too . . . shall we go home now?'

'Yes, we can, that would be nice . . .'

We left the others to it and walked quietly out of the airport, headed for home and peace. And into the longing that comes from spending time apart.

I walked into the hallowed stone building and stood at the altar were Kathryn and I had once stood. I honoured my pledge to Gary and offered a prayer of thanks. It was a gratitude that extended beyond the blessed pews and remembering walls; a humbleness that winged its way across the oceans. A nod from a tent on the ice, to the one who had waited. And the angels that kept us.

CHAPTER THIRTEEN

Maverick and Goose

This is our last expedition, our setting sun,
We'll steer a northern course though,
For to the ends of the earth we have been, together.
The compass begins its true swing and points to home.

Kathryn and I basked in the success of the Polar Challenge; the college hosted an awards evening to all the sponsors, serving up a grand meal based on the menu that Scott had in Cardiff before the Terra Nova Expedition started in 1910. I have a photo from the evening. A group of the sponsors are being presented with a certificate and an image of the team at the pole. Standing far right is Kathryn in blue blouse and black trousers. She had longer hair then. That smile is in her eyes, back when we were young, and the future was still being written; a story in progress. Yet all stories have their chapters of pride dashed in a fall.

After the lectures to schools and colleges about the Polar Challenge were over, so was my career at the West Notts FE College. I was to be made redundant. The person I had recruited to run the outdoor course was now doing the job instead of me, for over the last year I had been exclusively employed on the South Pole trip. And in retrospect in order to get us into a position to actually get to Antarctica I think I upset people. I thought outside the box and ruffled those that lived within. I steered a path that was geared solely to achieve the ambition of the pole. I didn't break the rules necessarily, but I made things happen. And that was my downfall. Six months after arriving at the pole I left the college. Di made sure I had a good pay-out, enough to give breathing space and plan what to do next. It was a hard time; in the midst of it, truly desperate. Yet, when roofs cave in, new horizons become visible.

As Kathryn had dreamed of doing things her way, free from the constraints of other people, so did I. I had wanted to carry on with more expeditions at the college, for the Polar Challenge was a great platform to launch from. We could have taken students all over the world; now I would just have to do it on my own, with Kathryn. In fact, I'd thought of the idea for an expedition company whilst I was still at university.

When we had arrived back at Patriot Hills, Mike Sharp, one of the owners at Antarctic Logistics & Expeditions, offered me a job working for them; I turned it down. Sometimes I think what that path would have led to; but it would not have led to our company, steering our own path in life. It would not have enabled Kathryn and I to share the journey together, a pilot and a wingman. Just like the iconic characters in *Top Gun*, the film she could never help but watch when I put it on; she was to be my wingman. She was Goose to my Maverick.

For the princely sum of £25 we registered Bull Precision Expeditions Ltd (BPE) with Companies House. We took no business loans out, did no business plan and formulated no long-term strategy. I'd hung on to a couple of speaking engagements about the Polar Challenge, yet I got cold feet. I looked at working with another company in Scotland, as there were stables nearby. Calling Kathryn and explaining she just said, 'We've got stables!'

Luck played a big part in what followed. We had been awarded a grant from the Captain Scott Society for the polar expedition, and in return I gave a speech at the annual dinner in Cardiff. It was like an old school officers' mess dinner. I used the Ladybird book about Captain Scott as a basis for my talk, and it went down well. In the bar afterward I met Peter Fuchs, the son of Sir Vivian Fuchs, the English explorer who completed the first overland crossing of Antarctica in 1958. He wanted to take teachers to Antarctica with his charity the Fuchs Foundation.

'Hello, may I introduce myself? My name is Peter Fuchs; son of Sir Vivian Fuchs who you may have heard of,' he said, approaching me at the bar in the same room Scott had stood in decades earlier before his last expedition.

'Hello, it's a pleasure to meet you and yes I have heard about your father,' I replied, trying hard not to look over-awed.

'I would like to say that your talk was excellent, and to also add I'm looking for someone to take teachers to Antarctica.'

'Thank you; I would love to hear more about your Antarctic plans . . .'

We talked late into the night and I forgot to call Kathryn.

I had an interview in Cambridge the next morning for a field assistant position with the British Antarctic Survey. Although I had turned down a job with Mike Sharp's Antarctic Logistics & Expeditions, I was keen to explore all options just in case BPE didn't take off. Yet given the fascinating conversations that night it was late when I left the dinner, and with only one hour's sleep I drove to Cambridge. Thoughts of Peter Fuchs and his father roamed through my head on the long drive. I fell asleep outside the interview room, and didn't get the job.

At that point, BPE was just a vehicle to do talks to schools on the South Pole and making dreams come true despite all obstacles. I'd led a four-week expedition in the summer for a well-known company sending schools on trips. I found Africa busy and hot (apart from a few glorious days riding horses across the Drakensberg mountains), especially after the ice of Antarctica, yet the team was fantastic and the teacher brilliant. It was to be the start of a long association with Chelmsford County High School.

Meanwhile Peter Fuchs got in touch; we met near his home and talked through his Antarctic plans for his charity. He wanted to take four teachers to the Antarctic and he wanted someone to plan and lead it; BPE could do this. After a few more meetings we were awarded the contract to recruit, train and put a team of teachers on a six-week expedition to Antarctica in 2007.

Around the same time the school I'd led in Africa got in touch and I was called to a meeting. Following a ten-minute discussion after proposing Patagonia as a suitable destination, I walked out to the car with a contract to take thirty-six students on a month-long trip to the south of Chile. Suddenly BPE had trips on its books, whilst we were operating out of the spare room with just a laptop and phone. Then a local school decided it wanted an Iceland trip. Quite suddenly we needed leaders, policies, procedures and lots and lots of kit. Kathryn and I set to the task at hand, with me writing procedures whilst she worked out the finances.

On the back of the Polar Challenge I was also invited to sit on the polar advisory panel at the Royal Geographical Society's annual Explore seminar, held in November, which aims to advise people wanting to take part or lead their own expeditions. It's a prestigious affair but good for networking. I'd been part of it before with the integrated expeditions, but being on the polar panel was a huge honour. Both Kathryn and I agreed it could only help and enhance BPE's reputation.

As BPE took off Cross Lane was becoming well established; it was just as well, for Kathryn now had to deal with all BPE's finances, be the company secretary and manage our air travel Operating Licence. Running a livery yard had been a steep learning curve for Kathryn, and so was setting up and running an expedition company. It was one thing to lead expeditions, but the curve climbed steeply when planning trips for schools and charities.

'It was a lot easier just planning the South Pole trip!' I said one night over tea. 'Putting multiple trips together is another level.'

I looked across from my chair to where Kathryn lay on the sofa fiddling with a crossword puzzle.

'I know, it's the same as running the yard; just looking after our horses is easy compared with Cross Lane. Sometimes I don't know if I'm coming or going, trying to please everyone and their horses,' Kathryn replied.

'Same with the trips; trying to keep the school happy, the participants happy, not to mention the parents and leaders . . . more wine?'

Kathryn grinned. 'Yes please!'

The key was to be able to make decisions, to attempt to balance all differing factors in an ever-changing situation. This was certainly the case with BPE and also with the yard as Kathryn was finding out. But, you have to do it your own way, trust your instinct and experience. BPE was based purely on what we did for the Polar Challenge, we would select the students or adults, and then we would train them well and most importantly pick leaders who we felt knew what they were doing.

Peter wanted me to lead the Fuchs trip; the Patagonia trip needed three leaders and the Iceland trip just one. With reluctance I pulled out of the Fuchs trip as BPE could not cope with me being out of the country for up to six weeks. I went to leaders I knew for the Patagonia trip and engaged them in the planning, and I led the Iceland trip myself. Two new leaders would be needed for the Fuchs trip. Yet amidst all this was a growing personal tragedy on the horizon.

Kathryn's mum got her into horses; my dad got me into expeditions. He once said all I was ever good at was walking, but outwardly he didn't think expeditions would prove to be a suitable choice for making a living from. He was immensely proud of my South Pole trip but unfortunately, he would not live to see BPE develop. After surviving a stroke on the top of Crinkle Crags and making it through a heart attack years later, it seemed God needed a bigger card to play to bring him home. So, my dad was diagnosed with pancreatic cancer. He lived through it for over eighteen months.

The week he died, a print I had ordered arrived, showing Peter Boardman and Joe Tasker on Kangchenjunga taken by Doug Scott, who had also signed it. Dad thought it was a fantastic photo and signed it too. Peter Boardman's dad also died of pancreatic cancer. Dad signed the photo on the Monday, and by Friday morning he was nearing the end. Not wanting him to be alone I asked the nurses if I could stay in his room, to be with him. They agreed, so I took my sleeping bag and some beers and settled down on the floor of his room. In the late hours I could tell he was on the edge, so I called the nurses and my mum. The most powerful moment of my life up to that point was in that hospital room, when my mum told her husband it was OK for him to go.

'Miles; everything is OK,' she said. 'You don't have to fight anymore. It's OK.'

My dad smiled back at Mum, and I will never forget the look in his eyes. It was as if he knew where he was going was good, and that it was OK for him to leave us.

As the years pass by, we begin to lose those we hold dear, who are the anchors in our lives. They may be human or they may be animal. We can either accept their loss and die with them or we can choose to keep walking, to take them with us on our continuing journey, until it is our own time to move on to what lies ahead.

Kathryn ran the Race for Life for Cancer Research with the

word Miles on her number badge on a cold day in Nottingham. She'd never been a keen runner but she wanted to get fitter so she ran for my dad. She would go on to run many races, fitting time in between riding to train. That first race was the emotional one.

Without my dad's approval we moved into new offices at Hexgreave Hall; and he never saw the Fuchs Foundation head to Antarctica for the fiftieth anniversary expedition of the first crossing of Antarctica. He would have got on well with Peter. The team of Phil Avery, Ian Richardson, Ruth Hollinger and Amy Rogers was given a big send off at the Royal Geographical Society with leaders Carolyn Bailey and Carl Alvey. Carolyn was selected to lead after joining the team for the Norway training, and Carl went as an assistant to gain leadership experience. For six weeks they explored the Ellsworth Mountains, remote ranges in Antarctica, undertaking science projects and standing where no one had stood before. The *London Gazette*, which claims to be the oldest surviving English newspaper, announced the expedition; a throwback to the heroic age as we had to get our own Foreign and Commonwealth Office (FCO) permit to conduct science field work in Antarctica. The Polar Section at FCO believed it was maybe the first since Scott had last been south. And the team delivered: deep in the Ellsworth Mountains they found a species of lichen that had never been found in Antarctica before. It summed up the ethos of BPE, and both Kathryn and I were immensely proud at the reception held at Cambridge University when the team returned. I wish my dad could have been there. Maybe he was.

The dinner jackets and posh frocks of old England became a memory as Kathryn lay in her tent, waiting for her group of students heading down from the Kinder plateau. She had completed her expedition leaders' course with ease, and was now working on BPE's expeditions. The way of the horse and the path of the mountain had truly merged into one. Kathryn was now equally as proficient at looking after students on the hills of Derbyshire as she was the horses of home. Sometimes we would work together on the hills; she would challenge me as I challenged her when riding.

And I liked the way she challenged me, she was the only one who could. At the end of one trip in the Dales she was photographed sitting on a bench, chatting and eating cake with a DofE assessor. Kathryn is gesturing with her hand as Brian, one-time platoon commander in the Parachute Regiment listens on. She had that rare gift, the touch that enabled her to engage as an equal with all souls. The bench is still there, yet the occupants and their cake are memories; only the crumbs are left. For they never seem to disappear, they linger for ever in hidden corners. In the back-of-the-sofa places of our mind and under the carpet of our souls.

CHAPTER FOURTEEN

To the Ends of the Earth

Light will guide, the shimmering flag of true home,
One band of gold for life, shall keep all love,
Each and every ship, will bear its storm to port,
So it will be so, for all souls. At the end of all things.

I spent three weeks in Iceland with the six students from the local secondary school; saw the magic in their eyes as they saw the truth of the wilderness. They didn't notice the increased tourism; they saw the landscape for the first time, through child's eyes. The thirty-six girls from Essex had an even remoter time in the Fitzroy National Park in Patagonia's winter; they too now saw the world with a different gaze.

BPE had become bigger, we had staff and we had offices and the cycle of getting work to keep staff employed had begun. Gone were the halcyon days of just Kathryn and I working on it. We could never compete with the larger companies, so we focused on quality and destinations for schools that were pioneering- and frontier-based. We gradually gained a reputation for such style of trips and built a small portfolio of established clients that came back each year, or on the two-year cycle that overseas school trips required.

There was still residue of recognition from the Polar Challenge when Carl and I were attending a presentation at the Royal Geographical Society one night. I had been a Fellow for several years, back in the time when you had to be recommended by another Fellow based on your geographical or expedition career. On our second pint in the bar, a lady introduced herself as Alexandra Shackleton. 'Are you related to the Shackletons?' I asked. 'He's my grandfather,' she said. Carl and I were both in awe clutching our glasses too hard. Several drinks later she asked me if I would be interested in repeating her grandfather's expedition, undertaking the boat journey in a replica 'James Caird' boat (the little wooden boat in which Shackleton and five companions travelled 800 miles to rescue those stranded on Elephant Island in 2016). It was a proposition I could not turn down, and I would get to know Alexandra 'Zas' Shackleton well over the coming months as I looked into the logistics of the trip.

Kathryn and I drove down to Falmouth one weekend for a dinner and fundraising event being held for an expedition that was following in the footsteps of Shackleton. The real James Caird was going to be at the National Maritime Museum there, and Zas wanted us both to see it, and meet a local boat builder who was going to make a replica for our trip. Henry Worsley, the leader of the Shackleton expedition, was due to give the after-dinner speech; yet for some reason during the dinner he declined. Kathryn looked as shocked as I did when Zas asked me to speak instead on Henry's behalf.

'Ladies and gentlemen. It's a great honour to be asked to say a few lines at this prestigious gathering . . .'

The rest of the words are lost, along with the menu they were written on.

Yet for both of us the highlight was sitting in the James Caird. Huddled inside its wooden memories, Kathryn and I felt like small children invited for tea with the fabled headmaster in his study. Shy in the presence of the heroic past. I still have the wine cork we found in the bottom of the boat, probably a stray cork from another dinner gathering in the past. And a great photo of Kathryn looking reserved on a sofa in the hotel; I think she realised at the time that the James Caird trip was not for us, because of our commitments with BPE. With great reluctance I pulled out of leading the expedition and in a little pub near Newark I handed over the project to a guy called Tim Jarvis; to great acclaim he went on to successfully lead the trip and repeat the Boss's boat journey and crossing of South Georgia.

Not long after the first Fuchs expedition to Antarctica, we began planning our second one to the continent, and Bruce also entered our lives. I was up in the Lakes working one week when Kathryn called to say that a black greyhound was coming to the yard; she missed Jack and so Bruce was coming for a trial visit. He ended up staying. The night before the Fuchs training trip in Norway he escaped out of the back door, we drove round for hours looking for a black greyhound in the night. In an unbelievable stroke of luck someone found him and took him to the vets, with huge relief Kathryn picked him up the next day as I flew north once more.

We left our little mews house for a larger house in Blidworth. It had the character we had always both wanted; stone floors and log fires and it was close enough to the yard for Kathryn to walk there if she needed to. I was working away when the moving date came, so it was Kathryn, her dad and my mum that moved all our stuff. She had labelled up every box and its contents to perfection. I don't think I thanked her properly for that.

The animals in our shared lives seemed to define us; the windswept lands held no life; home was sweeter with the wag of a tail or the stamp of hoof. The hearth of home isn't as warm without the ruggy coat of a tired hound on the carpet. The fields not so welcoming without a horse stamping its presence of breath on your neck.

On a good day the best feeling in the world is riding as one through woods and trees, through fields and stubble and up into the light. Enter Harlton's Field of Dreams, or Ollie for short. He wasn't an easy horse, so she picked him up relatively cheap; yet Kathryn liked 'problem horses'. He was to go on to become her passport to competing properly, the horse she always wanted. He's big at 17.3 hands high, and he's got presence; he's top dog of the yard. I view him as 'war horse' as when he was younger out hunting, he got caught up in barbed wire, his hind legs still show the scars. The incident upset him profoundly, but Kathryn had the right temperament for him, and they became a pair, a team that would go on to form an inseparable bond over the years.

Relationships we form with our animals are strong, so strong that when they break they can virtually destroy us. Otto died in 2011 when he was twelve years old. I was devastated. He slept on his chair with his teddy, and then in the morning he looked at me with the eyes that said it was time. The vet allowed me to give the injection; I didn't want anyone else doing it but me.

I made the mistake of not scattering his ashes straight away, despite Kathryn's advice. My depression came back and I struggled, I was at the mental ends of the earth. Kathryn and I had weathered our ups and downs as any couple does but we had a big blip then. In truth my depression had never gone away and I'd not faced my demons, just brushed them under the carpet. Direct and forceful as ever, Kathryn knew what would snap me out of it and force me to take action: she threatened to leave me unless I sorted myself out. This ultimatum scared me more than depression, so I sought help. With counselling and support over several months the depression was brought under control. Our relationship flourished once more. Kathryn had saved me again and our relationship.

After she had gone one of her closest friends told me that she had never ever thought of leaving; it was a bluff. A direct and bold bluff to look after the person she loved the most. It was one of those conservations that made me feel loved; despite her not being here anymore. In the end we took Otto to where my dad's ashes are; a windy wild spot on the moors of Derbyshire. Deep in the heather that my dad and Otto loved to wander.

We picked up a trip for the National Deaf Society, taking a group of adults to the North Pole and the Fuchs Foundation went across Greenland. With dogs we ran teams east to west and then back again. Carl, who had been on the college's Polar Challenge, led the team back across the ice. It was his first leadership test in the Polar Regions and a baptism by fire, which led to the next Antarctic trip in 2010 with Carl and Carolyn taking more teachers deep into the Ellsworth Mountains.

One day Mike Stroud asked if we could run a trip to Greenland for him and his family. In 1992–93 Mike had crossed Antarctica with Ran Fiennes. It was the first time the Antarctic had been crossed without support. Carolyn and I were both tongue-tied when he wandered into the office. Yet, she had a glorious time with Mike and his family on the east coast of Greenland; running sledges with dogs.

We developed a core of schools that wanted truly bespoke expeditions overseas; teams went out to Greenland, Svalbard and Iceland, spending four weeks at a time undertaking remote treks and project work. BPE gained a reputation for the arctic, teams were trained to camp and operate in polar bear country, safely and with good backup. The risk assessments and analyses were key for such trips, as a team we spent a great deal of time and research looking into the viability of sending students into an environment where one of the planet's most dangerous animals lives. We perfected a method for protecting and safeguarding the teams and suitable polar bear defence procedures. The procedures were tested in self-defence a couple of times over the years; one such incident involved Carolyn and her team of students when a bear approached their camp. The leaders fired a couple of shots whilst the bear was still far away, who then ambled off into the distance. With live rounds in the chambers of their shotguns and the safety catch off, the leadership team spent a very exciting few hours being directed by the on-call team to a safe location.

Risks and mitigating those risks was the core of BPE; I joined the committee for writing the British Standard (8848) on Overseas Expeditions. Saw first-hand the tragedy of the worst-case scenario after being an expert witness. Kathryn and I questioned the risks all the time. But life isn't fair, and risks exist in each and every waking moment. The students who sat on a glacier looking out for the white bear on the ice learned that.

Closer to home we ran Duke of Edinburgh Award expeditions, which proved just as rewarding for the participants as going to the ends of the earth. Students wandered the hills of the UK, gaining self-reliance and confidence. We combined the horse and the mountain and ran expeditions on horseback. Kathryn would train them out of Cross Lane and in the forests of Sherwood. Together we would work with them as they rode their horses over the moors of Yorkshire and the hills of the Peaks.

What neither of us realised was that BPE and Cross Lane were merging, the two entities were becoming one. BPE needed Kathryn to shape and hold her together, and in turn BPE would support and enable Cross Lane to function.

The field of dreams drew us in, linked us and combined us. The risks we shared and ran; ran with life in all its shortcomings and great hopes. Those risks she ran on Ollie also now, you couldn't ride him in a group of more than two, hunting was a real no-go and push him too far and he would object. He would stand like the mountain, tall and proud; daring the summit attempt. But there always needs to be the next day, the next step up the hill. The next year to ride. So, like the mountain in the mist, Ollie would be left in his field; dreaming. Whilst Kathryn waited for the storm to pass.

Competing in dressage competitions they reached the Intermediate standard, they show jumped and competed in working hunter classes. Eventually they progressed to one-day eventing, a combination of dressage, show jumping and cross-country. They became inseparable; he was the true successor to Strip, for eventually she had retired Strip with a great sadness. The highlight for her and Ollie was reaching the National Trailblazer 65cm show jumping finals held at Stoneleigh Park in 2013.

I never liked watching her jump, especially the cross-country jumps where there is no margin for error. I always felt it a little disconcerting that you had to wear a badge on your arm displaying your personal details and medical information; it was like going into combat. How many sports ask this of the competitors? Even the participants on our expeditions into polar bear country didn't have this.

Bruce left us in time, one day after tea Kathryn noticed a lump in his mouth. A visit to the vets diagnosed cancer of the jaw. There was nothing to be done, so Kathryn decided that when he went off his food it would be time. One evening he didn't come down for tea, just stayed on the bed. Hiding her feelings, she went and got him off the bed and we drove straight to the vet's. He was laid to rest next to Jack in the field.

As Ollie and Kathryn went from strength to strength so did BPE. We secured a large contract to deliver outdoor pursuits for the National Citizen Service, treating hundreds of young people to a taste of high adventure on the crags of Derbyshire. For many it was their first time under canvas, the first taste of life without concrete boundaries. They experienced the grass roots of exploration, as the overseas expeditions became the pinnacle. At the Royal Geographical Society's annual Explore conference in 2015, Phil Avery gave the keynote talk on why expeditions for young people mattered so much. Standing in the illustrious hall he spoke of his Greenland team, of what they achieved. Of the river that sets out young people on the course of their life. Of the journey to the seas of adulthood. As the BPE logo proudly stood next to that of his school; Kathryn squeezed my hand as we sat in the audience.

I could write a separate book about BPE's twelve years in operation. We were captains and masters of our own fate, and we explored the world teaching young people to look after each other and do the right thing. We didn't earn much money and spent all our savings paying leaders when times got tough, yet we did it together. We made relationships with people from all walks of life, at all points of the compass. I'd never been the famous explorer I wanted to be, but in reality, what's the point of that? Kathryn liked the fact that we made a difference and ran Cross Lane by the same ethos.

Life is about legacy and what you pass on, not what you take from the world. It's about the silence you leave for others to hear.

Romeo the greyhound entered our lives, as Kathryn wanted a new dog, so Romeo, the big black ex-racing hound, even bigger than Bruce, found us. On Sundays we rode out together, her on Ollie or a horse she was exercising and me on Oliver. On one morning though I rode Ollie, it was my third time and I had wanted a faster ride, as due to arthritis Oliver couldn't do much.

'How does he feel?' came Kathryn's words from behind me as we walked out of the yard gate.

'Fine; a bit big though.' I replied.

'Yes, he does ride big; you know maybe when Oliver is retired you should ride him more, as yours.'

'Let's see how I get on today! But that's a good idea.' I looked back and she was grinning with her eyes.

We went into the woods and headed for the black path, down by the lower fields at the end of the woods.

'Do you want to go first? Or shall I?' Kathryn asked.

'I don't know, is he best in front or behind?' I replied; it had been a long time since I had ridden fast.

'Ollie's OK either way,' she said. 'Just relax on him and let him go forward; you'll be OK!'

'I'll go first then,' I said, feeling slightly better about the prospect.

We turned onto the back path that curves in a long slow bend along the bottom of the forest. For a few paces we trotted, then cantered. I bridged my reins and felt the power surge under me as Ollie moved forwards. So, Ollie and I rode fast for the first time. Kathryn commented later:

Lovely ride and you and Ollie both did very well. it must be six years since you rode any horse except yours and he's not used to anyone riding him apart from me x

It would not be the last time I would ride him, yet I never imagined the circumstances in which I would ride Ollie next. Nor that the suggestion from Kathryn that I ride him as mine would come to pass. For there was a wind on the horizon and the grass in the field was stirring, events in our lives were out of our control. We all live each day thinking the days will never end, that there will always be another a day, another tomorrow. That the sun will keep rising and the moon following her in turn. But this is not the case, for there can be monsters waiting under the bed, and the darkness is real.

Kathryn and I approached 2016 as normal, full of optimism. We had walked Romeo on Boxing Day; we planned our holiday, went to a charity ball and lived each day like there would always be more days. That we would grow old, struggle with money and life's problems. I would probably die first and she would continue with her horses and dogs. Like virtually every couple we never talked about endings, we had no wills made and thought the pennant would fly in a forever sky. In ignorance that is the doom of all men and women we blissfully lived our lives. All was good in the world.

Kathryn's last diary entry was sadly poignant in its optimism. How many of our hopes and dreams in our lives come true?

Have brought on and sold four more horses so am actually achieving something that I wanted to do. My yard is full to overflowing with a waiting list, although I'm not exactly going to be rich – Steve now has his own business – an outdoor ed/ expedition company, going well so far and although he's busy, I think he's happy. So, all in all, life is good. Watch this space!

When we are in the midst of happiness, we don't recognise it and hold it. We think there will always be something better, that a distant horizon holds the key. We kept saying to each other that we needed to spend more time together at weekends, go for walks with Romeo on Saturday afternoons, or Sundays. But we never did, there was always next weekend, next Saturday. But sometimes next Saturday doesn't come.

She would get up about 6.30 each morning; she would reach over and pat the duvet that covered me. Sometimes she would say see you later, sometimes not if she thought I was still asleep, but she would most times pat the duvet or give me a kiss. I would hear her pad out of the room and the bathroom door would clang shut, followed by sounds in the kitchen. Sometimes she would leave a note to ask me to put the washing out; she would always make my sandwiches. Usually ham with a bit of onion and a packet of crisps, if I was lucky, she'd put some homemade flapjack in. Little did I know that very soon the Saturdays would end and there would be no more sandwiches made for me. That I would be coming home to find the sandwiches she had made for herself, left on a plate next to the sofa, with a half-drunk glass of water next to them. And Ollie would be mine sooner rather than later.

'Dark clouds draw down as the bow pushes forth,
Through black heading seas she pushes,
Heading out of my known port, my home,
My ship of English oak, built for a need,
I did not choose this voyage, but sail I must,
Out into the unknown, the setting sun,
Of all our souls and all our hopes.'

PART TWO

The Return Journey

'Great God! This is an awful place . . . Now for the run home
and a desperate struggle. I wonder if we can do it.'

Captain Robert Falcon Scott
Wednesday 17 January 1912
The South Pole

'Then I saw heaven open,
And there was a white horse.'

Revelation 19.11

I feel quiet tonight, so that's it. It helps to write to you – wish I could get a reply. It'd be nice to think you were writing back.

KATHRYN BULL

CHAPTER FIFTEEN

The Hunt in the Forest

She rose into the flags of all fathers and mothers,
All acceptance into a knowing of life lost and won,
In the noon of all belonging the thief and horse stand,
It's nothing and everything, it's you and I. As one.
The shepherd waits, while you're down the field.
A greyhound runs.
A horse canters.
A husband holds.
The field is all in April.

The moon disappeared for a few hours, the sun rose as normal; she awoke and patted the duvet as usual. 'Good luck with your watch,' she said. I smiled from the pillow; I'd catch up with her later. I heard her footsteps padding out of the bedroom. The bathroom door banged, then clicked open a few minutes later. Normal morning crashes and bumps came from the kitchen. In time the front door was unlocked and then shut with the usual whump. The Defender didn't fire up as she was in our old Peugeot (or '*Top Gear* car' because it often broke down). Kathryn drove up the drive and onto Main Street with Romeo in the back, then down the lane past the family field and onto Cross

Lane. She pulled up and parked, let Romeo out of the boot and walked to the front gate.

She would arrive at the yard about 8 a.m., and Bruno and Zak would be at the gate waiting; an unlocking of the padlock and she'd be in. Then it would have been a mad doggy hello as she walked across the outdoor school with the three dogs and onto the lane. A quick run around and then back onto the yard for breakfast. Two cans of dog food split among the three of them. They would then have followed her around the yard as she got the feeds ready, gathering each horse's bucket from their resting places, loading them in the barrow and then heading down to the fields to feed. It was a normal Friday at Cross Lane, a day Kathryn had done countless times.

I woke up just before eight; I was excited as I had a day off. And I was heading into town to pick up a watch. It was an interest of mine, an indulgence, a fascination with time pieces. The shop opened at 9.30, I knew the manager Andrew as my dad had done. I arrived early so went into Waterstones to have a look at the books; I found myself in the poetry section. There in front of me was the picture of a black greyhound running with a red banner in his mouth on the cover of *The Hunt in the Forest* by John Burnside. Inside, words spoke about eternal love, loss, grief and dealing with death. I bought the book and headed over to pick up the watch. I also bought a card for Kathryn as a thank you for letting me be me. Andrew and I chatted and after a while I walked back to the car, with a piece of time. Instead of going straight home I headed over to a friend's house. There I stayed and drank coffee and we talked watches, life and normal trivial earth-turning stuff.

At about the same time I was at my friend's house Kathryn was sorting out the horse list for the dentist who was coming that day. The list she wrote down was as follows:

Dentist – 29 April
Ollie – K
Riley 11.30 [crossed out] / 12.00
Ashley 11.30
Horse – K
Honey – 1.30
Speedy 11.00

Speedy's teeth had been done and so had Riley's and Ashley's, so Kathryn went down the lane to the bottom fields to get Ollie and another horse (whom I have referred to as Horse). Through the riding school gate, probably telling the dogs not to follow her, across the sandy outdoor school and onto the little track. She would have turned right into the fourteen-acre field and walked across the grassy patch that separated the upper and lower fields, to the field where Ollie and Horse lived. At this point she would have seen that they weren't in the top section but right down the bottom, near the tree line and gate that borders the fields and bridleway. In all likelihood she probably shouted for them to come as she did when feeding, yet it wasn't feed time so the chances are they didn't take any notice.

Meanwhile I left my friend's house and drove back home, turned onto the drive and parked up. It was time for a cup of tea and to look forward to a round of golf with the friend I always played with. So, I went into the back room which we called 'the posh one' and sat down with a cup of tea, opened the poetry book and put the watch on the coffee table.

Kathryn would have been grumbling that the two horses didn't come to her as she walked down the field, through the gap in the fence that separated the upper and lower parts of the field. Ollie and the horse were still in the bottom right corner. She most likely shouted for them again yet it looked like she would have to go right up to them, something she had done a thousand times. Two head collars, two horses.

She walked down into the field.

Stroked Ollie.

Put the head collar on Horse.

The phone rang in the kitchen.

The wind sung in the trees and the grass sighed. I walked into the kitchen and answered the call.

Ollie saw.

I love you. I've got you. See you later. x

Only two horses and Kathryn know what happened when she put the head collar on Horse. Horse knows and Ollie knows. Kathryn would have known what happened in an instant. Then she didn't. The horse she was attaching the head collar to bolted up the field. She was ripped out of life by a short lead rope attached to a horse that somehow had got around her neck. Frightened or scared by some unknown force whispering in the dreams of the wind, the horse took Kathryn with it. Kathryn died instantly, yet was dragged for an eternity as the horse galloped, bucked and ran through the waving grass of loss. She came up into the top of the field with Horse and they stopped, coming to rest on still dirt and green carpet as her Ollie watched from afar. He saw his master and owner die on the land she loved and cared for with all her heart. He saw the resting. She was only thirty-nine, yet she grew old and lived her whole remaining life in an instant as the wind blew in the trees and the clouds raced by above. It was everything in a corner of a field in England. God had painted a painting. It was all there was. Or as T. S. Eliot wrote,

'April is the cruellest month, breeding lilacs out of the dead land, mixing memory and desire.'

Back on the yard, Sarah and Kim realised Kathryn had been down the field a long time, so they called her on the phone; no answer. So, they followed her footsteps and found her in her field. They released her from Horse and Sarah tried to revive her. But it was all over. Time stopped and then carried on. The watch ticked its seconds into minutes. It was 13.34 on the watch when I answered the call from Christine.

'Are you at home?' she said.

'Yes.'

'You need to come to the yard.'

'Why?' I said.

'You need to come to the yard,' she repeated.

I paused. I felt her.

'OK, I'm on my way.'

George Michael sung about a 'Careless Whisper' on the radio, but the birds in the trees didn't sing back. The Defender steered itself. I felt sick to the core of my soul. I drove to the yard already knowing, her sister met me at the yard gate and her mouth said, 'She's dead.'

But I already knew that.

All time stopped.

The other side of the valley had seen the events play out in the field, the blue lights winking in sadness and the ambulances singing their tune. The theatre of wind, trees and Kathryn played out to a distant audience as the curtains closed on the afternoon's tragic play.

The rest of the day became a film where you're one of the main characters. The walk to the field with her sister, holding her hand. Trying to get into the field but the paramedics wouldn't let me. Not being able to be with her, to say hello or goodbye. Being escorted back to the yard and put in a police car, quizzed as to my movements in the morning. The yard on lockdown. Police, ambulances and paramedics. Bruno on a hay bale looking across the school and out to the lane. A movie set. Grief waiting in the wings, not ready to enter yet. A song on the radio that haunts.

The afternoon was a stark series of images. Her phone still contains messages telling her there had been an accident at the yard. 'Just calling to see if you're OK? There's lots of police cars and ambulances on Cross Lane.' Text messages that read, 'Everything OK? Ambulances at your place.' They record and hold moments in time that are now held in heaven's ledger.

I have no recollection of how I got the Defender back home, or how I got back to the yard to get *Top Gear* car and Romeo, although I do remember calling my friend and telling him I couldn't play golf that afternoon. Not even giving the reason why; just that 'something' had come up. Shock was dripping through the brain already. I have no idea of who was at Cross Lane, who said what, who held who, who cried. I think I called my mum, told her plainly. Informed her I was going to get drunk, the pub landlord tried calling me. It was around the village before I got to the pub where my brother met me. But I didn't get drunk; I think I just went home and sat on the sofa doing nothing. Two cheese and tomato sandwiches lay by the sofa, the water in the glass had gone stale; the lunch she had made herself before going to the yard still where she had left it. The walls walked into me and the ceiling crushed down in steady rain. It was too big for a drink. Romeo cried on the sofa instead.

I was plunged into the river of grief, high in the mountains I started at the source. In deep, cold waters that took me with them.

Kathryn was taken to hospital in Nottingham; I couldn't see her till the next morning. I think that was the hardest part at the time, just waiting to see her.

It felt like all the horses in the world had died and the proud colours of our life lay burned and frayed to all the southern winds. There were to be no more charges up fields of stubble, no more laughter together on wild horses. They all lay lifeless in endless corpses, swords and shields broken and bent. And in the midst of them all, there she lay with her big grey, fallen.

Ollie and Horse did not come in for the dentist that day. And I didn't sleep that night, and I don't think Kathryn's sisters did either. Nor her brother. Her parents were on holiday. Not due back till the Saturday night. The decision was taken to tell them when they came home. Like in all movies there was a soundtrack. It played on repeat; a lone bugle sound high in the distant sky.

Yet just as we seek, so are we sought out: at any moment we may slide into loss or be gathered in by some otherworldly light; at any moment, the angel of the annunciation may seek us out and demand some astonishing transformation.

Those words are from *The Hunt in the Forest* by John Burnside, the poetry book I bought on the morning she died. I am at a loss to explain how life works, like the way the spring breeze blows over long grass fields, or the way the wind moves trees and horses dance in fear and flight. Of great moments happening in fields no one knows about. Of life and death moving like tides flowing. The way the sun stops rising and the night comes in. Men in suits walking around doing their jobs, whilst people are crying, the ambulance man stopping me and apologising for not being able to save her. Of a horse watching the events and a dog waiting. Or knowing that it will never end.

Unlike the brave Oates: 'It was blowing a blizzard. He said, "I am just going outside and may be some time." He went out into the blizzard and we have not seen him since.' (Captain Scott)

Kathryn was my Captain Oates; yet she didn't choose to walk away from the tent into the snow. The field took her in a blizzard of green and horse. I felt like Scott left in the tent; the horseman had gone. And all I had left to look forward to was loneliness and a cold death writing sad letters.

It was yesterday, it was last year and it was a second ago. Infinity and eternity all rolled into one world, heaven in a flower. The church where we married is still there and the bells ring out for newlyweds. Horses are ridden and the dentist comes to check their teeth. I like the photo where Kathryn is stood on the lane outside the yard best, she's holding Strip in one hand and Otto and Jack are next to her. Or maybe the selfie of her with Strip. And there is the one of her and Ollie jumping out of water at a one-day event. Yes, that's the best one. It doesn't really matter though, they are all yesterday's images. Just like the time we stood in church together and the bells rang for us. The tolling of the bell never ends, grief and love ring out loud together, just as the images of an unfinished life never stop coming, in their past story-time way. Like all the yesterdays and unsaid words. It's all now and it's never there tomorrow. And outside the tent there is nothing but a void of dead snow; no more calls to a girl on a sofa waiting at home. No more notes left in a book for a boy to read.

CHAPTER SIXTEEN

The Hardest Walk

The car won't rumble fast down the drive,
This is alone, the non-return from the expedition,
A telegram of moon fall, freight train standstill,
Lone dark pummelling, or a steady creep of
The dawn slug, the glistening inch over stone floor,
It's the fire without flame, cramp in warm feet.

When times were tough, or we'd had a bad day, lying in bed at night, just after we had both snuggled up, covers over, lights out end-of-day feeling. Either Kathryn or I would say to the other, 'I've got you.' It was the single most important thing we said, apart from the three words that everyone says to each other. Or should do. We had been through tough times, and our three words, our own words, meant the world to us.

The sun rose the next day and I went to the yard. At least I think it did. I hadn't eaten or slept. I wanted to crawl out of the tent into the blizzard, after Oates. But the tent flapped and whistled, moving became instinct for I needed to go to the yard. I had the overwhelming sense that I needed to move forward. Get out of the tent and start walking, not crawling, for to stay still meant to die. There was no other choice, one way of life had abruptly ended and a new harder one began. I made no conscious decision to do so; it was just the right thing to do. And if I didn't get up to do the horses, I would have felt like never getting up again. I knew nothing about running a livery yard; I'd left Kathryn to it. Yet, I felt something deep within me even then and from somewhere else that this was the only path for me to follow. The reality of the situation had not hit, the shock of reality had not sunk in, and so the first day was just one of pure adrenalin. I have no idea or comprehension of what the rest of her family were feeling. The continuing sense of being in a film was all-encompassing, yet no film I'd ever watched.

Friends of Kathryn's, most notably Charlotte and liveries showed me each horse's feed bucket, what they ate, where the feed was stored. I think I labelled feed bins and buckets with what was in them and which horse had what. To be honest though I can't remember a lot about that first morning as the yard was secondary to what was coming later; seeing Kathryn. I think we fed the horses after I'd written the end lines of Tennyson's 'Ulysses' and lyrics from a Springsteen song, 'No Surrender', on the feed room wall. I'd just written what feeds were which in black marker on the wall but I needed words to steady me for the fight ahead, for I was about to drive to my brother's. He was taking me to the hospital, to the Western Front and all the horror that could be summoned up.

What happened over the next couple of hours was the hardest thing I've ever done and will ever do. Anyone who has lost someone suddenly will know what it feels like. You can't explain what it's like. You feel forever detached from the rest of humanity, you are alone and at a distance from all those around you. It is as if you have become a leper of death.

The walk from the car park to the hospital reception was not too difficult, relatively speaking, yet everything around me was blurred, as if it existed in another space in time. I saw myself from a mountain top, a little shambling figure moving over grey stone. I met a police officer and someone from the hospital to escort us to the mortuary, for Kathryn had to be formally identified by a relative, hence the police presence. We inched across no man's land. Or to the summit of the unknown mountain. Each step then became harder than the last; it was like pulling a 100kg pulk through heavy snow on the Polar Plateau but without the fatigue. The legs just didn't want to move, as if my feet were stuck in concrete. And why for the love of God do they put the mortuary in the very depths of the hospital? So, you take a walk when all reality you have ever known goes south and to the wind. No one exists, nowhere in the world.

Like in a set from *Alien* the corridors in the basement of the hospital were dimly lit, some lights flickered and some didn't work. There was litter blowing on the floor and all the doors steel-like and shut to life. The escort didn't know the way that clearly so we trudged through another world to the room at the end of the world. I've never done so short a walk that was so physically or mentally hard, nothing in Antarctica, nothing in the Arctic compares to it.

Faltering steps; walking to the ending of all things. Fumbling, faltering, on the walk no one should ever do. It's away from the light of men. It's the collapsed heaven's gate. It's a walk of darkness. It's the knowing that the end is real and that the demons exist. Every fight you ever fought, every ounce of determination has to be summoned; called upon in one final effort to pass under each neon strip light. The mortuary walk is one you do alone. My brother was there but not. The mortuary walk is a solitary walk of hell.

Eventually we arrived at a darker grey that seemingly stood out from the walls; maybe it was a door. Maybe a gateway. A ring on the buzzer and we were shown into the waiting room, a room with a couple of chairs, small round table complete with tissues and a leaflet stand with pamphlets on loss and support. It's a room with no sun in it.

And then there is the door, the door to the room at the end of the world, the door to the end of all things. There are no words written to describe the courage needed to open it and step through the opening. You are told, 'whenever you are ready, in your own time'. You will never be ready. There is no more time. In a split second that lasts an eternity you walk through the door into a room you actually now never want to leave.

To see a world in a grain of sand
And a heaven in a wild flower,
Hold infinity in the palm of your hand
And eternity in an hour.
William Blake

There she was. And there I was. It was everything. It was eternity. You cry, but it's not normal crying; it's a wail. The moment you stand in is so intensely personal and powerful it exists only with you. It sears you with the intensity and emotion. I saw my dad die in front of my eyes, and at the time that was the most powerful thing I thought it was possible to experience. Yet there was wonder in that in some strange way; when I saw the peace in my dad's eyes as my mum told him it was OK. My grandfather I saw just after he had passed, yet, he was an old man and had run a full course of life. Kathryn was not yet forty.

She looked as if she was tucked up in bed, all quiet and peaceful. But there would be no cuddles and no more patting of the duvet. There was nowhere to sit next to the bed, so you stand. You do what you need to do. I said words and stroked her hair. I promised her that I would look after her yard for her, her horses and dogs. I vowed through tears. Kissed her and felt the cold. I am forever standing by the bed and Kathryn. She looked like she was asleep. A quiet, deep, long sleep. But a lonely sleep, for the room didn't have pictures of Jack in it, or little greyhound statues and paintings by her dad. Or horses made from china. Chipped in places, but still standing proud. There were no clothes drying on the radiator. And she never stayed still that long, she always fidgeted lying in bed, rolling this way and that; kicking the covers. The covers stayed in place where she was lying now. And that broke my heart. So, I left it there with her, under the covers.

Walking to the room was hard, stepping into the room was harder, yet leaving the room; well that was another level of hardness. I could have stayed in that room for the rest of my life. I think I went in and out of the room at least four times, you walk out the first time and have to go back in. Even now, I just want to be back in that room with her.

Yet, all things in life end, and so did the time in the room at the end of the world. I asked for her wedding ring and the kind woman who waits table at the room of endings went in and got it off Kathryn. I left with her ring on my wedding finger. I'd never had my own, as when we got married we decided Kathryn would just have one. I wore my dad's after he died, but Kathryn's fitted like a glove.

Cars and people in them drove around on the roads, the sky with clouds in it moved around above us and we drove back to my brother's house. I can't remember driving back to the yard. Perhaps I wasn't fit to do so, but I didn't care. For there was only one thing to do, that had to be done and needed to be done. To ride Ollie.

The field was all quiet, there were no blue lights and men in high vis jackets with sorrowful looks. There was just a grey horse standing on the grass, alone. We were both alone now. I got on Ollie and we rode; with one of her friends, Charlotte; we rode for all time. We rode through the fields, down the paths, along the bridleways and up hills. We cantered through narrow paths lined with trees, round corners and up banks. We rode for Kathryn.

That night, social media kept me and Kathryn's brother going. A post announcing Kathryn's loss eventually reached over seventeen thousand people, and the messages and comments kept coming all night. Yet, her parents were due back and Andrew went to meet them at the airport. My brother-in-law Stuart stayed with me in the bleak empty house whilst in an airport private lounge, Andrew broke the news. I think my walk to the morgue room, and stepping into that room, must have been easy compared to what they had to hear from their eldest son.

I felt consumed by guilt; I wished with all my heart and being to change places with her. I still do.

I went to see her parents the next day and I just burst into tears when her dad held me. And I held him. And there was nothing in the world to do but hold her mum, and for her to hold me.

We sat at the same kitchen table where I had asked for her hand in marriage. Her dad said how excited she had been. My heart kept breaking as I'm sure theirs did. I never questioned why she was taken when she was, or the manner she went. I decided early on there was no point in that. No point at all, for she was already gone. Yet, now as time passes it's hard not to wonder why. As Christmas tunes play out over the pub stereo and couples and groups enjoy looking forward to time together, it's hard to accept the hand that was dealt. Yet, the very thing that had taken Kathryn would save me. Horses gave me a reason to wake up and get out of bed. I was in shock for a long time, still am. I still think I'll wake up one day and it will be just a bad dream. The door will bang and she'll walk in the house in a dash of Kathryn. Our empty house haunts me in its solace and space.

The owner of the horse that brought Kathryn up the field was distraught. I stood with her in the field, I might have held her. 'It's not your fault and it's not your horse's fault.' The words echoed again and again to an empty sky. Because it wasn't the horse's fault. Nor was it the winds or even the trees' fault. It was no one's fault. Sometimes bad things just happen. And good people die. We can do everything right and the roof will still fall in. It's part of life, and we either accept it or we die too.

Later that day the mobile rang in my pocket; the number showed it was from a satellite phone. I picked up and the line crackled; 'Hi Steve, it's Carl . . . I've just heard. I can't believe it. I had to call.'

I heard wind rustling on tent fabric, felt the delay in time and space. I knew Carl was in his tent in the middle of the Greenland icecap.

He felt my silence and continued. 'My mum heard the news and got in touch with me; I wish I was there with you . . .'

'Thank you, Carl, I can't really talk much now; but thank you so much for calling; it means a lot . . .' I mumbled.

'Take care Steve, I'll come and see you once I get back . . . take care . . .'

The signal died and the phone whistled in the distance between us. I thought of my calls to Kathryn from the icecaps and wild spaces. I thought of the love that bounced from a phone in a tent, into space and to a phone at home; I thought of the warmth those calls meant. For when the air has that summer cold burnt smell and the swallows have left, we need to hold on to love. The love that was and still is.

CHAPTER SEVENTEEN

Back to Church

The congregation came and left, only to come home,
Life continued on the same and not the same,
He carried on in life; she carried on in death,
Both working towards a meeting place. Mary's Place.

The next month was actually easy compared to what was to come. The focus in the early days was all about the funeral, all about the inquest, all about learning the basics to run the yard. About riding Ollie. I started a diary the day she went. It's a snapshot now; of raw loss in its infancy:

29 April. Hell.

30 April. Saw her at the hospital. Rode Ollie.

1 May. Parents. Yard. Rode Ollie.

2 May. Hospital with her mum. Yard. Fixed electrics. Played Bon Jovi.

3 May. Vicar. Yard. Ride with a friend of hers. Kathryn loves me. Work. Environmental health. Tough. Did field.

4 May. Yard all morning. Meeting about Cross Lane. Funeral man.

5 May. Yard. BPE meeting. Golf. Yard.

6 May. Bank. Coroner. Funeral people. Health and safety visit. Spent.

7 May. Tack shop, Cheshire. DofE. Hitting home.

8 May. Ride with a friend. Mum. Slept instead of golf. Tough.

9 May. Feed. BPE sorted. Ride Oliver. Coroner call. Reporter. Sort her dress for funeral.

10 May. Feed. Fetch her truck. Banks. Vicar.

11 May. Yard all morning. Rode. Funeral meeting.

12 May. Getting harder. Church again. Met Christine. Rode Ollie.

13 May. Car mot. Counsellor. Rode in school. Friend jumping. Got truck on road. Struggling.

14 May. Rode, got clipper blades. Vets with cake. Golf.

15 May. Rode both horses. Tired.

16 May. Anger.

17 May. I can't remember. Jump clinic.

18 May. Funeral directors. Kathryn.

19 May. Berry's. Printed final speech. Rode alone. Funeral directors.

20 May. 3 weeks. Funeral prep. Saw her the last time. Rode. Golf one hole. Par . . .

21 May. Funeral.

22 May. Fed, then back to bed. Rode with a friend felt better.

23.May. Bad day.

24 May. Picked up her ashes.

25 May. Springsteen concert in Manchester.

26 May. Can't remember.

27 May. Scattered ashes.

Those were the first days on the return journey, when the load was at its heaviest, the way forward was so dark and snowy, I was stuck at the pole; at the ends of the earth. The return to home was just a daze in the distance. I needed to walk forward to survive. I had started the walk back. The diary is not like Scott's, for posterity; but it gave me a reason to get home each day. To just write a couple of words, it means I made it back to the tent each night. That I had covered the distance I needed to each day. I lay on the sofa with *Star Trek* on the TV, Romeo on his sofa and I wrote the daily log. It was my comfort zone at the end of the day's walk, when the stove was on and the wind whispered in the tent.

I made a very basic list: Yard, BPE, Kathryn. There was a family meeting at her parents' house where the question of what was to happen to the yard felt like the elephant in the room.

'I'm going to run the yard,' I declared.

The family faces looked at me, all in disbelief.

'Yes; I'm going to run the yard, I promised Kathryn in the hospital. I'm going to look after her yard, her horses and her dogs . . . I told her I've still got her,' I stated. For that was the truth.

'You don't know anything about running a yard,' someone said.

'I know that. But I'll learn. I didn't know how to get to the South Pole once. But I learned. If it takes me years then I'll learn. But that's what I'm doing,' I declared.

And the silence remained until the conversation moved on.

I'm stubborn when I need to be, and it was probably that single quality that enabled me to face up to the task ahead. The yard needed sorting and to be kept running, BPE needed taking into a very busy summer season of overseas expeditions to places like Iceland, Greenland and the Himalaya and UK programmes, and a funeral needed planning. There was also the inquest and the investigation to contend with. A friend read about Kathryn's inquest in *The Times* on his way to work on the train, but there was no Robin Hood to rescue the maiden from the sheriff. Accidental death was the conclusion. Because she died at work there were lots of issues to deal with; and also, her mum wanted to go and see her. I don't think anyone else could face it, or maybe they wanted to remember her in the fullness of life.

We sat in the café at the hospital in silence and watched people walk by in their bubble lives. I did the walk to the room in the basement one more time and experienced the same feeling of not wanting to leave. But harder, the second trip took something from my soul. I have no idea what was going through her mum's mind, I can only try and imagine; but surely there is nothing worse than losing your child. She looked at Kathryn for a long time. I told her there were no rules, no right or wrong on what to say or do. We drove home, and I think we had a Sunday dinner at some point, and I was starving.

BPE was relatively easy to sort at first; Steve Stout the overseas manager took over complete control of the company. He had to contend with the fact our company secretary and financial director was no longer there. Kathryn was the only one who knew about the financial side of BPE, the ATOL licence and all the invoicing. Plus no one knew her passwords. Steve faced a logistical nightmare, and I cannot think of anyone on the planet who could have done it easily. But he did it. We would meet once a week to talk over things as the summer progressed to see how we were coping in our little capsules of difficulty.

It would take three weeks for Kathryn to move from the hospital to the chapel of rest at the funeral directors; opposite the pub we used to meet at, and the one where I'd wait for her ahead of parties we'd go to together. I couldn't wait for her to arrive at the chapel, despite the bizarre decisions as to what dress she needed, what shoes to pick for her. She would be there for three days, three whole days to see her. So, I went morning and night. It wasn't her though. It was just her body, but I would sit in the room with her and tell her that her dogs and her horses would be OK. I made the promise once more to her, in case she hadn't heard it the first time in the hospital. Despite whatever obstacles would be thrown our way, I would look after her animals and her yard.

I can't remember how we ended up with our funeral directors, but we met and started planning the funeral. It's surreal being shown the brochures of coffins. Is someone playing a joke, you think? When is Russell Crowe going to walk in and declare the true emperor is dead? You are asked to choose a dress and shoes for her to wear, big decisions clouded with emotion. It was also a time of isolation. For some reason the planning fell to me, the order of service, the songs, hymns, the where and when. The list seemed endless, yet it was also a strange blessing for it gave focus to a life without meaning. But like Kathryn when she planned the wedding, I made a simple list to start with: '*Church, hymns – words to say.*'

'I Vow to Thee, My Country', 'Jerusalem' and 'Make Me a Channel of your Peace' formed the core of our wedding. Hymns Kathryn and I had planned together. So that was the core again. Fergus agreed to be my best man just as he had done before. It was essentially the wedding service again; that was my reference point. There were people to carry her into the crematorium and then a memorial service at the church we were married in. On a long drive into Cheshire to buy some new boots for the yard I sought through songs to enter and leave to. Gradually the arrangements took shape. I had no plans to involve horses, yet somehow, they needed to be there. Louise, a local riding instructor whom I'd never met stepped forward and offered her two Greys, Duke and Jaylow, to provide an escort from the swimming pool. We met at her house and planned the horses' journey to take Kathryn home. The songs were one of the hardest choices; even now I hope she thinks I got it right. I just wanted to be on a mountain once more with her, to bathe in all the sea and as the song says, lie with Kathryn for ever. Until every sky falls in.

The yard was all about hearts and minds, it was a shattered place. It had lost its captain, owner, and in truth its soul. The colours flew tattered and frayed, for Cross Lane was Kathryn and Kathryn was Cross Lane. Everyone at the yard rallied round in the first weeks, the support was truly amazing as I thrust myself into a job I knew nothing about. It was a jigsaw puzzle with no reference point; just fragments of corners. I relied on the snippets of information I had picked up from Bloomsgorse, from friends in the industry and from everyone at the yard. Kathryn guided me through her close friends; Charlotte was invaluable, Tasha helped beyond measure, Fiona too, as did many others. I rode Ollie at every opportunity, on my own, with no phone, with people from the yard, and in all weather and conditions. I was a ghost rider on a widow maker. Out of control seeking no solace but the plains of the forest. Death fed off me and I longed to be consumed.

The 21 May was the date set for Kathryn's final journey in this life, a Saturday. The day before I saw her for the last time after picking up the flowers for the funeral with her friend Fiona, then driving by her old house; which had a sign in the window saying 'love'. Finally to the church to make sure all was ready.

I sat on the same seat in the church where it seemed like only moments ago I had waited with Fergus for Kathryn to come down the aisle. A female vicar saw me.

'Hello there. How are you doing?' she asked kindly as she sat down next to me.

'I don't think I can get through tomorrow. I don't have the strength.'

I started crying.

'It's OK, let's ask for some help to get you through the day,' she said as she put her arms around me. And then she prayed for me and for Kathryn. To get us both through the day, together.

'Thank you. I think I'll be OK now,' I said, after the prayer. 'Will you be here tomorrow?'

'Yes, I will, I won't be conducting the service but I'll be stood to the left of the dais; look for me if you need to,' she said with a smile.

She made a difference and gave me the courage to face the hardest day.

Ollie and I rode out in the early morning, and for the first time in all the years I had been walking in the woods and riding in them I saw a deer. It stood on the track in front of us, looked at us and then bounded off through the fields and into the forest. The deer seemed as a symbol, of the hunt that forever goes on in the forest. The hunt we all beat our drum to, the drum of life and death. With the yard done, I and all those going to see her off headed home to get ready.

Kathryn's funeral was a big day. People lined the road outside Cross Lane and threw flowers on the hearse. The driver commented that he had never seen that before. Kathryn went up Rickett Lane past the field where Oliver and Strip live. As if in recognition, Strip Cartoon was stood at the gate. She turned onto Cross Lane and Bruno, Zac and Romeo were waiting with one of the new liveries. And there were the people; lining the road and all the little yards on the lane. With flowers streaming off the hearse Kathryn headed to the crematorium.

Kathryn was carried in by her sisters and brothers, two friends and me. Family and close friends gathered to see her go. She was held aloft to the backdrop of Springsteen's 'The Rising'. I read my poem, 'Today God Painted a Painting' that I knew she had liked. It went like this:

Early in the morning god woke up with a purpose, for there at the bottom of his bed was a blank canvas, of such purity and white clarity he knew he had to paint. God was not a great painter, occasionally he sketched; sometimes wrote, but painting; no. After tea and toast he sought out his tools, deep in a lost chest lay god's brushes and paints. So, he started. He painted, he painted in watercolours of such breath the canvas sang.

The sky was so blue you could see through it, into the blue that lay behind. He painted the morning, a morning of trees, all in one; browns and yellows and sort of browns, running water paint that dripped and swam into one colour, it was the colour of late sunshine autumn. He painted bells ringing, an echo of sound ringing across the valley blending into the days being. And people played in the grass and the churches, painted into the canvas.

Lunch was a brief affair of cold ham and bread, for god wanted little time put to waste, moving on to the afternoon the colours faded a little, with a deft of brush and faint of hand the day wore on. The golds and blues lost not any brilliance, they faded into the memory of home and all that is cosy about slow steady walks towards the oak fire. And the planes danced on air in streaks of white, balloons rose on nothing, all over the canvas life lived its purpose.

It was tiring work, so he broke for tea and toast at just after three, girding for the last hour of light. The time when all painters lay down the finest and most important painted words. So, with hand aching he picked his finest brush; with a committed hand he drew the silver strands of dew and web streaking across all the meadows, fields all over told tales in the waving lines of dreams he conjured on his canvas. And at this he realised his pallet was drawing empty, the day was drawing.

And then at the last moment he paused, he remembered something, the reason for the day, as the sun set he grabbed his pencil, A quick sharpen with wood falling in curls to the dusty floor, in the bottom left-hand corner he etched them in. A couple. Hand in hand. Walking through heather into the setting love. Two pencil dogs ran in laughter, one short-haired, one fawn. I reckon that's perfection he said to himself. He added his signature, an afterthought, as a big grey leaped in joy.

So, the canvas had a painting on it, a picture to match the backdrop, and god sat back with tea in hand, lit his pipe and looked at what he had painted. But he could see no painting, instead he saw the day as we saw it. The dance of colours in the leaves, the sweep of sky so blue it hurts, the crisp heated air of warm autumn and the joy of such a day spent in good company, it was a special day, a day to remember. It's not every day god paints, he is not known for his brush skills. But when he does, oh my Lord; he can't half paint a good picture.

I think the poem went down well, I don't know for sure. I deliberately tried to detach myself from the day because it was the only way to get through it. As Springsteen's 'Mary's Place' played out I stayed behind and left a rose on her. The BPE flag with its Latin motto *fortitudo et fides* (strength and honour) lay on her too. I watched her enter the fire as she went from this life and into the next one. The close group then headed to the church for the final scene, the celebration of her life.

As the cars passed the swimming pool, Louise's two grey horses stepped out onto the road. The power of the moment was beyond emotion; word-failing equine beauty stood there in salute. For a moment of eternity they stood there, then they turned to lead the cars all the way to the church in a troop of perpetual love. Majestic and proud, they rode through the streets taking her home. Steel hooves heralded her arrival at the church.

Fergus led the way for me as we walked into St Peter's to pay tribute to Kathryn's life, and God's house was standing room only. There was just one person missing. So, I held her ring and kept her heart in my heart, and like before there were only really two people there.

Just off to my left, a quiet spirit watched the day unfold and held my hand.

I wore the same suit I was married in, the same shirt, the same shoes and same socks. The same tie and cufflinks. The only differences were a few comfort items in my pockets. A wooden cross, her engagement ring and eternity ring in a little bag Andrew from Berry's Jewellers had given me for the day. And the watch. The clasp on the watch has what's known as the Calatrava Cross; in memory of a Spanish religious order that in 1158 defended the Calatrava Citadel against the Moors. I needed to feel her by my side, defending me like she had always done; and the feeling that I would be now defending her for as long as I lived.

Friends and her sister Emma spoke; they led the way. Gave me hope I could speak too. I trusted the vicar from the day before.

Holding the sides of the plinth I stared out at the faces before me.

'To all those at Cross Lane and BPE, you have been beyond words. I am forever in your debt. She was as much of BPE as me, we were a team. I now will be as much of Cross Lane as she is.' Faces stared back at me in the crowded church.

I carried on. 'Death has not parted us. It's actually made my bond with Kathryn stronger. So, to you all, don't worry about death. It means nothing; it's just a small thing.'

After struggling through a poem I stepped down and thought of the wind in the field when she died. Of a girl and her big grey horse, of our love. Of a bond that is bigger than death. 'Living on a Prayer' by Bon Jovi sounded out through the stone pillars. The vicar quoted poems that felt surreal in their connection to Kathryn and me. We were playing the bugle and laying the colours to rest. It was the place we remembered. I don't think she could have had a better farewell. 'Because We Can', also by Bon Jovi, signalled the end of the service.

I went outside, sat on a bench and reflected. The friends who had been there at the wedding joined me and friends from Bloomsgorse. I took Kathryn's hunting hip flask out of my pocket and we toasted her with sloe gin. We called the ride home, were the little band of brothers who were there in the beginning.

'From this day to the ending of the world, but we in it shall be remembered' Shakespeare said about such days. But this wasn't St Crispin's Day that Shakespeare referred to and the cavalry didn't stamp their hooves around us. This was a day that would suspend us in time, for the actions of such hours are indelibly marked on our soul. There is no going back and no glory, no uncurled flag and no country; only memory.

Funerals are strange; family members you rarely see turn up, never to be seen again. Most of the people who stood in our front room I've not seen since. Why is that? Is the darkness of tragedy too hard to face? Or do those of us who live it turn people away in our grief? Friends become bigger friends only to disappear later. People know you really well; then don't know you ever again. People come in and out of your life like leaves in autumn.

Her mum and dad thanked everyone for coming, a handwritten note which they asked me to post online: *'It made us very proud to know so many people thought highly of her.'*

The yard was done later; I went and fed the horses, detached from their warmth and touch. A few people met for a beer later in the local pub. Some I didn't know at all and haven't seen since. It was a lonely heart-breaking meeting. And then it was done. A very close friend from a long time ago, Sue Dawson, and her husband came back to the house, but didn't stay for long. I needed to be alone. To get ready for the battle ahead.

The film had not stopped playing; it had just started. The city was in ruins and the sofa was forsaken. This was the lone. The jet was without a deck to land on, out of fuel. No goose. I felt the shivering shock of a falling horse onto frost-ridden grass; of the solitary years ahead, without glimpsing the sleeping nose or quiet eyes bathed in a warming sun through closed curtains.

Everyone that has gone through such a day knows that it takes away something from you. Something that can never be replaced. I wanted no hugs, no sympathy and no love. For to accept that would have made it impossible to make it through the day. You pay a price for the day, for the strength it takes to endure the loss and the saying of goodbye is only given by giving your heart and soul. A part of you dies with your wife.

Is this true of all losses, or only sudden ones? I only know from experience. When my father was ill with cancer, we all knew he was going to die. So, you slowly prepare yourself for the loss. Bit by bit you adjust, so when it happens it's not so shocking. Yes, it's heart-wrenching and desperate, but you've had a chance to say goodbye. Sudden loss doesn't give you that. It just takes and keeps on taking, leaving nothing.

Diaries are private things, as was Kathryn's. Years before her last journey she wrote down words that I only found in the months after her funeral.

My other train of thought was funerals – mine, actually – I'd like to be buried, and I'd like two songs played – for your Savage Garden's

Truly, Madly, Deeply and Dido's Thank you. I'd also like a poem read, by you if you like, or someone else if you prefer (family if poss) – Remember by Christina Rossetti.

> Remember me when I am gone away,
> Gone far away into the silent land;
> When you can no more hold me by the hand,
> Nor I half turn to go yet turning stay.
> Remember me when no more day by day
> You tell me of our future that you planned;
> Only remember me, you understand
> It will be late to counsel then or pray.
> Yet if you should forget me for a while
> And afterwards remember, do not grieve;
> For if the darkness and corruption leave
> A vestige of the thoughts that once I had,
> Better by far you should forget and smile
> Than that you should remember and be sad.

Having said that, I always assume that you'll go first. Morbid tonight aren't I! Love you, Kathryn xxx

On a mild day not long after the funeral, the immediate close family gathered as we laid Kathryn to her final resting. Her ashes were scattered into the winds and the sky, the fields of grass and the views of home. A piece of stone I'd found in the forest marked her name with a single kiss. Jack is buried at the family field along with Bruce, Ellie, Scarlet and Penny. I read out one of my poems.

As each close of God's play and waking of dew's dawn, your hair tangles the pillow of our sleep. And as the leaves fall to be consumed by the earth that created them, my love grows.

It was to a pillow with no weight on it that I whispered a quiet 'I've got you' that night in the darkness of May.

All life returns to the hearth in the end, and I wait to join her on the grass mound overlooking the places we rode together. When I do go, I hope someone carves my name next to Kathryn's on the stone, that they scatter my ashes and lay my heart back down with hers. I can't think of anywhere better in the world to be.

CHAPTER EIGHTEEN

Entering the Arena

Many a long winter and summer have passed,
Since wandering eyes befell on the kingdom of home,
So now all ropes are straining and the deck singing,
As a tired bow plunges homeward,
Chasing rampant horses down white chases.

As I stepped down from the ladder the wind whistled into the marrow of my bones. Snow drove in tiny particles across the ground, gaining pace until it cantered into my face. The Ilyushin transport plane's engines hummed in silent protest at the vastness of the last continent. Yet, I was ready. Ready in my heart of hearts for this great expedition. A violent laughing gust of ice and hay caught me by surprise. I grabbed the ladder for support. Then I realised; there wasn't an expedition transport plane attached to the ladder. It was a tractor. And I wasn't in Antarctica about to walk to the pole and back. I was in the field; and it wasn't winter at all. It was the end of April, and the cold was the quiet feel of grief. Suddenly I was uncertain; there was no note in my pocket from her. Only the scale of the quest ahead. I left the pole behind, kissing the ring on my finger. Took the first steps homeward as a lone robin danced in the air.

A ring of gold is a symbol, a complete circle of unity that binds together on itself. It's not broken, it lasts for ever. I had put Kathryn's wedding ring on and it fitted perfectly. Which was strange, for her hands and fingers have always been bigger than mine. In *The Lord of the Rings* the main character questions the ring coming to him, Gandalf summarises that we cannot choose what happens to us, we can only make the best out of the time we have left. So, Kathryn's ring came to me; I did not want to wear it. Yet, I chose to accept it and continue the unbroken circle that we exchanged in church. For as long as I wear the ring, she is alive with me and I carry her forward with me. I've got her.

In church in front of everyone I had promised I would be there for Cross Lane, I knew it would be hard and probably the hardest thing I would ever do. Yet I never realised how difficult it would actually be. I hadn't agreed to run a marathon or climb Everest, a singular event in time; for my Arthurian task was to have no known end. An ongoing monastic quest each day and then another day, until the setting of the sun on my life. And to try and do it in the grief that consumes you, becomes a rage and an anger that tries to destroy you from the inside out. You rage at others who haven't lost. You begin to despise yourself and what you have become, an empty hull of the ship that once was. Then the anger sets in, anger at life and all those who are happy. This was to make trying to run the yard like swimming in sand over the coming months. A slow-motion drowning in loss.

The easy path was to continue with BPE and expeditions, in the beginning I thought I could do both, manage BPE from afar and have someone running it day to day. But it soon became obvious that I had to decide. Cross Lane or BPE.

Kathryn hadn't made a will and we had never talked about what we would do if one of us went suddenly, who does? At thirty-nine you think you will live for a long time, the unthinkable doesn't cross your mind. When Ran Fiennes' first wife Ginny died, they had already discussed what he should do. She gave him her blessing to remarry and have the child they always wanted. And that he did. For my part; I had the promise I had made to Kathryn at the hospital and the vague conversation we'd had that one day Ollie would be mine. But when the world falls in you can only act on blind faith. I had no idea what Kathryn would have wanted me to do, I only knew what everyone around me wanted me to do, and in the expedition world they wanted me to carry on with BPE. Kathryn's family probably thought I was doing the wrong thing; they didn't say so out loud, yet their belief that it couldn't be done hung in the air like solid grey clouds. Yet, as I drove away from the office one day, I knew the answer; it came down to one thing, one act of faith and belief. If one day I was to see Kathryn again I could not look her in the eye and tell her I'd sold her beloved Cross Lane. So, I made plans to sell BPE instead.

We went into the summer season in 2016, God knows how. Everyone at BPE did wonders; in fact, I think it was her finest hour. We had one major incident when a student got altitude sickness in the Himalayas. The team had done everything right, acclimatised correctly, taken their time. Yet, sometimes the deck just stacks up against you. One little incident builds on another, and over the course of twenty-four hours a minor incident became a major one. Both Steve and I thought he would not survive; that would have ended us both. He was burnt out and I was in the depths of grief; we got lucky as the student pulled through. It was the first serious near-miss in BPE's history. In retrospect it backed up the decision to focus on Cross Lane; I couldn't face the prospect of loss anymore.

The toll of Kathryn going meant I had no reserves left. I concentrated on the yard. At the same time the inquest was rolling on, first of all they needed to 'open' the inquest. Apparently the bereaved don't usually attend these, but I wanted to go the full distance with Kathryn and the coroner had implied it was just a name-calling-out exercise. I misunderstood and went alone to the venue in Nottingham, it wasn't just a name calling out, and as I sat alone in the rather large serious room they went through every detail of the accident, the post mortem and its findings; I was given copies and I read them. *Christ, how do I get through this?*

I have read the documents once, the post mortem report in all its detail is a hard read. I know all her weights, each part of her body, all her details. They are written down in black and white. I once saw a post-mortem when I worked at the hospital. It still haunts me now. I can't watch police dramas or anything to do with hospitals; it's too close to home.

The parting was so brutal, so sudden in its entirety that sometimes I can't believe she was ever here. Or, that she ever went. Surely the drive will rumble any minute with the sound of a silver Defender horse-box pulling in. The bleep of a vehicle alarm, a sound of a bin being put out, the clash of the front door opening.

'Hello,' she would loudly shout. 'I'm just going to do Netties,' or, 'just taking Romeo round the block.' This was normal. So not to have it must mean it never was there in the first place. This is how it feels.

That's the cruel nature of sudden loss, there is no goodbye. There is only high water and hell, the slow-motion drip of another reality. Her lack of existence was destroying me. I felt as if I didn't exist in some ways, half of me left with her. And what was left of me was trying to follow a ghost, live up to a legend.

Did Kathryn exist? Yes, she did. I wear her wedding ring, I own her horses. Friends remember her. Did she die? Yes, she did. It's the sudden tearing away of the life that makes you question that very existence though. I would find shards of frayed rope in the field; heartbreaking real reminders that she was here; coarse touches to the hand of her last walk. I raged at the horse.

I knew someone once who used to be a counsellor for Cruise, the bereavement specialists. According to her, sudden traumatic loss is the hardest to deal with. All forms of grief are terrible in their sadness, yet there is something cruel and desperate about sudden loss. If someone loses a child or a parent, or a husband or wife loses their partner, then they face the toughest challenge a person can face. Kathryn's parents know this challenge. They know its name, face the raging each waking sunrise. Face the questioning of the existence of a precious daughter.

The utility companies also seemed to have difficulty in believing she was gone; they wanted to speak to the 'account holder'. Every day became an exercise in falling down and trying to stand; an insane battle with energy companies, phone companies and every utility and bank provider because I didn't have the list of passwords. I lost count of the times I put the phone down on officialdom and bureaucracy. The house insurance ran out, phone accounts ran out; the account holder wasn't home. In the end I was forced to take out new accounts on almost every aspect of household management. The one company that did the right thing was the National Farmers Union (NFU). I'd picked her car up as it was in for service when she went, I knew I wasn't insured on it and eventually found a three-year-old letter from the NFU. Upon calling them and explaining the situation the lovely women said, 'I'll look into it and call you back in two hours.' On the dot two hours later she called back and explained Kathryn insured her car, trailer, horse and business through them; she informed me she had transferred the account into my name. It was the only company to cut through the red tape and make a logical and humane decision. They were in direct contrast to most companies, the worst being a high street bank. The commercial bank manager Michael was brilliant; he went above and beyond to sort and help stuff out; yet the 'official' people have been difficult at best.

Whilst I was trying to sort all of this out I found the last photo she took. It's a screen shot on her phone of Zac. The date is Friday 29 April 2016 and the time is 12.35, an hour before

Christine had called me with the news of her death. In the top left-hand corner, the signal is displayed as 'no service'. I find the combination of that image and that time very difficult to comprehend. It's something I wish I could have conveyed to the huge corporations when trying to get the bills and paperwork sorted out. Yet death is a business and the personal side of loss is something left for the families to deal with and cope with.

The fact that she had made no will and was the sole director of Cross Lane was a huge issue, but gradually Christine who managed Cross Lane's finances made headway and began the slow process of sorting out the probate and all the paperwork that involved. Whilst I immersed myself in a world of horses Christine drowned in paperwork. She had ridden every Saturday with Kathryn, but to this day she has still not got back on a horse.

A few days after the funeral on the 25 May her brother Andrew accompanied me to see Bruce Springsteen in concert in Manchester. Kathryn and I were supposed to be going together. It seemed the right thing to do at the time, try and carry on as normal. Vainly I tried to get a request to him to play two songs; 'The Rising' and 'Mary's Place'; on social media the response was amazing including Radio Manchester appealing for the songs to be played. I don't think he got the requests, and it didn't matter anyhow. He played 'The Rising' anyway followed by 'Thunder Road'. It seemed appropriate, yet the stadium felt like an empty place. On the drive home I snapped at Kathryn's brother Andrew; I was selfish in my grief. He'd lost his sister but I felt I'd lost everything, my wife, my career and my life. The house was desolate and cold when I got home; there was no glory at the end of the day. No Kathryn, only slugs on the stone floor at midnight.

For me the way to cope was to face death and the loss head on, to go to the yard and try and learn Kathryn's job. I think in retrospect it was the hardest way to deal with it, if she had worked in a bank and been killed in a traffic accident in some ways it would have been easier. Yet she had her business and was co-owner of BPE. Whichever way I turned I could never escape, save leaving everything and living on a desert island. That would have been running away, and I've never run away from a challenge in my life, but every day I wanted to, the scale of the challenge was at times overwhelming. I had also inherited her role as chairperson with the local Blidworth and District Riding Club, which gave young riders a place to practise and have fun, free from the pressures of the show world, plus I'd started the Kathryn Bull Memorial Trust on the back of donations given in church. Its aim is to give grants to local riders to help them with competitions or training. Then I'd enrolled on a horse management course with a local training provider, and to top it off I had Ollie to get to grips with. The way to beat the devil was to engage idle hands.

But still it was the start of a descent into the deepest grief and complete and utter loneliness that is possible to comprehend. Little did I know then that the first six months were the easy days, people asked how you were and spoke about it. Two years down the line it was to get even harder; for by then everyone else has moved on. And you are just on day two; grief becomes a lurching stumble between anniversaries of missing. You are caught between not wanting to live and not wanting to die. Time hangs on the drips of tears. Every day I would go into the field to work and feed the same horses who were with her when she died. Every morning I would kneel down in the school and take a small handful of sand in my palm. I tried to connect to the earth, to her. To cleanse the dreams that threatened madness in the night.

Dreams so vivid I thought they were real. They seemed to be in the nether land, between sleep and waking. I came home from work to what I thought would be the usual empty house, yet I heard dog bowls clanking in the kitchen. Kathryn was feeding Jack and Otto. I went into the garden as for some reason I needed to look for a golf ball. It was a hot summer evening despite it being mid-winter, Boxing Day night. So, I had no top on. She came into the garden and stood slightly above me as I looked in the ditch for the ball. She looked down at me with such a look of love it was home again. And then she kissed me. Held my head and continued to kiss me. She had never gone away. It felt as if she had realised I was lonely and alone and came to me. And I knew she would always be there, waiting for me in the garden. She would always be in the garden.

Then you wake and realise.

Sometimes on a mountain, deep in cloud and visibility at zero with steep drops only metres away, panic rises. It's a feeling of stomach-churning dread, cold sweat and fear; but then your experience and training kicks in. You get the map out and work through the problem. There is no map to loss though, and the momentary feeling of panic you have on the mountain lasts all the time in grief. You have no idea how to find the map that will guide your way out of grief, never mind how to use it. It would take me a long, long time to find the map, and then longer still to begin to learn how to read it, to realise what she had actually left me. To finally see the map as her gift.

The pervasive sense of being on a film set haunted me; a cross between *Gladiator* and *We Bought a Zoo*. I felt like I had been shoved into the arena, to fight for something I never wanted to fight for. I was alone; too used to support and backup. Now it was gone and the armies of the north were far away. I was fighting to get back home at the same time as working with her dream and her horses. I was trying to uphold our beliefs of strength and honour, but caught in a loop of unreality. Trying to keep Cross Lane running in the midst of all the heartache. I was Maximus and I didn't want to be, I just wanted to be at home with Kathryn and for the nightmare to end. I wanted to be in the garden helping her sort the flowers out or at the garden centre buying a little plant. She was the head gardener and I was her helper, I needed her hand to hold mine as I walked into the crowds and the dusty sand school of death.

I felt that whilst everyone was moving upwards and forwards, I was sinking. I wondered if the worst was to come; what prospect a lonely future? Chris Bonington the climber remarried less than two years after his wife of over fifty years died from motor neurone disease. He had found someone he could share his life with a second time, realised that we need to make the most of our time here on earth. A year after Kathryn left I was still dealing with bills and phone companies and the red-tape nightmare of loss. I can understand why someone would remarry because the nights are so dark and so stripped of life, you want to feel that warmth once more; to share a life with all its unexpected problems, joys and smiles. To feel the closeness of another person telling you it will be OK, that the monsters under the covers and in the cupboards will go away when the sun comes up. But on your own they don't. The monsters are still there in the sunlight.

Seeing someone I used to work with in town one day rocked and upset me, although he didn't see me. I wanted to go over and speak to him, but he was with his wife and son. But to say what? I stood behind a market stall and watched them instead. It's a side effect of the loss, you withdraw into yourself; afraid of talking about the loss, afraid of explaining how you really feel. So, you walk quietly away on the other side of the street. Whilst others carry on their normal happy lives.

Mallory the Everest climber described climbing as spiritual, 'To struggle and to understand – never this last without the other.' He could quite easily have been talking about grief, but maybe he was; coping with loss is like trying to scale the highest mountain.

Not long after Kathryn left, her sister's horse Ellie was put down. She had laminitis in all four feet and in the end the decision to end her suffering was taken. I think it broke Christine's heart again. She was buried in the family field; Pete a local farmer dug the grave with great skill and care; as I watched the soil cover her, death came back again, punching with even harder blows. New losses tend to trigger old losses; they remind us in sharp kicks to the ribs of what we have endured. Of what we don't have any more, of the sadness that only consumes the grief-stricken. Then a few months later someone called about their horse. His name was Cap, and he was retired. Kathryn had promised the owner a place at the yard if they were ever struggling, so the decision Kathryn made was honoured. Cap went into Ollie's field but he had Cushing's disease and his time was limited. Late one afternoon the vet came out and he was put down. I think this hit me harder than when Ellie went, for I was still in deep shock from losing Kathryn.

I led Cap out into the top field and there under the Land Rover's glare he was put down. Horses land with a thud. I covered him with a tarp and arranged for him to be buried the next morning. Pulling off the tarp on a cold damp misty morning was like pulling the rug off Kathryn in the hospital. Climbing down into the hole to take the webbing straps off that had lowered him down was like walking to the room in the basement once more. Standing ten foot down in a hole in the ground with a dead horse, I questioned my sanity in trying to run the yard.

Liveries on the yard were truly amazing in the early days, I clung to them like a drowning man does to a lifebelt. They were souls that saved me in the fresh waters of death; Charlotte, Tasha, Sam, Tracey and Alison, to name a few. Yet over time they drifted away, maybe the loss of their friend was too much. And the yard too full of ghosts. Maybe I was so caught up in my own self-pity and dark clouds I drove them away, maybe I just upset them without knowing it. The death of Cap and Ellie was compounded by the loneliness of these lost relationships. I tried to do what Kathryn would have done, smile and carry on, yet at times I failed. The simple fact stood clear, Kathryn was Cross Lane. And I wasn't.

I found myself in between worlds, wanting to be here in ours and wanting to ride after Kathryn. I struggled to hold the line. I have met many people in the course of my life: people in foreign lands, explorers on icecaps, soldiers and officers, dignitaries and royalty, but no one has had the dignity, honour and sheer love of life that Kathryn did. I couldn't live up to that. I do what I do out of love for her memory. The belief there is such a love for all of us.

We are sometimes presented with opportunities or choices in our lives that can either define us or consume us. To either live by the words and codes we believe in or walk away from the fight. At BPE our motto was 'strength and honour'. Do those words mean anything? They kept Kathryn and me moving forward. The strength for me was the ability to keep getting up each morning in the early days after Kathryn left, and would continue each day as an exercise in getting hit to the ground, getting back up and then falling down again. To feel the pull of Kathryn as I lay there, the pull to stand.

Honour. In some ways an old-fashioned word these days, it's about doing the thing that is morally right. I also think for me it links to our marriage vows; 'to love, honour and obey'; we had chosen the traditional vows specifically ahead of the wedding, vows I think were key in taking on Cross Lane. I wanted to honour Kathryn and the purest way I could do that was to keep her yard. To try and keep her legacy moving forward I am honour-bound to Kathryn.

'Honour-bound' represents the 'sword' and the 'shield', words Kathryn wrote down early on in our marriage. During the time of my depression, she used the words to motivate me. They form the armour to withstand loss, to force back the shadow of grief. She also talked of a horse, now I had her horse; and a means to wage war on grief.

As time went by though, I sensed that some people ignore you if you have been touched by death, either because they don't know what to say, or because they don't want to be touched by death. Or they think you are ignoring them because you are so focused on just breathing. And because you don't smile or wave cheerfully, they think you don't like them. In reality you just want them to say it's going to be all right.

This is something I've particularly struggled with over the months; that life moves on; it has to, for the sake of the living. These words by Jim Crumley hold true to my experience. He talks of a swan he observed for years, who then dies:

A small mound of white feathers
Lies on a tussock of grass
Made grey by a Highland winter.
It is all the monument there will
Ever be to the life of a swan.

That's sudden loss from a husband's perspective; she existed, then she was gone. Life moves on, people move on. The husband hangs on to the white feather for a long time, maybe for all time, even when the swan is just a feather on the grass. And he is the tussock.

There was no way I could ever replace Kathryn in terms of running Cross Lane, yet I could try and keep it going. Cross Lane felt like an outpost of grief, detached and deserted far from the nearest cavalry. Lonely despatch riders would arrive and help sometimes, liveries rallied round and the frayed flag flew over the lost captain. The yard kept running though, alive for her memory; for as long as the yard runs then some small part of Kathryn lives on.

The health and safety investigation wound through its course, and the police finished their investigation. No blame was attached to Kathryn or the yard. It was a minor victory, but one none the less. It was a small breeze of warm wind on the edge of the Arctic tornado.

The summer rolled by and we cut the hay with the baler at the family field, by far the hardest physical thing I have ever done. Far harder than any expedition day, for moving bail after bail in the steaming sun is arduous. The bailing machine leaves its little particles of wrapped hay all over the field, all 300 of them. They are then lifted into the trailer by hand, probably eighteen in one load, and then also moved by hand into the barn. And you repeat until the field is clear. Pete the farmer and Bill (who had always cut the hay for the field) gave guidance on when to cut the hay and local people helped when we got the hay in. It had rained for days and the hay lay down in the field, yet by a miracle we got it all in. Kathryn had never failed, and I viewed it as some kind of test for me; I couldn't fail. What would she think? At the end of the day though, the bales of hay sat in the barns, safe and dry. It was a small miracle I thought as I drenched myself in the shower late in the evening.

The conclusion of the inquest was easier for me to deal with than the opening: it found that Kathryn had died as a result of a freak accident. Family and friends gathered in the large important room and listened to the script of death and tragedy. The pathologist talked through the mechanics of the accident and explained what he'd said in the report I'd asked for. Was she killed in an instant? She was, he declared. It was cold comfort.

The media focused on the rope that got tangled round her neck, pondered why? But even the forensic investigation couldn't find an answer; it wasn't like she died in a car crash where the tell-tale skid marks and debris pattern provide clues. Only horses knew the answer and the truth of the day. BBC East Midlands came to the yard and carried out an interview; they wanted to discuss how she died. I said, 'I'll tell you how she lived,' and we sat on the upturned empty water trough next to the field with Ollie in and talked about a life. They say that things get better with time, yet I found it to be the opposite. The distance from the start and the last time I saw her became greater and unreality started to sink in. Her family didn't seem to talk much about her, and I began to withdraw into a world that was just me and her. In some ways you can only relate to the people that were there on that day, at that time. I imagine it's like soldiers who have been in battle together and lost one of their own. Counselling then becomes a lifesaver because the person who listens is separate from the trauma, is not part of the family or a friend – because after a while you don't want to burden those close to you with your grief. And time just makes everything worse, especially when the 'firsts' start approaching.

Firsts are like freight trains; you can hear them and feel them approaching. Everyone knows they are coming. I even bought her a birthday card for her birthday on 5 October, a date I struggled to remember when she was here. The actual day was hard but adrenalin kicked in and it wasn't as bad as the day after, when you have used everything up and all you can do is sleep. Firsts in the expedition world were nowhere near as hard as the first birthday without Kathryn, or the first Christmas. I wanted to spend Christmas alone yet I was drawn to her parents; it was the only place to go. We sat round the family table in an awkwardness that was palatable; the air was heavy with loss and missing. We toasted a daughter, a sister and a wife. It was the best we could do on the day of the first Christmas without her.

I decided to sell my Land Rover; I couldn't justify keeping two Defenders and had always thought about getting a Golf; a GTI to be specific. My favourite photo is of Kathryn in the passenger seat of our red GTI at Honister Pass on our honeymoon. Newark VW had one on its UK stock list; it was red. So, the Land Rover went and my mum took me to pick up the red car. My mum said it was the first time she'd seen me smile for months. Driving the Golf made me feel like Kathryn was sat next to me; it still does.

On our wedding anniversary, I took the Golf to the Lake District for a couple of nights. I drove her up to Honister Pass and just sat there remembering. It was definitely the hardest and saddest first despite being in the Lakes, and required a lot of sleep the following day. Another card bought with no one to open it. And the yard was now in the depth of winter, the season when some of the liveries at Cross Lane started leaving. As Valentine's Day approached the days got harder and the climb seemed hopeless.

I felt like Boardman and Tasker with the whole North East Ridge of Everest stretching ahead of me. Like Oates lying in his tent and thinking of the day ahead on frozen feet and gangrene setting in his leg. I was riding into the Russian guns and knew I would not make it back.

BPE was sinking; my whole world seemed to be ending; even Ollie and I were having issues. Everything was a quicksand of lost hope and there seemed no light ahead in the tunnel. I had found someone to buy BPE, but they only wanted to buy the overseas section, and due to the way BPE worked as a small company some of the overseas money had been spent. Kathryn juggled the finances each year, making it profitable. We were forced into bringing in the liquidators or I would have had to undertake the planned 2017 overseas trips alone without staff or an office. I was back in soulless offices facing bankers. It was as if each room I stepped into was a morgue, the room in the basement. Part of me had died when Kathryn did. And another part died when BPE sunk into the deep sea. It was hard to find something to hold on to that was me. Kathryn had gone and within six months so had BPE. All that was left were memories. There was just the dark moon blowing through the windows at night onto the lifeless duvet and empty pillow.

CHAPTER NINETEEN

Field of Dreams

I'll stand by the colours once more,
And I'll ride.
Ride the grey into the dawn.
Home.

Memories are strange things, they come and go like waves on a shore, they ebb and flow. Sometimes surging forward, sometimes just trickles on the sand. One of my strongest memories is Kathryn pushing a barrow up the track from the field, loaded with empty feed buckets. In her right hand was a lead rope attached to Ollie. He was plodding gently behind just off her right shoulder. I was standing halfway down the track seeing if she was coming. We walked back up together. She tied Ollie up and washed out the buckets, turning them upside down to drain and dry. One day a little pony was having his feet trimmed. I can still see the look on Kathryn's face today as clearly as a wave surging on the rocks at full tide when I asked her what the pony was having done.

I had ridden Ollie three times before she went, the last a fast ride down the cinder path. Kathryn commented I rode him well, seeing as she was the only one who rode him. He wasn't an easy horse, yet in the first few weeks after she left Ollie and I rode, we rode in all weathers, we rode slowly and we rode fast, in high winds and in early morning fog. We rode. We mostly rode alone. It was a sort of honeymoon period, for a new partnership. One we didn't really want.

The only thing I looked forward to now was riding Ollie, yet that was proving difficult. For the first four weeks I rode him without a care in the world. I didn't care about life or living so I just got on him and rode without fear, thought or reason. I rode on memory and instinct. It was the best thing and the only thing that connected me with Kathryn. We rode on Fridays, to remember the day. I took no mobile phone, I rode to die, to join her. I became the ghost rider in the sky. Then on a ride with Charlotte and Tracy everything went wrong; one horse spooked and then another reared up throwing Charlotte to the ground. Ollie spun and reared too; he then dropped down and spun again, rearing once more. I decided discretion was the better part of valour and jumped off. I suddenly realised I didn't want to die just yet.

And that was the start of a rocky road for me and Ollie. Kathryn had spent years learning to ride him, now my learning began. I began to ride a new friend's horses in order to get my confidence back; to enable me to ride Kathryn's big grey properly. Louise had supplied the greys at the funeral; she has three competition horses, all grey, fast and big. So, we rode together, and her horses taught me to ride with the leg again, to be soft on the hand and strong in seat. After years of just riding Oliver I was rusty riding other horses, for riding one horse all the time doesn't make for a good effective rider. Just like walking up the same mountain each week doesn't make a robust mountain leader.

We rode for hours into the woods and on the roads; I was learning again the art of riding fast responsive horses. We rode in drenching rain and beating sun. Louise and I discovered we have the same birthday so on a January day we rode in high winds; both glad to get back home safe. I wanted control, control of what killed Kathryn. I wanted to tame the demon in me and the darkness that lived on the fringe. So, we spent hours riding in controlled trot, slow canter and changing paces. Regulating paces with leg and seat, holding and giving. This was the key to riding Ollie. For in a strange way my happiness and well-being was linked to Ollie. He provided a light at the end of the tunnel, the key to life once more. But he would test me, there was a reason Kathryn didn't let anyone else ride him, he reared when under stress and he could be difficult to ride. But when it went well with him then I could see a reason to live and a way out of the abyss. I didn't know it then but I was riding to get back the control, the control sudden loss takes away from you. I was riding to beat back the reaper and regain the colours. I rode to live.

We went back to basics, riding her horses without stirrups, then without saddles we went back to the beginning. We then progressed to jumping on Duke, little lessons in allowing the horse to move freely over the obstacle. Then one day when I was on Ollie, Louise put a jump out. Not big, just a little cross pole.

'What are you doing?' I exclaimed from the other side of the yard.

'It's just a little pole, don't think about it. Just come around in trot and put your hands forward. Trust Ollie, trust yourself . . . feel Kathryn's hands.'

'No one's jumped Ollie since Kathryn last did!' I shouted.

'Well, then it's right you should be the first isn't it?' came the reply back.

It made sense I thought as I approached the tiny jump. I relaxed and felt Ollie leap forward and upward. We landed and I smiled, as did Louise. The feeling of jumping Ollie gave me the first glimpse of a path out of the darkness. It felt like a continuation of Kathryn jumping in some sense. It was a pivotal moment. The future wasn't going to be plain sailing, what is in this life? But I had set myself a new goal; one that I felt was achievable in the near future. With renewed confidence I entered my first ever competition, a dressage test with the Blidworth and District Riding Club.

After a week of practising on Ollie and one of Louise's horses, Farn, I thought I was ready for the test of walk, trot and canter. Yet on the Saturday afternoon before the test doing one final run through on Ollie, he felt too big for me, too strong and too much horse. I got off him and told Louise that was it, I couldn't ride him. I stood in the sand of the school and the loneliness and fear swept through me and I couldn't escape it.

Something made me get back on.

'You're not alone,' said Louise, as I walked round on Ollie.

'I am,' I replied, and trotted round in floods of tears.

'I AM ALONE!' I repeated to the sand and the sky.

'Feel his neck, feel his mane; you're not alone . . .' the voice standing in the school whispered.

I felt down Ollie's neck, tried to feel the belonging. Find the whisper of home, searching for the map.

Kathryn was gone and here I was trying to ride her horse, but maybe I wasn't alone; maybe. We completed the practice test, yet all night I didn't sleep and just wanted to get in the car and drive away. Drive away from horses and the yard and go back to the way it was, watching Kathryn competing Ollie. To just turn up at a local venue and watch her warm up, get changed in the trailer and jump on from the Defender's bumper, take a photo and then go and play golf.

Despite all Kathryn's expertise and experience she was killed by horses that knew her, and she knew well. I've read the reports and know it was a freak accident; but that doesn't take away the fear that it will also happen to me. In the past, being around horses never scared me but now I fight the fear all the time. I know the 'mountain' too well now. If someone we know dies in a car crash, we would get back in a car. Or if a friend dies on a mountain we would continue to climb; it's an acceptance of risk and consent to put ourselves in harm's way, for cars, mountaineering and riding horses are dangerous. I always knew I'd never die on a mountain or on an expedition. I suppose Kathryn believed she would never die from a horse-related accident. I don't have that same feeling working with horses. They are too unpredictable. There are too many variables involved.

I made it through the night without running away, I felt like Rannulph Junuh in the book *The Legend of Bagger Vance*, trying to find my place in the field. I was drawn to the yard and Ollie. The plan though was to get on him straight away and just get through the test. Prelim 11 is a dressage test consisting of walking, trotting and cantering within the confines of a 20m by 40m arena. Dressage has its roots in schooling horses for battle, control of pace and control of the horse in all three gaits. It seemed appropriate that I was entering such a test, a battle of grief and loss. Waged in a sandy school on her horse.

Ollie and I did the dressage test. I wore Kathryn's hunting stock and hat cover plus her gloves. I had her hands in mine. And I can honestly say that for me it felt like a bigger achievement than reaching the South Pole. It was beyond anything I've ever felt on a horse. I burst into tears as we both stood there in the sand school of Cross Lane. A few minutes later I rode Farn in the same test and came second in the competition. Yet riding an ungroomed Ollie was my biggest achievement in the time since Kathryn had left. Ollie and I came fourth out of eight riders. It felt like the gold medal in the Olympic Games. Someone later commented that it was the first time they'd seen me smile since Kathryn went. It was also the beginning of not feeling truly alone, for there was Ollie. It was the start of knowing there was a map, a map she had left hidden. I just had to seek it out.

Horses are just like people. Some you like instantly, some it takes time to get to the liking part. Some are stubborn and hard, some lovely and gentle. There are horses that like to lead and those that are happy to follow. Some are intelligent and some just aren't. Just like people they have baggage that they have acquired over the years due to issues they have faced. Some don't have a great start in life due to circumstances beyond their control. They each have their own personalities and characters, just like us.

Ollie is a character, he is a loner and he is the boss horse of the yard, he would probably be pack leader on any yard and in any field. He's a one-person horse; just like people who are happiest with only one other I think the same can be said for some horses. Ollie is like that, he loved Kathryn with all his being; that was obvious. He is strong physically but not emotionally, he needs total security from his owner or rider. In reality he is emotionally insecure which is why he is so bossy in his field with the other horses. I sometimes wonder what impact Kathryn going had on him, as his head collar and lead rope were found on the ground. What did he see? How did he feel? How did he react? What ghosts does he see in his mind's eye?

And what memories does he have?

So, the long process of getting to know Ollie began, for him to know me and accept that he had a new person in his life. He didn't accept this easily, for he tested me with his rearing, insisting he was in charge, that I wasn't his true owner; yet one long week of hard work with Louise giving guidance saw a breakthrough. Ollie finally accepted that there was a new person in his life. My own horse Oliver took a back seat; I rode him a few times but, in the end, decided to retire him fully. His shoes came off and he went to grass and the hearth that exists for the good horses of our lives. He was my Strip Cartoon, my horse of a lifetime. Ollie took over, for it was a battle now and I needed a war horse on which to ride into it.

As Ollie and I sought the truth in each other, autumn blew in with golden leaves. October 2016 saw the first Kathryn Bull

Memorial Show hosted by the Blidworth and District Riding Club. It was the busiest show of all time; people came from all over, lots of riders and their horses. I struggled to talk as we awarded the Kathryn Bull Memorial Trophy to the rider and horse who best demonstrated Kathryn's approach.

Horses and their riders stood in the field, the field that had seen so many acts, plays and scenes ridden out in the dusty school. Storm clouds drifted on the horizon. All were tired and weary, yet one had ridden with Kathryn's soft hands, kind manner and effective way. As the memorial trophy was awarded emotion ran in rivers and the rain began to fall. It was a great day, and I think she would have been proud of us all.

The yard was changing; brown leaves were replaced by frost and white grass. Winter was hard, but not as bad as I expected. It was more wet and damp than full on snow and ice. I didn't attend the yard Christmas meal as I just couldn't face it. It still felt like Kathryn's role, not mine; despite the fact I'd now taken over doing all the jobs that needed doing and was inch by inch finding my feet. I had the quixotic hope in the early days though, that no livery would leave. How naive I was then, for people did leave. It felt like they had left Kathryn and the flag that was her life, yet the truth was they left because people move on. And ultimately I didn't have Kathryn's expertise, way with people or smile.

Those that stayed or came to just say hello, helped the trust, the riding club, made a cup of tea on the yard, they became knights in my heart, kept my world turning and made it OK to get up in the morning. They were the foot soldiers on my front line, the climbers on the North East Ridge; the explorers in the darkened tent on the ice shelf.

I was learning a new job in quite exceptionally difficult circumstances; I made mistakes and needed time to adjust. I was learning that the equine scene was full of people that knew everything about horses; the hard bit was actually trying to figure out who knew what they were doing, instead of just talking a good talk. In expeditions it was easy, people can navigate or they can't. If they can't they don't get to the top of the mountain or the pole, the tent doesn't go up or they can't light the stove. Every horse person I came across had a different opinion to the next person if something wasn't right with a horse, which bit of tack, a way of feeding or what rug to put on.

Many people would play a part in this last expedition, offer invaluable guidance in navigating the mists of the equine world. Some names stand out: Louise would become a vital link into getting to grips with Ollie. Zoë Grant, who introduced me to the world of the horse; many moments ago in the heart of Sherwood. Jayne Martin who taught me to ride with soft hands and soft eyes. And of course, Kathryn, the most effective rider and overall best horsewoman I've ever known. All of these, each different in their own way, all effective and all united in their love of the horse I look up to. Each one with a track record of end results; for that is the only way of judging if someone knows what they are talking about in the horse world; indeed, any world.

Expeditions were becoming a distant memory. The mountains and moors were far-off places now, destinations it seemed strange I'd ever been part of. And for the present they could stay distant memories, the prospect of being away from the yard was panic-provoking and too much to contemplate. People would always ask me what my favourite place in the world was. Antarctica cannot be beaten for its sheer magical appeal and the feeling of being in a lost kingdom, but my favourite place was always the Lake District; Buttermere and the surrounding fells a particular high spot. The moors above Hathersage in the Peak District were also special places, tramping heather and soggy peat places I loved to walk. Yet now my most treasured place in the whole world is the field where Kathryn last walked with its free-flowing grass, the bank of trees at the bottom, home to hoof dents in the turf.

It's also home to Ollie, George and two other horses. I'd have thought it would have been my worst place, but the opposite is true. The top section is often split into two to save the grass and has the water trough, where hay is put down in the winter. The field gently slopes down to the bottom section, fenced off with post and rail. It's also rested in summer as there's too much grass, yet in winter and into the spring months it's open for Ollie and his friends. It's in the far-right corner of this section that Kathryn left, down by the trees that protect it from the wind and the rain. To the right is the bridleway that leads into the fields and woods.

It's all part of the map that Kathryn left me. A map she didn't even know she'd left hidden. It's a map that shows the path back to happiness, and that is in essence what home is. I would find little notes at home:

Only two things stand in stone. Kindness in another's trouble, courage in your own.

Words by Adam Lindsay Gordon, written down by Kathryn in an old notebook.

Or sometimes it's the sun glinting down on the field at the right time. In the beginning the map was hard to read, for the grief got in the way, like trying to read with glasses on in hard rain. But when you wipe your eyes it becomes easier to see.

I could sit for hours in the field. The grass has a deep peaceful atmosphere and the slope that gently heads down to the stream beyond the tree line beckons to home. On a sunny afternoon with the light fading it's the most tranquil place I ever stood in. Elysium hangs on the lone red poppies. Dew stands out on spider's whispers as they weave over the grass, the trees sing in long slow voices, red kites drift on the breeze; and a peace descends into the heart. It is to me the field of dreams. In a way it's Kathryn too.

CHAPTER TWENTY

A Different Kind of Expedition

I climb on his back,
As the fjord stretches ahead of me.
Deep unseen depths filling my hands
The horse swims, cantering crawl.

There are images of Kathryn on mountains in the Lake District. She is always smiling, either with her mouth or her eyes. She is on Green Gable in the snow with Great Gable clothed in winter finery behind her, she's next to Buttermere on the path up to Haystacks, water bottle in hand. A big smile is on her face whilst she sits on top of Binsey, again in the snow. We stayed in pubs or hotels. She was a competent walker, strong uphill and steady going down. She always commented how fast I went downhill. But over the years she got better at descending. It must have been hard for her doing a physical job and then undertaking a walking holiday that also involved hard work albeit without horses. She liked it except when it poured with rain, but then who does like walking in the rain? Walking in the Lakes is not the same now. There's no wingman anymore. No Goose to talk to.

Winter at the yard was passing into February and more firsts loomed, namely the first time I went back into the hills and worked with a group on expedition. I had done one walk since she went. Wondering which book to take, I picked up Maria Coffey's book about the loss of her partner on Everest and out fell a note:

Steve

Thanks for the kit and expertise. Thanks for the time and patience. Thanks for the inspiration. Thanks for looking after Jack. Love you, miss you. Take care, Kathryn xxx.

The note felt like coming home, I'd not seen it since I first found it many years ago. I cried as I read it again, but warm tears; not cold lonely ones. I'd taken a day off from the yard and headed to the Lakes, staying at a lovely pub in Troutbeck. I walked up Clough Head and with tears in my eyes flew the pennant that Dave Tait had intended to fly at the top of Dhaulagiri in the Himalayas, the little white prayer flag that bore Kathryn's name. It flew in a strong breeze at the top of the Lakeland Fell. I missed her more than I wanted to be on the hill. Looking out over the Cumbrian vista it struck me that, as far as I could see, the horizon bore no Kathryn at the end of it. The world was completely empty of her and the mountains just echoed that sense of loneliness. The places that had felt home to me all my life now just felt like hulks of rock. There was nothing there.

I had some work booked in with a local school, I'd trained the teacher in expedition leadership and he had been on the same course as Kathryn. He was taking his students for some training in the Peak District, an overnight camp in Edale. It was a huge hurdle for me as I was starting to get anxious about being away from the yard and the field. I pitched my little green tent in a familiar but now strange field. The same feeling of the hills being impostors came back. And the prospect of being responsible for a group of young people on the hills terrified me; I simply did not feel emotionally secure to be responsible for young people on an expedition. I barely felt responsible for myself. I had a quiet word with Chris and asked if I could work with his group rather than be in charge of them, to which he thankfully agreed. My little green tent felt soulless and cramped, its fabric whispered nothing to me as I lay curled up in my sleeping bag. There was no Romeo downstairs, no Ollie in a field five minutes' drive away. Just the bulk of the hill behind me in the darkness, with its peat and groughs shrouded in cloud.

I was in the ocean of pointless, a great sea of grieving; looking into young people's eyes, I could only see the futility of it all. Leave school, get a job, and get married. Die. What was the point? I could not see the point in getting worked up about making sure you navigated to a little sheepfold in the middle of a blank grass moor. In truth what did it matter? But it did to Chris and it does to all the people who train people to lead in the mountains, who train young people to be safe in hill skills and camping. It did to me in another lifetime.

Being touched by a tragedy and death, especially if the person you lose is so close, so integral to your life, marks you indelibly. Home becomes so far away, so long ago. And each step forward breaks your heart. Life is just about days; days to get back. It didn't seem to matter if I got to the top of a mountain or I stayed at the bottom. Horses had replaced the mountains. Because it mattered if they weren't fed, they needed feeding. The mountains don't need anyone.

Yet I did more work for Chris's school, a couple of days out training more students, and some DofE work. Gradually the feeling of panic became lower over the horizon, rather than an all-encompassing gulf. There were days in the Peak District supervising students as they worked to complete their final training and a three-day trip to the Yorkshire Dales on a Gold Practice expedition. It rained like the flood of Noah and the

Dales felt like the end of the earth. There was no sun and there was no Kathryn on the end of the line. I slept in the van as I couldn't face putting up the tent. I've never felt so far from home. The yard was three days away and the field was all I thought about. I'd started calling Kathryn's mobile only to get the disconnect sound. I'd text her to say I missed her. I searched for answers on the moors drenched in rain.

Chris asked for my advice on the route as I was the most experienced. I suggested a low-level route which he agreed to. So, the teams tramped along paths and roads until we called a halt to the trek one night early. Somehow, I found it easy to make the decisions needed, for I reverted back to memory. It was easier than deciding which field we should use next at the yard, which rug to put on Ollie, decisions Kathryn would have found easy. Even so, I relied on the decision-making skills used on expeditions when trying to run the yard. I used the same Norwegian Met Office app we used at BPE to decide when to cut the hay, for example, or to decide what rugs to leave on the horses.

It was becoming clear that I couldn't live off the yard exclusively. The DofE work was vital for substituting what money I took from the yard; I paid myself what Kathryn did, £260 a week. Yet, BPE had covered our big costs like the mortgage and the main bills. Michael the bank manager explained the reality in all its starkness.

'Cross Lane is a hobby business; it could function the way it did because of BPE.' The words rang home as the closeness of our two lives stared in from the bank walls. I now had to cover everything with £260 per week, and broken down over seven days the hourly rate wasn't great. Cross Lane needed to be full of horses, ideally twenty horses and their owners. And I began to feel pressure to keep the yard full, in order to keep the bank manager happy.

Suddenly I so wanted to be on a mountain somewhere, anywhere but the yard. The place I wanted to be the most was becoming the worst place to be. Distant lives called me home, but the pull of the field drew me down each morning. In due course new faces would come; new horses would walk the fields. But for a time, it was a struggle to hold onto the dream. All I wanted to do was stay in the warmth of my grief.

Dreams can run through our fingers like sand. I struggled with my decision to run the yard and get involved full time with horses. I was used to the expedition world; that was my comfort zone. In the horse world everyone seemed to be an expert, everyone had an opinion and I was a stranger in a strange land. Kathryn though, she put truth first and looked after people. At times she would put other people's horses' needs before her own. She always told it how it was, what you got was what she said. There were no false pretences, no hidden meanings. If she thought I was riding badly she'd tell me, if I was good then she would compliment me. If she said she didn't want a Christmas present or big birthday present she meant it. She gave me a note once that thanked me for listening to her and not buying her anything huge or expensive.

Dear Steve,

Thank you for my birthday present – it's perfect. I appreciate you not getting me anything else today, but don't forget we have our Spanish Riding School tickets. Looking forward to seeing you in a bit. K xx

My previous circle of friends and my life as I knew it had ended. Every routine and way of life had changed beyond any form of recognition. The house was full of expedition kit and clothing, maps and hardware, the remnants of twelve years' running an expedition company. Yet each day I would get up and do exactly what Kathryn had done. Wash up, make sandwiches for the day, sort Romeo out and then put on the yard boots. Load Romeo into the Defender and drive down the lane to the yard. If it was a week day, I would let Romeo into the yard then go and put the hay out for next door's horses. Then fight through the gate as Zac and Bruno jumped on me, dash to the school gate and walk the dogs down the little lane. I would serve up two cans of dog food for the three of them and then prepare feeds for the horses, load up the barrow and head down the lane to feed. It was just like walking up a mountain, walking down the lane. A barrow instead of a rucksack. Buckets instead of waterproofs and maps. Horse feed instead of a flask and Mars bar. Bringing horses out of the fields in the right order instead of deciding what compass bearing to walk on, what route up the mountain to take. Lightweight rug or medium weight? Waterproofs on or off? Getting through each day, to get home and curl up in bed with Kathryn's old fleece. And then do it the next day. Leading expeditions and working at Cross Lane were physically demanding, and after a few months at the yard I had dropped from a 36-inch waist to a 32. I had eaten and drunk the same, yet the daily exercise meant I lost weight. Now I suffered the cold more as my fat levels had reduced. And home felt so far away, so long ago. Each step forward broke the heart a little more.

It felt as if I was on the return leg from the pole, a damned struggle to get through each day and make camp. Each night's sleep was a welcome respite from the daily distance that needed to be covered. I would wake each morning and feel like I was Oates in the film *Scott of the Antarctic*, the scene where he stares at the flapping canvas of the tent in the polar wind. I was 'Soldier', as Oates was nicknamed by his fellow explorers. He was employed to look after the expedition's nineteen ponies, to ensure they helped lay the depots on the way to the South Pole. To ensure they had a way back. I was trying to get back home, just like Oates was. I was sacrificing everything for the horses. Would they help? Would they help me on the return journey? Just as Oates had hoped they would him.

When the weather was bad I used to offer to help Kathryn at the yard, but she'd always decline my help as she said it would take longer to do, as she'd have to explain everything. I wish I had been more persistent, but then Kathryn was a persistent person herself. Instead I would make sure the tea was cooked and the house clean for when she came home. She would comment how great the tea smelled if there was a chilli in the pot or a cottage pie in the oven. Now I say hello to the empty house, maybe one day she will answer.

When Kathryn went on her expedition to Iceland, to ride horses down the south-central aspect of the island she left her note in Maria Coffey's *Fragile Edge*, a book about loss and expeditions; impossible north-east ridges and quixotic goals. Coffey travels to Everest with Peter Boardman's widow to seek answers to unanswerable questions. It seems to me strangely and heavenly weird that our roles are entwined. That I would go on to do Kathryn's day-to-day expedition, working with horses, each day living her dream. Facing a new Everest, walking and riding with ghosts of the past. Sometimes I feel Kathryn's hand in my hand, when I'm too tense on Ollie's reins, or a horse needs taking charge of on the ground. Sometimes I think she's with me. She guides me through the expedition that was her life, making sure I make the campsite safe each night. I take out the compass that one of the liveries Amy gave me for Christmas with the inscription 'Every day is a step closer to home'. I think of the steady plod to happiness once more.

All my life I had dreamed and hoped of undertaking a big expedition; the attempted Greenland crossings were large expeditions but were in preparation for doing some huge polar exploration. The South Pole trip we did was ground-breaking in terms of taking young people on a frontier wilderness trip and for that I am immensely proud. But I always thought I would have liked to cross Antarctica or do a similar big journey. There are still lots of fantastic exploratory trips in Antarctica to be done, not necessarily to the South Pole, but in the unexplored mountain regions, where a team could carry out field work whilst undertaking a self-supporting journey. Yet that life and that dream are not for me anymore, and instead I find myself on a very different expedition. An expedition in the fields and grasslands of home. It's an expedition that goes on each day. Sometimes I wander across the sandy school and imagine my footfall rests on the snow like it used to. Or in the fields I am walking untrodden ice and that a note will be waiting in a book, for me to read in the tent.

All you have to do is keep putting one foot in front of the other. Day after day, week after week. Take one step further each time and you will make it. Kathryn x

Polar expeditions and high-altitude expeditions are exercises in repeating the same task each day. It's a simple life. Melt water in the morning, eat breakfast and prepare for the day. Dress and drop the tent then pack the pulk. Ski slowly in one direction for several hours with regimented breaks. Reach your campsite and pitch the tent, securing it safely for bad weather. Melt water and prepare the evening meal. Consolidate the day and check your progress, followed by a check-in with base camp. This you repeat for the entire length of your journey. All exercises in patience and living each day at a time; for the scale of the expedition is likely to sap the morale if viewed as an entire trip. It may be a month, or longer, but it won't exceed more than a hundred days for that's as long as the expedition season lasts in Antarctica.

Cross Lane has replaced the glaciers and the icecaps. It's a day-to-day exercise in patience and getting up each day to repeat the same process. Feed dogs then horses in the morning, clear the fields of horse muck and then get ready to feed and sort the horses in the evening. Yet in order to participate in this new expedition I had to learn new skills, just like the apprentice served in polar expeditions. The only difference was I didn't have the time I had before; this was on-the-job training, which on the face of it seemed a simple task, just like skiing in one direction to the South Pole. Yet skiing to the South Pole is one of those 'how hard can it be' jobs, for in reality there are lots of skills required including the ability to make daily decisions that are only gleaned from years of experience. Kathryn had spent years learning the tricks and trade of her job of running a livery yard, as I had in learning to lead expeditions.

There was one key similarity: people. Managing the expectations of the people on the yard, on any livery yard, is pivotal. Just like an expedition where a person's expectations and their own personal goals for the trip need to be managed. Everyone wants to get to the summit or to the pole. On a livery yard it's no different; the pole is replaced by a horse, the summit by a pony. The biggest single aspect to execute is getting the right horses in the right field; but it's not easy. A rule of thumb for land and horses is one acre per horse; with approximately twenty-one acres Cross Lane can sustain about twenty horses without decimating the grass, for it's all about the grass. People don't want their horses in fields without grass. Or they don't want too much grass. Just like a mountain, sometimes the summit is hard won.

Some horses go well together, become best mates; some horses don't. And some people don't fit well with others; just like on an expedition. Initially I struggled with this complex issue, especially when we had new liveries join the yard. For as people left, new horses and their owners would come. In the early days I would explain that it was Kathryn's yard and talk through what had happened, yet most knew already. The horse world is a small one.

Anyone new coming had to buy into the philosophy that it was run in Kathryn's memory and I was new to the game, learning as I went along.

I gradually got better at selling the yard as people came to look round; as time went on I was getting to know the ship, for want of a better word. I was also getting to know how to run her and what she needed. Getting to know the feel of the deck. I learned which horse came out of the field first and in what order they needed to be fed, when to order hay and haylage in winter, how long the bails lasted and the best way of getting the large bails down to the fields.

Maintaining the fields is another part of the jigsaw, moving the horses around from summer paddocks to winter paddocks and making sure fields are rested, so we don't go into spring with no spare grazing. Lots of people helped in this to start with, yet over time Mel and Lucy's (both livery members whilst Kathryn was here) quiet words by the stable door at night became a constant. Gradually over the months I became able to make decisions on my own. Others helped too, yet Mel and Lucy accepted me for who I was and what I had inherited, and defended the battered flag that flew over the yard. They became my new expedition tent companions. There was moving the muck heaps to get my head around, spraying to deal with and mending fences to get to grips with. Kathryn's dad Ian showed me how to put posts and rail fencing in. He must have found it hard that I was running the yard instead of his daughter, but to his utmost credit he never told me as much.

I learned to muck out, a new skill for me; it was mainly Amber's stable to start with, and Lucy her owner was very particular. Lucy had been at Bloomsgorse as a child and now kept her horse Amber at Cross Lane; she had been there several years and is the longest serving owner. She had also become a great confidante at the end of each day, along with Mel. I would stand outside her stable as she mucked out and learned more than she will ever imagine about running Cross Lane from chatting about how Kathryn did things. A phrase I soon got tired of was, 'Kathryn did it that way or this way'. It was impossible to fill her shoes; I had to find my own way, yet in the same spirit as Kathryn. One night Lucy was busy digging out her stable. It was already dark and the yard lights were on. There's something special about stables in winter and the soft glow of the yard lights. It's perhaps the closest feeling of true Christmas there is. It's the manger with the wise men watching. No shopping, no neon, just a horse stood by a stable, feed waiting, rugs hung on the old door.

'You're the best person to run the yard, and no one else could run it as close to Kathryn did as you do. You run it like Kathryn did,' Lucy remarked.

'Really? Do you mean that? If so then I can't tell you what that means to me.' I replied.

'Yes, I mean that, you're doing a great job and Kathryn would be proud of you.'

I've had many compliments over the years, from John Major on receiving my Winston Churchill Medal, to Ran Fiennes when he asked if I was '*the* Steve Bull, the explorer' but the comment from Lucy beats everything. I like to think Kathryn would have agreed.

I felt that many people judged me because I was Kathryn's husband and not Kathryn. This, on the one hand, was always inevitable, but hard to live with on the other. Just like being on an expedition I was seeing the best of people and the worst; mainly in myself; grief is no judge of character. However, I had made the decision to take on the yard, so I had to learn to deal with the situation and the circumstances I was in; it was in effect the bed I had made myself. I needed to accept the crumpled covers and lumpy pillows. Accept that the way out was with a grey horse who was as grumpy as me and use the negativity as a spur of steel. Even so I spent many hours thinking about running away; a nice remote house in north-west Iceland would have been ideal. A cottage in Scotland? Perfect. I searched the Internet for hours looking for houses in remote corners of Norway and requested brochures. But deep down I knew that going to Norway wouldn't get rid of the grief; I'd just be transferring it to another place. All things considered it was best to stand and fight on home turf, I thought, but help was needed to do that. So, I did what Kathryn would have done, sought help, from local farmers and people who had been working the land for years. They gave me guidance and support. They knew I was struggling. So, they helped, as they still do. Her friends stuck around; some helped with the accounts, events at the yard, or the running of the yard; and the family field. And some just came and talked by a stable door as the sun went down and the moon rose over the fields.

Leaving the stable doors behind I went away to work on a Gold DofE in the Lakes for a week. It seemed like an eternity. I'd done a couple of Bronze training trips locally; drank too much when I shouldn't have done. I was not always the hero Kathryn had believed in and written to me about. I struggled when interacting with the teams and the teachers, felt detached from normal life. In the Lakes the teams moved slowly over the rough hilly terrain; a sign of the times. It rained hard at the wild camp below Scafell Pike, the desolation took my mind off the absence. The tent comforting me in its green warmth as the stove purred away in its orange heat. Even so, I couldn't wait to get back to the new life at Cross Lane which was slowly becoming a happier place, and the new liveries who knew no different.

My main motive to get out of bed in the morning now was Ollie. Louise commented that he was the one to pull me out of the quagmire of grief. I don't doubt this. I think it's about facing the ultimate fear. All my life I have taken part in various outdoor pursuits and challenges. I hated heights, so found rock climbing and abseiling very hard. A free fall parachute jump was also tough, as was caving and trying cave diving a couple of times. Horses never really scared me until Kathryn went. But it was this fear that drove me forward, that and memory.

One winter the snow lay thick and deep. Kathryn and I tried to get Ollie and Oliver through the bottom gate and into the woods. We carried our tack down to the fields and tacked up on the bridleway, leading our horses over the little bridge and into the fields. There we spent half an hour trying to get on before deciding it wasn't the best idea after all. We laughed as we walked back into the fields of home, about the failed adventure and the madness in our ambition.

In winter the clear frosty sun-burst days are rare at the yard, and when they come, they are glorious; just like being on a mountain top with the polar wind on your cheek. Spring brings new life and fresh grass; the horses are happy and lively. The swallows return from their winter migration, flying into the same stables they left months ago. In the summers the sun beats down on parched land.

When the days are bad on the long road home, when the yard is empty in the depths of winter, I call upon memories imprinted in a laughter of snow. When it takes three hours to just feed and water the horses, I fiddle with the gold band on my finger and accept that I am now paying back for all the times Kathryn looked after my horse for me. The fear and the wind and Ollie in his field are part of the ring.

It took me over two years to realise that I needed to start sorting Kathryn's clothes, and one morning, with Mel's help, we managed to clear out one carrier bag of her clothes. Whilst we did this Everest of a job we talked of the past and the present; the creep of time. We found Christmas presents that had lain untouched from 2016. That was another move forward; one giant leap to a smile.

The counselling has helped; it enables you to talk about the really dark stuff. Early on I went to see Cruise, the grief specialists, but they showed me into a room that felt like a morgue. Next door was a huge park which I suggested would be a better place to talk. Yet it wasn't allowed due to health and safety. So, I see someone called Deanne; we sit in her conservatory overlooking a garden. She gives answers where she can and smiles when she can't. She understands that it's silent now and red carpet empty for me, in that old stone building down in town. That the photographer has long gone; but I'm still stuck at the door with eyes lingering in time. Sometimes I am drained by the sessions, for the weight has been lifted for a bit and the relief is intense. Counselling goes hand in hand with riding Ollie and walking deep lonely moors. Searching for the ghost in the darkness, facing the fear that rides in the mind. Inching and crawling to the smile and belonging once more. Seeking out the beaming summit, the pole of life that lies in the mist.

CHAPTER TWENTY-ONE

Keeping the Light Burning

The calling was coming from a place not seen,
It was and is hidden from all mortal souls,
Life was living in a corner of grass, days hidden,
Darkness was banished in a light so heavenly,
Even the moles crept off to hide for the day.

She loved the birds and the bees; the week before she went a friend gave her a bee house. A place where bees could live and be happy. It still hangs in the garden. Yet, the garden isn't as lovely as when she was here and I find it difficult to find the time. But I do put bread out for the birds as they seem to be everywhere. Every morning as I have a cup of tea in the garden before going to the yard, I look for the white dove that flies over. Most days she comes. And down in the field there are always lots of birds, blackbirds and thrushes and the red kites. Two live in the woods near the fields and I am followed by robins all over the yard. Swallows nest in the stables; they come back each year, swooping into their old nests as if they've never left. Everyone's lives have moments that transcend the day-to-day struggle to get back to the house each day, in some ways just like swallows.

It wasn't just the garden of the forest and fields Kathryn loved, she adored all forms of garden, even expressing that she would have liked to be a gardener. We once found a secluded secret garden, deep in the fens of Norfolk; walled off from the rest of the National Trust garden we were visiting. I can't remember the name of the estate, yet we did get in trouble when we got lost in the house. We wandered around the public avenues and walkways of glorious trees and flowers, never hand in hand for that was not our way. She loved the garden, but away from the guided tour was a walled secret with a broken wooden gate. Kathryn led the way through, and there lay an abandoned garden, old potting sheds and broken pots. Long-forgotten beds of flowers, dusty earth not tilled for years. Kathryn wanted to see it in its glory; to see it returned to the garden of shining flowers and shrubs. In one corner there stood a new barrow, with new seeds in it, ready to be planted. A purposeful fork leaned against the wall; signs of new life about to be grown. 'I'd like to come back here one day,' Kathryn said. One day I'll go for her, forget about the horses and see another field. I'll know she's been, because there will be a robin on a fence post watching me.

We are all part of the poetry that is human existence; in all its sad glory and fleeting glimpses of ecstasy. All entwined in the garden of light that lives on. It's about ordinary lives that are sometimes touched by the extraordinary. 'For God's sake, look after our people,' Scott wrote in a blizzard at the edge of the world. His companions Bowers and Wilson lay each side of him. Which is in effect what we do when our nearest and dearest die; we try to look after their memory. Yet do any of us join our loved ones when we die? Is that why we keep the fire burning for them? Mel has been at the yard several years, goes about her business quietly and is highly respected. Together over a stable door as she grooms her horse Soul, we've talked about this at length. Of keeping a light lit, for the flame does guide us when all lights go out. It gives comfort and hope and allows our soul to regrow; to move on with their love in our hearts.

Like the swallows returning, arriving safe at home each night is one thing; it's the act of getting there that is the hard part. Churchill was right when he said, 'When you're walking through hell; just keep walking.' My dad once said to me I was best at walking, so that's what I do, keep walking. Friends drop flowers off in the immediate aftermath of death and social media is awash with notifications of love and remembrance. Families keep going with old-school perseverance; the keep calm and carry on attitude is their way of keeping a fire lit. People say, 'She wouldn't want you to be unhappy.' Why not? Would I be upset if I was in heaven, seeing Kathryn happy without me? But we need to be happy for those that have gone. So, life rolls on and time passes. And soon two years have passed, then three, since they left. And all moments are just one in the wind.

There is a second-hand bookshop in Keswick. We would always go in there, Kathryn on sufferance for she didn't seek out second-hand books like I did. But she wasn't with me on this visit; it was over a year since her accident. I wandered into the smell of old read pages alone. On a pile lay a book about the faith of Edward Wilson the Antarctic Explorer. I took the book to the man behind his desk who owns the shop; 'Just come in this one; quite rare,' he said.

I'd gone back to the beginning, to the hotel where we went on our honeymoon. Over the course of my five days and four nights at the hotel I read the book, about faith and hope and believing in a higher purpose. Reading the book and staying in the hotel where we spent our longest holiday together gave me new strength. I walked for a day in pouring rain, crying as I walked. I got lost in the mist and the moors and struggled with mountains. The third day I parked next to a little church and went up onto Helvellyn; it was a glorious day and I felt happy in my own company for the first time in months. But I don't think I was alone. I sat in the church afterwards and listened to the stones and wood the church was built of. On my last day I walked with an old friend from the expedition days; again, it was a great day, and I sensed that there were three of us on the fell that day.

I believe in keeping the light burning in the place of faith, of hope and love. There is one other drastic alternative that is too terrible to comprehend. One of the last great taboos; suicide. In the past when I had looked into the face of suicide, Kathryn had saved me. And in the months following her accident, as time went by I looked at its face again. The prospect of the rest of my life without her at times felt too much to bear. To me it seemed the fastest way to get to her would be to end it. I thought it through and had a plan – a quick turn of the car wheel into a wall and in seconds the pain would be over. Yet I decided Kathryn would be exceptionally mad with me if I turned up just after her; leaving Romeo, the horses and our families. And the time she saved me all those years ago would have been wasted. The author Cory Taylor examines taking your own life in stark detail in her memoir *Dying*. She concluded that it wouldn't be fair on the person who found you, and that she didn't want the stigma of 'suicide' on her death certificate. Yet, the best reason she gives is this: '[A]fter all, suicide is dangerous.' I can't argue with that. During heartfelt counselling sessions we've talked through the darkness. In order to understand why people choose suicide you need to have faced the darkness, lost the colours and be cradling the dead as the enemy on wild dark horses gallops down upon you with sabres of fire.

When the bond is so strong and it's cut in a second, an instant, the pull to follow is hard to resist. And to be honest we have to fight the pull. I fight the pull each sunny day. That's when the love that was given so freely steps up another gear, defends us from the darkness. Helps us live our lives and wait till the time we are together again. And now, today, this month is not that time. Kathryn knows that. I really believe that. And she also knows that life is hard, yet I have to face it to make her proud. To pay back the faith she gave me, the reason why she chose me to be her husband. For that's the path now, the route to the top of the mountain, the compass bearing to the last pole. The path south from that place.

One day Louise and I were riding out in Sherwood Forest. I'd ridden through Ollie's rearing a few months ago, so he didn't scare me as much as he used to. I was comfortable with him; relaxed. She was on her horse; Duke. It was a normal work day about mid-morning. There was no one else about.

'I wish it was Kathryn riding with you and not me,' I commented. She looked at me shocked, but before she could answer I carried on, 'But you know what? I can't change that. What I can do is choose to follow the map she left me, and the gift she gave . . .'

Louise nodded. I carried on, aware the words were significant in some way; 'She left me the greatest gift in the world, her horse Ollie, and the forest to ride him in, to remember her by and her dog to go home to. So, I think you and I, right here right now, in this field have won the lottery of life. Kathryn couldn't have left anything more precious to me.'

I looked across at Louise, maybe thinking I'd said too much. But she was smiling still, smiling with her eyes.

'Shall we trot?' I said.

'Yes, let's . . .'

Two grey horses moved forward across the ground and headed for the forest. And the two riders smiled as they saw the forest ahead. I sensed a third horse with a quiet rider to our side, but didn't mention this to Louise. The fields waved their corn and the sun bounced down over the trees, the grass shone like only it does in Sherwood and the pulse of the horses beat through our bodies. To ride your own horse out through the woods of home in the sunshine and glow of life, despite the death that surrounds the flag is a special feeling. For our sense of belonging lies in the events of our own hearts and the places they beat in.

By keeping the light burning, the purity of life shines through. For in the end we have nothing except each other. And that having doesn't end when one of us goes, if we believe in the love we have. During our honeymoon there were only six other people in the whole hotel, so it felt like our own private house. I would sit by the fire on the sofa that faced directly to the grand staircase and watch Kathryn walk down the stairs in her dress, smiling shyly. So, don't tell me there isn't a heaven, for I've seen it already. And one day I'll see it again. One day I will sit on a red sofa whilst a fire is lit. Two drinks will be served on the low wooden table before me. And she will walk down a large staircase in a red dress, with a pearl necklace on and just a hint of makeup and red lipstick. And her smile.

CHAPTER TWENTY-TWO

The New Enterprise

So becomes the enveloping night,
Wiping clean in fell swoops the memory,
Setting down the score for tomorrow,
Giving reason to keep waking, in hope,
That new rain will tread in dawn's light,
Leading the glow into action and to
Bring the talking west wind into play.

I used to joke that BPE was like the Enterprise in *Star Trek*, we had a bridge and a crew and we explored. It was an analogy that seemed to work. We'd had a tough year, and I emailed everyone saying that we were battered, and the ship had been through a lot but she was OK. Kathryn emailed back, with just three words; 'Shields holding Captain.' I loved that. She knew the most important thing to say at the right time. She was the Starship Enterprise; the ship you'd do anything for. Somewhere that email reply is saved, either in the cloud or on a server somewhere. Words written down in another time. But the shields are still holding, Kathryn.

I was on Ollie in the outdoor school when the mobile rang. I don't like the ringing of the phone anymore. Nor the voice that may give bad news. Yet, on this occasion I answered it. Andy Utting the owner of Terra Nova Equipment was on the line. He hadn't been in touch since Kathryn had left, and had decided to call and see how I was. I'd known Andy for several years since his company sponsored the South Pole trip. I brought Ollie to halt so as to talk with Andy better.

'Hi Steve, how are you?'

'Not bad thanks for asking,' I replied as Ollie fidgeted.

'OK, great; sorry I've not been in touch before, I wanted to give you some time. Are you still involved in expeditions at all?' he asked tentatively.

'That's fine; no – I'm all done with expeditions. I've got nothing left to offer I'm afraid.'

'OK, I understand. If you ever want to chat, just pop in for a coffee one day.'

'Thank you, I will. I'd better go now as Ollie is getting bored . . .'

At that time I wanted a quiet life away from the madness, to live out a quiet reclusive life at the yard and down the fields of home. But Andy had sown a little seed, he hadn't pushed it, he'd just left a door open. After a drive out in the Golf one day I was passing Terra Nova, so I pulled up outside the back entrance and rang the bell. Over coffee Andy and I chatted about work; the simple truth of the matter was that I still needed to supplement the income from Cross Lane. So, I asked if he could give me any work; but nothing associated with expeditions. He agreed to think about it; but did offer work in the warehouse packing at any time. That would suit me fine; no mental work, nothing to think about. Just pack and move boxes.

I went back a few weeks later and Andy had produced a list of possible work; ranging from warehouse work, selling tents, helping design tents; and at the bottom of the list was 'set up an expedition company for Terra Nova.' He wanted to get involved in doing expeditions as well as making tents for those that went on them.

'Good luck with that one,' was my answer.

I never found the time to go and work in the warehouse, I was given the task of speaking to schools to try and sell tents but I couldn't bring myself to do it. Then I was offered the chance to help re-design some of their tents. Yet, the fields and horses kept me from venturing back into the real world of business and meetings. I couldn't make the break away from the yard. Finally, I was supposed to go into a meeting, yet the farrier was due at the yard, so I called Andy and said once again I wasn't coming in; he offered to come to me. That night I thought seriously about working for Terra Nova. I needed a way to make working at Cross Lane viable, just as in some way Kathryn had done.

With the farrier's clang of hammer on horse shoe in the background, we talked.

'So, you'd like to set up an expedition company then? Take schools and adult groups on overseas trips?'

The anvil sung to steel, ringing out around the yard.

'Yes, that's the plan. But I have no experience or any idea how you go about doing it,' Andy honestly replied.

The mobile forge in the back of the farrier's van continued to beat out heat. Phoenix flames, maybe. I watched Calum preparing the shoes, thought of Kathryn working at BPE to help me, and how I would keep her yard secure and safe.

'I can give you a day a week to start with,' I said. 'I'll set you up an expedition company that can go anywhere in the world. But my heart is here, on this yard. As long as you understand that?'

'That's fine, I understand,' Andy said with a smile, and we shook hands. In the background Calum finished nailing the shoes onto Ollie.

A week later, in August 2017, I went into an office environment for the first time since Kathryn had left.

After each day at Terra Nova I needed to rest, to regain the strength to face the past all over again. My plan was simple though, I was just going to reword all BPE's policies and procedures in Terra Nova's name. The new ship was called Terra Nova Expedition Services, yet in all truth it was and is a new BPE. Over several weeks I put in place the structure to make her fly. We were granted the Adventure Activities License exceptionally quickly; once I explained it was all our old policies rebranded. The insurance was granted on the basis of my past personal experience.

Hannah Vasey who had worked at BPE had just handed in her notice at her job; she'd worked with the company that took over BPE's trips. She agreed to come and work for Terra Nova as our expedition manager. All the old leaders that were the core of BPE also agreed to lead for the new company. It was a touching tribute of loyalty not only to me but also Kathryn. The strength and honour of the past was being repaid as the old commanders came back.

We needed customers to send to the ends of the earth. Individual teachers called me – they had heard on the grapevine about Terra Nova – and others expressed interest. I was being drawn back into the arena. The sword needed to be picked up off the sand and wielded once more.

I now know what Kathryn must have felt like, trying to run her yard and also keep BPE ticking over. It's a juggling act of horses and expeditions. In more ways than one I was living her life; rushing to do the yard in order to get to a meeting at the office. Apologising to those in the office for being in mucky boots and smelly-horse clothing. Dashing off early to get back in time to feed before darkness drew down over the fields.

BPE's logo was an image of Captain Scott's sledging flag: in the heroic age of polar exploration many explorers had flags based on family coats of arms, and like knights of old they flew them from their sledges as they strode off into the whiteness. I didn't ask Andy to incorporate this into the new Terra Nova Expeditions logo, but in a marvellous gesture he suggested the shape of the BPE flag be incorporated into the Terra Nova logo. It's a phoenix statement. Out of the ashes of destruction rises a new BPE, the new enterprise.

Meanwhile, the fourteen-acre field was coming up for sale. For many years Kathryn had rented it from the farmer who lived at Providence Farm. Kathryn had desperately wanted to own it. It was and is the key to Cross Lane; it's where the big horses live. And it's where Kathryn died. Harold Smith had given Kathryn first refusal on it years ago, and holding true to his word he offered it me as Kathryn's husband. It was a lot of money. Fourteen acres of prime grazing land on sand soil, on a slight slope next to a bridleway and leading into Harlow Wood; Robin Hood's old hunting ground. Other people wanted the field, yet maybe not more than I did. The bank manager agreed we needed to buy it. I had managed to raise half the money and I needed a loan to raise the rest. But the bank declined on the basis that the consultancy could end any time.

The initial refusal devastated me; I was down and knocked back once more onto the canvas. I thought about being back at BPE, when Kathryn and I had faced no-win situations, when the cash flow had run dry, when the bears were circling a team in the Arctic. We always found a way, angels always came when the wagons were down and we had to circle them.

So, I walked into Andy's office and asked him for a full-time permanent contract; to my complete amazement he agreed. Half an hour later I walked out of his office with a signed contract, which was promptly dispatched to the bank. The next day they agreed the loan. Terra Nova had provided the key to get the field, Kathryn's field. Just like BPE had provided the key to get Cross Lane in the first place, alongside our parents' support.

A weight was lifted off my soul. Finally, Kathryn had her field. It was and is the greatest single thing I could have done for her yard.

Phil Avery of Bohunt School and I started planning the 2019 trips, we looked at maps and thought up crazy ideas, and it was just like the old days. At night we ate in the pub we always ate in. I stayed at the same hotel we always stayed at. Yet, the absence was incredible; there was no one to talk to about the proposed trips, no one to bounce ideas off. The phone sat in silence.

Hannah, Andy and I drove down to Bohunt School for the launch night; the night when we would present the trips to the students and their parents. I'd spent ages thinking about how the presentation should look and feel and Phil wanted the BPE history to be mentioned. In the past I've never had any issues with public speaking, in fact I've always enjoyed it. Now there felt such a weight of expectation and history about the presentation, for the first time ever my hands were shaking and the legs felt unsteady. The presentation needed to honour the past and move forward into the future.

The receptionist welcomed us as the team from Bull Expeditions (which BPE was sometimes called); and parents came up to me expressing their thoughts for Kathryn. They had never met her, yet had had other sons and daughters go on previous trips, so they had dealt with her. Kathryn handled all their finances and payments, so she would have known them also. The hall was full with over 350 people in attendance. Loudspeakers and three separate screens waited for the opening of the presentation.

I couldn't watch as the end lines from Tennyson's 'Ulysses' scrolled through to music that we used from the old Polar Challenge presentations, followed by a huge picture of Kathryn jumping Ollie and then the words 'Dedicated to Kathryn'. The mood changed with a compilation of images from all the previous Bohunt trips, with upbeat music heading into the wilds and the north winds. I forgot to mention details like how much the trips were and how long the expeditions took, yet I don't think I did a bad job all things considering. We went for the usual meal afterwards and the hotel was again the same. All things the same, all things different. I went to sleep having drunk too much, with the image of Kathryn jumping out of a water ditch on a large screen at a school in Hampshire she had never been to. Students signed up in their droves, it was the most successful launch we had ever done.

Following the launch at Bohunt, I found myself in the head teacher's office at Chelmsford County High School. I'd meant to wear my best interview trousers, but they no longer fitted. So, feeling decidedly underdressed in jeans from Tesco I sat in her office and went through the formalities. I was humbled beyond words when Nicole and her deputy agreed wholeheartedly to go with Terra Nova on their next expedition.

I drove home, and this time there was no Kathryn to head back to. But I was slowly starting to accept this. I remembered driving back from the first meeting at Chelmsford. The feeling of excitement and fear all mixed up in the same breath. Now I was heading back to a yard of horses, and Ollie and Romeo. And the feeling of the return journey was starting to make some sense; that life finds a way. That even without Goose, maybe I could fly again one day.

CHAPTER TWENTY-THREE

Good People Die

With eyes blinking and breath catching the world returned,
As they moved onto the road that would lead them home.
And so it was the ride all too soon came to finish,
Perhaps it would not be the last, but if it was so, then it was good.

We never know when the last time will be. The last hello, the last argument or the last touch. We always tried to ride out together on Sunday mornings; sometimes Christine came on Ellie. The last ride was like any other ride, Kathryn did the yard first and I got up later and went to get Oliver, walked him down from the family field to Cross Lane. As Kathryn walked up on her horse I took some photos; I've not taken photos on a ride we both went on for years. I can't remember much about the ride; we would just have walked and talked. It was a normal Sunday morning. It was the 3 April 2016, our last ride together.

They say it takes at least five years for a spouse to come to terms with sudden loss. Once playing golf I met a man who was always with his wife, who I'd played with a couple of weeks previously. I asked him where she was and he replied that she had died suddenly of cancer. She had gone to the doctors on the Monday morning and by Friday she was dead. I felt shock and sympathy for him as he wandered off down the fairway alone.

Now I know what it was like for him as he walked off into the distance; not knowing why he was playing alone now.

I'm sure golf and horses were the last thing on Shackleton's mind as he stood ninety-seven miles from the South Pole in 1909 with his companions. He knew the pole was his and with it, immortality. Yet he knew he couldn't get back alive, so in today's terms he made what is called a dynamic risk assessment; he was on the ground, knew the condition he and his men were in and he knew what food and fuel supplies he had left at his depots on the way back. So, he turned around and headed for home, leaving the pole behind him. 'Better a live donkey than a dead lion,' he told his wife.

On a cold, icy day at the yard far away from Antarctica; riders were debating whether to ride or not, the ground was hard and frozen, snow lay on the grass. Why even consider it, given the risks? They can ride any time all year round, the snow and ice does not last for long in Nottinghamshire, and the ride would only be in the school or through the woods. Shackleton had one chance and he favoured life.

One year a friend and I were in Chamonix training for an expedition. In the two weeks we were there twenty people died in avalanches on Mt Blanc, none of them were local climbers. They live there all year round and know the mountain isn't going anywhere. Yet, the foreign climbers were on holiday so they pushed when it wasn't the time to push.

There is a time to go for the summit and there is a time not to. Just like there is a time to get on the horse and a time to leave the saddle in the tack room.

Sometimes maybe the prize is worth the risk, Mallory probably thought so when he and Irvin were last seen heading to the summit of Everest in 1921. The first to climb the highest mountain in the world could be deemed as a time to push the limits, or not. Boardman and Tasker were pushing to be the first to climb Everest via the North East Ridge in 1982; they never made it back, last seen on a high pinnacle moving slowly. Years later Peter Boardman's body was found in the snow. Did they know they were pushing too hard? They were known for bold adventurous climbs; yet did they realise on that fateful climb that they had gone too far? Or were they committed and had no choice? No one will ever know.

Scott knew the risks when he went to the pole in 1911, like Shackleton he was aiming to be the first at the pole, he didn't turn back though and pushed on to reach the pole with his four companions; only to be beaten by Amundsen. The story of his return is well documented: a series of errors and unseasonably cold weather ended their hopes of returning safely. First to the South Pole? Worth the risk? Scott thought so.

When Kathryn walked into the field that Friday it was something she had done hundreds of times before, she knew about risk and she knew about assessing risk dynamically. She had often refused to get on a horse, or she had got off a horse if she had felt the horse was dangerous or she didn't have the skill or experience to ride it safely. She knew her limits with horses and how far she could push. Horses are large and heavy and can be unpredictable, and they can be 800kg of killing machine: Ollie weighs 753kg. Sometimes she had not turned horses out or brought them in because the weather was too bad or there was something else that made it unsafe. She didn't have to get the two horses in for the dentist if the conditions weren't right, she would have left them where they were and booked them in for the dentist another day. So, she must have thought nothing of it as she walked down to the bottom field where Ollie and the horse were. Even as she approached the two horses she would have been analysing what was going on about her; she would have done it subconsciously. Her experience was engrained in her.

Riding horses is dangerous. Fact. They have a mind of their own, and even the most placid of horses can do something unexpected. They can jump to the side, spin around or run off. Every horse can also react differently to different situations. Handling horses is dangerous, that's also a fact; for the same things can happen on the ground. 'It's one of the more dangerous sports, even though the safety equipment is very good,' quoted the editor of *Horse and Hound* for BBC News in 2009. She goes on to say that there have been a number of fatalities over the years, yet 'the reward and thrills more than make up for it.' Do they? I cannot agree nor disagree; I think we do feel more alive when we engage in a risk sport. The greatest thrill I've ever had when doing a sport is going flat out up a stubble field on a Boxing Day hunt. After a free fall parachute jump I was on a high for a week. Getting to the top of a hard climb gives the same feeling. Entire books have been written on the adrenalin-seeking and the pursuit of risk and the thrill it provides. Whether the threat to our life is real or perceived, it does make you feel more alive.

Professor David Nutt noted that riding contributed to ten fatalities a year and 100 traffic accidents a year. And Dr John Silver, an emeritus spinal injuries consultant, found that many accidents resulted from 'a mismatch between the skills of the participant and the task attempted'. Silver wrote a paper; 'Hazards of Horse-riding as a Popular Sport', citing a study that suggested motorcyclists suffered a serious accident once every 7000 hours but a horse rider could expect a serious incident once in every 350 hours. I think the statistics are interesting but they don't give the whole picture. Many incidents aren't reported. (The reported deaths of riders on our roads between 2010 and 2018 is a grand total of thirty-nine, with 230 horses also killed, noted a British Horse Society survey.) Riding horses on the modern UK road network is very dangerous, as both Louise and I know only too well having braved the main street in our village many a time.

In comparison there is one 8000m peak in the Himalayas; Dhaulagiri; where for every three people that summit, one dies. A far more startling statistic than riding-related incidents. Yet, polar expeditions in the modern era are not the high-risk trips they once were; maybe with the exception of some of the current 'sport endurance' treks across icecaps where the human body is pushed to the limits of its endurance.

At Bloomsgorse some of the clients that came always exaggerated their experience. In my world of expeditions everyone played down their experience; keeping their powder dry. Yet, for some reason people out riding on the fast rides often played up their ability. Maybe eighty per cent said they were better than they were; this led to loss of face at best, danger at worst. A mismatch of ability with a partner on a mountain can make death a far likelier outcome.

It is this mismatch of skills that is the key to success or failure. People may buy a type of horse that is not suitable for them; they then become what is known as 'over-horsed', whereby the horse requires a higher level of riding skill than their owner has. And the horse gets left in the field or is ridden sparsely, because they are scared of riding such a powerful horse. In the outdoors world people don't normally go and climb a difficult rock face on their own if they haven't climbed for a while. It's the opposite in the horse world a lot of the time. Like an English climber on holiday in the Alps when the snow conditions aren't right. Common-sense and reason get left in the stable.

In the time I have been running Cross Lane, I have on three occasions been lucky not to have sustained a serious injury or been killed. This was purely down to luck. Each time I was doing the correct thing with the horse as taught to me by Kathryn. Yet, due to some unknown reason the horse I was with spooked and each time I was lucky not to be crushed or jumped on. Kathryn herself had been stood on, run over and fallen off numerous times. When hunting she had suffered concussion a couple of times due to bad falls over big hedges.

In one particular incident I became over-confident on Ollie, and one morning whilst jumping him over several fences he went one way and I the other. It was a classic mismatch of skills. Fiona came running over to where I lay in a heap. Her first thought was that I'd broken my neck. After we had established that my neck was working fine, in the bizarre tradition of horse-riding culture, I got back on my horse. Ollie and I did three more jumps before I decided that my leg and hips really did hurt. I went home for a rest with great difficulty driving the Defender; it didn't get any better lying down. With great reluctance I went to hospital.

X-rays and CT scans revealed I'd broken my pelvis; it would be several weeks before I could ride Ollie properly again and it took all my effort to get down the fields each morning following Anna as she pushed the barrow of feeds. It was a slow road to recovery, but gradually the pelvis healed and I got back to riding Ollie. It had created a fear that had not been there before, but in time it would pass. Initially though, Kathryn's accident was brought back to me in stark colour every time I got on him. It had been a close call, a mistake on my part that led to coming off a 17.3 hand horse at speed. I could quite easily have seriously injured myself or worse. And that's the risk and the inevitability of the work with horses. I was a statistic to be recorded, part of the number of riders that have had an incident.

If I'd bought a motorbike my mum and dad would have gone mad when I was young. Yet when I bought Oliver, they loved him. It's all about perception of risk versus the real risk, and what is accepted by our current society. Parents buy their children cars; steel vehicles capable of travelling very fast, on roads with lots of other similar vehicles. On an expedition launch night parents would always ask about the risks, the risks of travelling to certain countries; of contracting diseases; of terrorism; the risk of being attacked by a polar bear. Yet, the greatest risk statistically was travelling from the school to the airport by bus. The greatest terrorism risk when BPE finished trading was probably in London. Parents think nothing of sending their young children for pony riding lessons; the young girl in turn dreams of owning her own pony. This is turn leads to the young girl growing up in the culture of riding and horses; they may not get taught by a qualified instructor. The equine industry is well-regulated in terms of its structure and the British Horse Society's registered instructor scheme, yet this is not always accessed as much as it should.

Anyone can buy a horse or pony and stick it in a field. Anyone can buy a motorbike, but at least you need a licence to ride it on the road. You don't need a licence to ride a horse on the road, and although the Highway Code urges drivers to 'be particularly careful of horse riders' and to 'treat all horses as a potential hazard', it doesn't state that a horse has priority over vehicles on the road. You don't need any form of licence to ride a horse anywhere. Nor any form of licence to own one.

Kathryn made sure that Cross Lane was insured and as safe as it could be; yet it's not a riding school, so riding is at each person's own risk. She intervened only if she thought someone was doing something unsafe on the yard or in the fields, as I do. But we all have to die from something; we all have to live a life. The two are at odds together and also linked like sleeping spoons. We can't have life without death. Captain Scott in one of his 'last letters' wrote that the journey was hard and tough, but far better than lounging around at home. As he lay freezing and starving in his tent, his implication was that he still preferred that to achieving nothing at home. The expedition and what he wrote was used to inspire troops in the trenches of the First World War; to show that Englishmen could face overwhelming odds and die like gentlemen. Death was glorified and society accepted losses and loved ones not coming home; in public that is. Oates' mother never got over the loss of her son, and spent the rest of her life in mourning. Some people never accept the loss, the futility of life despite the public false glory that can be attached to it. The men who died on Scott's expedition were glorified to such an extent they eclipsed the achievements of Amundsen and his team who were first to the South Pole.

Maria Coffey visited Everest with Peter Boardman's widow. They both tried to find a peace. Eventually both of them would go on to marry other men; they would both find love again. In her second book, Maria explores in detail climbing and the effect on those left behind when the climber dies in pursuit of their hobby. Because ultimately that's what climbing is: a leisure activity. It is carried out for the pleasure it brings to the person doing it. It just happens to be an extreme sport. Yet, it doesn't cure cancer, banish poverty, save lives or house the homeless. Neither does riding horses.

I don't buy into the philosophy that if someone dies doing the sport or job they love then that makes the loss easier to bear. Each person that has died would (I believe) far sooner come back from the expedition or pursuit they are engaged in to see their family and loved ones. Those of us who are left say 'at least they died doing what they loved'; it gives us comfort in the small hours when the fire has gone out and the candle wax is cold. Yet we are desperate to find meaning in loss, that 'what doesn't kill us does make us stronger', even though it may take time to find the strength. And that's all part of the return to peace.

In the end there is very little that is worth dying for; life is too short as it is. I would die to get Kathryn back; I hope I would give my life to save another person in distress. Those are the exceptions I think; but I don't want to die riding a horse or falling off a mountain. I gamble that my experience, knowledge and skill will keep me safe in my job. But it's only a gamble; and

I'm not as experienced, skilled or knowledgeable as she was. So, my odds are not as good as hers. On an expedition I always felt the odds were in my favour, I had experience, skill and years of practice. With horses I think the odds are stacked the other way.

After falling off Ollie, my lack of mobility did make the office work more bearable. I spent most of my days writing the procedures for Terra Nova. Writing risk assessments for expeditions in foreign lands as the risk of riding horses stared back at me from the reflection in the office window.

I rationalise the risks because I have no choice; I feel this is the path that was chosen for me following the day Kathryn went. Each day I choose to live the life in a way that Kathryn would be proud of me. I accept that Ollie is a challenge; but he's my challenge and he's now my horse. I am cautious in what I do with him; but at the end of the day he's a complicated horse. Like Frodo Baggins' ring, Ollie is my band of gold. We all have a ring we must accept in order to live the life we have left. I believe that our paths in this life are governed by forces we know nothing about. Yet, under extreme hardship, if we ask for help, then those forces hold us and keep us safe, or they comfort us in our darkest hour. This is something I have found difficult to grasp in the journey so far, because it goes against cause and effect; however, when I have been totally down and out, something I can't define picks me up. Or guides my hand, or just comforts me in the darkness.

On the second anniversary I struggled immensely leading up to the day for I knew what was coming, and I was ill for several weeks beforehand. On the day in the dawn of the field I laid two roses on the grass. I whispered 'I've got you' to the dust by my boots. Ollie maybe sensing something walked up and nudged me with a comforting force. As I stood there, he bent down and ate one of the roses in one. Then he looked at me with a cheeky horse expression, not unlike a smile. I burst out laughing in the field as the sun rose over the trees. The diary entry for the day was surprisingly upbeat:

29 April 2018

Day 367. Yard early. Jobs done by 8.30. Ollie ate a rose. Laughed; rode him. Good. Louise came and Mum. Lunch at parents. Poo picked the field. Spoke to liveries and Nichola. A good day considering.

Sometimes the feeling of being touched by a sunbeam is palatable, as if she is holding Ollie's reins, or pushing the barrow in the field. T. S. Eliot wrote:

There is always another one walking beside you
Gliding wrapt in a brown mantle, hooded

The one that is always there. When I'm really down, Ollie seems to know it, and he walks over and nuzzles his face against my shoulder, just like on that morning of the second year.

I believe there is life after death, and it is here on earth if we have the courage to open our heart and let the love in. The third person is the love in our hearts from those that have gone.

Ultimately none of us have a choice as to what happens to us. We think we do; but in reality, if the wind blows the wrong way, and the sky goes darker unexpectedly, the roll of the dice will fall against us and then we have to adjust to a new life. We can't always decide what happens to us in this life. We can have dreams and ambitions and try and act them out, yet sometimes fate deals us a hand that is hard to fathom. All our dreams and hopes eventually become dust in the grass, futures are scattered to the four cold winds. So, it's not always about what we achieve in this life that matters, it's how we deal with what is thrown at us. For as Rocky Balboa says in the *Rocky* films: it's all about moving forward no matter how hard life hits us. It's a great metaphor in how to deal with great loss.

So, if we can't change the dice, life is all about doing something worth living for; that may be climbing a mountain or trying to cross a continent encased in ice. Or it may be working with horses. Kathryn did something worth living for. That's what it's all about. Standing by what you believe in and who you love. Even when the mountains fall. It's about doing an honest job, whatever that may be. Coming home and being in love; working at a relationship. And living life to the fullest, to live life as though we have the eyes and hands of those gone before us. Of never giving in. Finding, striving, seeking and never yielding.

CHAPTER TWENTY-FOUR

The Rides of All Our Lives

For all things come to pass, as the field gate shuts,
Leading us into empty paddocks, the shut-down grass,
All we can do is tempt our belonging.
To strive for our place in the lone field, our authentic home.

All days dawn with a beginning. The rising of our sun and the sleepy, slow joy of our eyes opening, with the banishment of night and the dreams we had lived. Kathryn would always wake first; sometimes the phone would bleep if it was an early start. Yet the seventh day was our day, and if I was not away on an expedition we would ride. She would pat the duvet and wander out of the bedroom, thumping into a doorway with an 'ouch'. I would relish the space in the bed, stretch out and enjoy the time in bed alone. How desperate are those thoughts now? What would we all give to relive the times in our past that have gone.

As the front door clanged shut I would roll out of the double bed and shower. It takes only a few minutes to take a Land Rover from the house to the stables, the time it takes for Springsteen's 'Glory Days' to sing out its tune on the Defender's old tape player. A steep pull out of the drive that overlooks the forest of Blidworth Bottoms, turn right at the church where Alan-a-Dale, the minstrel from the Robin Hood legend, is buried and follow your nose along Rickett Lane. After half a mile is the family field where Oliver and Strip live; they would be standing at the gate as I drove by, as if waiting. Pulling up at the yard the dogs would welcome me as I pushed through the gate. There would be livery members on the yard, a couple of hellos as I walked to the tack room. No sign of Kathryn as she would be down the fields finishing her morning jobs.

This was our Sunday morning start, each of us going about our ways of being, finding our way on the day. It was ordinary, it was our ordinary. Our family day, our roar of simple life.

We mostly arranged a time to meet at the yard, a time to saddle up and mount our horses. I'd always be on Oliver, she would mainly ride Ollie, and sometimes it would be someone else's horse she was exercising. In the early days it would be Strip Cartoon. She would do the yard, feed the horses, turn out horses and muck out those that needed it. All I had to do was get Oliver.

She was always late up from the fields, and I was always impatient. She admitted to me that she would go deliberately slow finishing off her jobs if I was already sat on Oliver. I don't blame her now, for I was sometimes a pain in watching the clock. With her jobs done she would inevitably groom Oliver for me, as the dust of his coat would sometimes make me sneeze, and I would pick out the hooves of both our horses and get the tack. Then we would wander down the lane and into the heart of the woods. It was like being back at Bloomsgorse when we would ride together on Fridays.

Our rides together merge into one now, the horses a combination of Strip Cartoon, Oliver, Ollie, Scarlet, Penny and Gordon. We would ride through the gate past Providence and through the little strip of trees and into the fields, some days up the bridleway to Lindhurst, trotting or cantering, dogs running ahead. In sun and rain we would ride out in the forest of our youth, our single days and married days.

Talk would be idle chat about the week gone by or the week coming ahead. Arguing about work and normal couple stuff. And of course, how to ride the horses, mainly my riding. Kathryn's voice echoes down through the years and the trees. We trotted the deserted roads, country lanes with wide open fields that stretched as far as the eye could see, and that if it had snowed seemed like the icecaps of Greenland and Antarctica. Before expeditions the rides were more special, a time to be with each other and settle affairs before the weeks of separation.

Through dale and dip they went, for in Sherwood they belonged, and for King Richard's land they rode, they covered ground as only they could do. Up the hill and into the light.

'The Ride' was written for Kathryn, about her and Strip. It was a favourite of hers; as she reaches the family field the ghosts of her greyhounds act as guardians. They keep her and Strip safe.

She watched as he walked down the field into a glowing sun, Heading for the big grey and all that he knew, as the Tan and black guardians watched; over both him and she.

Now Kathryn is one of the guardians, with our greyhounds Jack and Bruce. As I write this, Strip enters his thirty-second year and is one of the last links to my rides with Kathryn. His history stretches back to the early days at Bloomsgorse, to the deer glades and forest tracks of the pines. He is the link to the expeditions, to satellite phone calls home from a wind-blown tent on an icecap.

Now my rides are about following the memory, a grey horse that is always ahead of me or behind me. I ride in the knowledge that love never dies. It just changes in its form. I can accept that now. So now I ride for both of us.

CHAPTER TWENTY-FIVE

Robins Will Come

Let it begin then; the climb from despair
The crawl back up to the height of belonging.
For the bird will act as our beacon, upon his castle.

On a cold day in deep winter Kathryn took Otto and Jack to the local park:

8 January 2004

I saw a swan in the park today, not one that lives there. The usual pair were on the lake, with the two remaining young from last year. As I approached, the Canada geese all waddled off toward the pond, leaving behind a single mature swan. As I walked down the road, almost home, the lonely swan flew overhead. I wonder where it went next.

They say swans mate for life. Was it flying home to its mate? Or was it truly on its own? Destined to fly in search of something, from park to park and pond to pond. Searching for something. I have spent my whole life in the belief that we live, we die and there is nothing else. But the past couple of years have taught me differently. I wonder now, as Kathryn wondered.

In the midst of great tragedy, it's easy to see things that are perhaps coincidences. And to turn those coincidences into meanings that give us hope in our darkest hours. On our South Pole expedition there were so many coincidences that linked the trip together it was hard not to believe in something else that was guiding our path. 'Angels' playing at significant moments, not to mention Gary's bible finding its slot just where Gary had said it would. Shackleton spoke of the third person as they crossed South Georgia ('during that long and racking march of thirty-six hours over the unnamed mountains and glaciers of South Georgia, it seemed to me often that we were four, not three'), now referred to as the Third Man factor, and Wilson and Scott also spoke of sensing providence as they lay in their tent. We all seek out a light to hang on to. When times were tough on the expeditions there was nothing better than hearing Kathryn's voice. It's the most significant improvement in exploration. How grateful Scott would have been if he could have got out the satellite phone and called his wife, just to tell her they were in a tight spot.

I find myself wondering if Kathryn felt anything down in the field on her fateful day. I saw the look in my dad's eyes when he went away. I knew he believed, sought the light and found it. Did Kathryn know the light as the calling came? I like to believe.

After my dad had died, my mum was lying in bed one morning when she heard my dad say to her, 'Jennifer, you need to go and see the doctor.' By the afternoon she was in hospital, diagnosed with cancer of the womb and was operated on immediately. The surgeon asked why she came in when she did, as if she had left it later it would have been incurable. She didn't tell the surgeon the truth. The cancer was removed and she made a full recovery.

Those that have stood in Scott's hut at Cape Evans say you can feel the presence of those that lived there. That there is the expectation the explorers will walk back, hang up their jackets, take off their boots and settle down. Light their pipes and talk of the journey south and the winds that blew hard. Since Kathryn left there have been instances that have also been hard to explain. They are glimpses, little rays of light most of the time; yet they are unmistakable in their directness. On Ollie I have had the strangest sensation her hands have taken hold of mine, helped me when I've needed her. Sometimes on the yard I have a feeling that someone else is there, it's only a feeling, but it's there. Warm pockets of air exist where they shouldn't, they hang sometimes on the lane, then they are gone. Objects move sometimes and low hellos are heard over the grass. I have dreams that are so vivid I wake and feel that I am still dreaming. I dreamed of her by the pond in the garden, except it was much larger and deeper. I said I'd been looking after it for her, and she smiled. Then the pond lit up with life and flowers of every colour and kind. She thanked me for looking after the garden, said she was going to ride and she was sorry I couldn't ride with her, but I wasn't allowed yet, I had work to do; to look after her yard, Romeo and Ollie. As she turned away, she told me she would see me in a bit. That morning the yellow buds of the new daffodils poked through the snow.

Once, she was next to me, saying 'I've got you'. It was as real as these words. I leaned over to kiss her, and I woke alone. But the feeling of her being there was so powerful it brought the sun down on me.

Well you're back later tonight. I'll hang on to last night's phone calls, when you said you just wanted to hear my voice.

We all hang on, hang on to the last night; a last call. The hard part is letting go. But if we stand still then no return journey can take place, and we feel guilty about being happy. Part of us wants to wait in the place of sorrow, but we must move into the silent storm, take the step down the mountain, push out across the plateau. Push hard for that happiness.

Couldn't decide whether I should wait up or not – made right decision in the end though! Love you, see later, Kathryn xxx

That was for a phone call from a man on the ice to his wife back home, a robin flying across the ocean. With hindsight I know the return from the journey isn't to a place in heaven, it's back to wherever we think of as home. It's to the heart of the knowing smile of everlasting love.

In the afterglow of dawn's light as I pause on the patio, tea steaming into the air, doves fly over me. Kathryn's surname was Dove. They normally come when I'm feeling down, not looking forward to the day. Most of the time it's just a single dove, white, flying high and then turning as it comes over the house. Sometimes the birds sing. On my birthday there were no birds in sight, I despaired for a moment and suddenly there was a chorus of doves.

They say that robins are like angels; they come to us and guide us when times are hard. The winter of the second Christmas was especially hard physically as well as mentally. Hard weather tried its best to beat me, the rain came down and made rivers of the fields, and the mud couldn't decide whether to be sticky or just wet. And then it froze, followed by snow. It was the first time all the taps froze and we had no water for four days. Then the boiler at home broke, so for ten days it was cold showers until it could be fixed. It was truly like being on an expedition. Hard physical work in cold conditions, and going home to cold water. After spending three hours one afternoon just putting feeds out in the fields and topping up the troughs with water, I sat on the bench in the yard exhausted. I still had horses to fetch in. That's when the robins came; several of them started walking around me. When I went to wash the feed bowls, they followed me. When I brought the horses in, they were there. On the gate, on the stable doors. They followed me everywhere. Her presence was in them and with them. The robins gave me strength.

I think now that so many of us walk through life without really looking, without seeing the little things that give comfort and remind us of our loves. I know I will see her again one day, and what stories I will have to tell. She will be mad and proud I think, but she will also laugh at the crazy idea I had to run her yard and ride her horse.

She'll also know that when she first went I would go to sleep asking God to make sure I didn't wake in the morning. He could take me now, I was done; all in. All cards played, I wanted out of the game. I prayed that he should have taken me and not Kathryn. I felt I was forcing a square peg into a round hole trying to run Cross Lane, and it was an uphill struggle to convince people that I could make it work. It took God a long time to reply, and when he did, he didn't take me. One day I woke and felt that I was being held in the arms of the hugest love I've ever known. Faith, hope and love held me, held Kathryn, joined us. The pages of the story were bound in the love of the morning.

God's not been back like that again. I think I needed reassuring to know that Kathryn was all right, so I could carry on and run Cross Lane. That despite all the knockbacks, all the heartache and hard work, I was loved. And that I would never be alone. His answer is in the soft light, the robin on the fence post, the dove over the house and the nuzzle of Romeo. The respect of Ollie. In the quiet background, the ring on my finger, the soft light of the candle and the peace of sleep.

I felt Kathryn with me on the moors one day, tramping through heather. The wind blew from the south-east, the ground had frozen and the earth was mine. On the horizon a large cairn stood like a beacon on the fringe of the world. Sometimes she was behind me, just a quiet figure in shadow, walking along in her blue fleece, black trousers and red hat. Blue gloves on. At other times she was beside me, just off to the right. She was never ahead though, for she didn't want to leave me. So, I walked over the hills in peace and love, I could have walked far into the distance and beyond that day. Out of the Lake District, across to the Howgills and into the Pennines, past the yard and Ollie and the dogs, down the length of England, and through the rest of Europe. From one continent to the other I would have walked, for I didn't want the good feeling to end. Past the South Pole and across the ice that lay there. Then on to the last horizon, following the dimming southern stars until the world finished. For that's where we would both stand, as the world finishes, and all dreams are hope and just sunlight. We would have walked the life we led together and it would carry on for ever. As an eastern wind blows on the face and the birds sing on the drifting air.

CHAPTER TWENTY-SIX

Kingdom of Horses

The fjord is castled in by mountains,
My grey carries me through the water valley,
Steel-made hooves pay their way,
There's no one else to pay the price,
A price we pay.

I wonder now how many times we rode out together, how many miles we covered together on our horses. Riding in the wind, laughing in the rain and soaking up the sun on our faces. Endless forest tracks we rode down, in walk or just trotting along. Cantering one behind the other, galloping up stubble fields, through the early days at Bloomsgorse, the hunting days in Lincolnshire and through our own woods. All the days at competitions before returning to the grass of home; the hearth of the field.

One day, when the field was glowing in the soft light of late afternoon, Harold shouted hello from the bridleway. We met by the steel gate that borders the fields and his lane. He shook my hand as usual.

'It's good to see you,' he said. 'How are you doing?'

'You know she lived for these horses, this land,' I said, looking around me.

'Let me stop you on that point, Steve. Do you know what she told me once?'

'Go ahead,' I said, in some ways dreading his reply, for I'd had so much hard news by then.

'Kathryn sat on Ollie right there, just by where we're standing and she said, "Harold don't tell anyone, but all this, the yard, the horses, everything I have, I do it for Steve." Then she bid me good day and rode back up the lane on her big grey.'

Harold smiled and held my hand, and I held his. I held his hand like it was the last one on earth.

Under the bed there are boxes of rosettes, dated in years in large black ink. Dozens upon dozens of rosettes, won in all sorts of competitions. Some are for dressage, either at the local riding club she ran or competitions in the local area. There are some for show jumping, again from all over the local area. One-day events; a combination of dressage, show jumping and cross-country. The bookshelves have trophies on them, first place, second place; sometimes third. More rosettes hang in the kitchen; they are the more prestigious ones like the National Trailblazer final at Stoneleigh Park. She also kept all the dressage test sheets she entered, the records of Ollie and her progressing through the years. Scores and numbers, the judge's comments on how they both rode. They are the memories of a person progressing through a career in horses, of a love between one person and their horse.

In a corner of the bedroom by the crime novel bookcase is her bag with her best riding clothes in. It contains her eventing colours; the hat cover and silk top, blue with white stars on. Her ID card for cross-country and her stock and pin for hunting. And they will stay where they are as I use her stock when I compete on Ollie at dressage now.

At the start of each year Kathryn would sit on the sofa and plan her competitions. Laptop open, pen in hand and a little notebook resting on her leg; she would look for the best events and the right dates that fitted in around Cross Lane. The money she made from clipping other people's horses – which allows their coats to dry faster and stops them sweating too much – she would use for the entry fees. In her silver Defender with its white roof she would load Ollie up in the Ifor Williams trailer and head off at weekends and compete. Many times I would turn up and watch, then head off as soon as she had finished riding. Osberton, Speetley, to name but a few of the venues she went to. At the Southwell Ploughing match she competed in the Hunter Class, Ollie jumping big and proud over the rustic fences.

All the events now lie on the top of the sofa in an unfinished photo album; pictures Kathryn put in of her and Ollie competing over the years. Each photo is pinned in place with the venue and date and position she came handwritten underneath. It's not a digital album, it's an album put together by love and feeling and most of all pride.

The dates she competed on had to match in with the days she ran the riding club. Once a month on a Saturday the riding club where she was chairperson, treasurer and secretary held a jumping day, on similar Sundays it would be dressage. After doing the shopping I would stop by and leave a cake in the microwave for her, wave across the school and leave her to it.

It was just the same with the riding club committee meetings. I would go to the local pub at 7 p.m. for a couple of beers. It's a habit I've never got out of from the RAF, when we would always have a drink before dinner in the mess. Riding club meetings were also held there. The meeting would be in full swing, Kathryn engaged in conversation, as I silently held my own counsel and opened my book or responded to work emails. Yet, she would always smile and look over at me with her wet hair, as she was always late for the meeting. Afterwards she would sit on the sofa typing up the minutes and sending them on, just as on Saturday evening she would be typing up the results from the show jumping and posting them online. She had become the British Horse Society's Local Access Officer and was looking forward to getting to grips with the role. It combined her love of horses with the landscape and maps, and helping out and giving back. This was Kathryn's kingdom of horses; she was respected, liked and loved by most, if not all. She had touched so many people in the horse world, not to mention the hundreds of horses she either rode or handled over the years.

The rosettes and trophies sit alongside the expedition photos; images from Greenland, Iceland, Norway and Antarctica. The riding boots slump next to a saddle, the planning sheet with her 2016 show dates remains uncompleted, just as expedition plans lie unused in maps. There are skis that went to the pole, with Kathryn's name on the front. And in the bathroom is the pulk; 1.6m of plastic and fabric that contain all the planning information and my personal clothing from the Polar Challenge. They are mementos of a previous life. They link the past life into my present life; trying to fit into Kathryn's kingdom of the horse.

It's a kingdom that has shaped the world we live in as we know it. Our very culture is based on man's taming of the horse. From Genghis Khan on the steppes of Mongolia, all the way to the plains of north-west America the horse has shaped the destinies and futures of those that lived there. In Africa and South America horses have shaped the way the countries have developed. Even in Antarctica the horse was pivotal in the exploration of the continent. Scott used them to get to the Beardmore Glacier, following the example set by Shackleton. Both used ponies imported from Siberia in an attempt to conquer the last kingdom; Antarctica.

They all sit now in various guises in a cabinet in the hall. Each Christmas Kathryn would buy me a model horse with a rider onboard; first they were 7th Cavalry figures, galloping to the bugle John Wayne was blowing, charging to save the day in their glass-enclosed display. Then the Scots Greys joined them in a dash to the French guns; cantering alongside the western comrades. I loved them and it was good for Kathryn, as she was rubbish at buying presents. So, a defined list to follow each year was brilliant for her. When the Scots Greys were finished in their charge she moved on to the Crimean War and the Russian guns. The Light Brigade ran with the greys and the 7th Cavalry in one big kingdom of model horses. If you walk round the house now, it's full of our horse figures. They depict the horse in all its forms, as a weapon of war, as a form of entertainment and leisure, and as a machine of industry. The horse has been all those things.

Part of this vast equine lineage, at the tip of the empire, is the riding club's summer competition. On show jumping days I stand by Alison leaning on the gate, just like Kathryn used to. I stand where Kathryn used to stand. I think it's important, it's part of the ongoing chain; it means the journey is a return in itself, the fire that needs to be kept burning. It's a carrying on of the kingdom, for right or wrong.

'I couldn't have done it you know,' Alison whispered one day whilst a horse leapt over the jumps in the school.

'Done what?' I replied looking at the stopwatch.

'Come here, run the yard the day after; you know . . .' She turned and looked at me.

'Thank you, that means a lot Alison. Now I've messed the timing up!' Alison just smiled as she said, 'Nothing new there then.'

The riding club is an important part of Cross Lane and Kathryn's legacy, the committee is smaller now, yet still dedicated to carrying on the ethos of Kathryn. It's all about people coming to have a go at show jumping and dressage in a small friendly setting. Cakes are baked and we have a laugh. After I set up the Kathryn Bull Memorial Trust, funds came in straight away, mainly from all the people on the Blidworth Horse Owners

Facebook page; and we bought a bench in memory of Kathryn, which we decided to put in the main yard at Cross Lane. 'To rest paws and eat cake' is inscribed on the bench; which mainly means that Zac lies on it dreaming of food.

Two awards have been made so far by the trust, one to a local rider to work on a horse ranch in Africa, the other to a rider wanting to compete in Tent Pegging; an ancient equestrian sport. Riders gallop and try and spear hoops and rings, I think Kathryn would have loved to have a go. Yet, the most important part of the trust's calendar and indeed the riding club is the Memorial Show.

Cross Lane carries on, and as I write she is full to bursting with a waiting list. The winter is hard and long, but spring is around the corner. I try to do the right thing and keep Cross Lane a nice, safe and happy place to be for the horses and their owners. Some of the horses Kathryn would recognise. Nibbs is still here, along with Amber and Soul and George too, who lives with Ollie. Little Sunny she knew for a short time. The new ones like Prince, Bella, and Flicka to name a few she didn't know in person but she would love them all too; be tough with them when they mucked about, comfort them when they needed it. Zac and Bruno still stalk each other on the yard. It's the same and it's not the same.

At the end of each day in the week I go and do our horses Oliver and Strip just like Kathryn did. There is a peace to the family field that I appreciate. When the horses are done Romeo and I wander the fields if it's summer, to reflect and think before heading home. It's also time to spend with Kathryn, to just sit and talk with her face to face as the sun sets on another day of the return path. One of the last photos Kathryn took was of the baby pigeons that nest each year in the little tack room; she'd taken the photo on the morning of her accident. It's a connection to the ongoing circle of life and death that we are all part of.

Death seeks us all out and the day of death hangs low in the sunset; it's how we face it that defines who we are though. And we have a duty to those that have gone before us to live a life the best we can; we owe that to the departed.

Before attending a show, she would work out exactly how long the drive to the venue would take. She would wear over-trousers over her jodhpurs, with the aim of keeping them clean; yet somehow, she would always get a little muck on them. The trailer would be her changing room, the Defender the tack store. My job was to take photos; normally I'd get one good one which she put on social media. After tea she would sit on the sofa and keep the computer on, every time someone liked the photo she would comment, 'Another like!' I would nod and smile and she would go back to her crossword. Ordinary days and nights that now seem extraordinary. None of us know when they are happening, when we are living in them, that these are the momentous days. The kingdoms of our lives. Kathryn riding Ollie on a windswept field, jumping out of the water ditch, or coming down the hill on a Hunter trial. On those days she was part of the ongoing chain that is our relationship with the horse. The chain that can't be broken. Those were the days of her life.

I wonder often now what it must be like to wear someone else's hands for the day. Kathryn's hands were imprinted with her life with horses and fields. It feels like her hands are mine now. I would like to live in someone else's hands for a change, to feel a different future, one without loss and longing. I can't break the chain of our entwined hands, yet perhaps someone will lend me theirs for a moment, to feel the ongoing love. To be able to teach a child to ride, to feel the gritstone on a climb once more, or to hold another's hand. To carry on the chain of life.

Old friends have visited the yard, and the circumstances of my life now seem very different to theirs. Dave is a group captain and station commander of the regimental depot, Rich is an air commodore at the Ministry of Defence in London. Other friends are head teachers and my brother is dean of a large university. Yet, I would not swap places with any of them. They are all happily married with great children (apart from Dave, he's still single; but he's too busy climbing and enjoying life to be married). But I will take my past, my love and life with Kathryn for all of what they now have tenfold and more. I'll take the new horse kingdom and accept my hands. In time I think they will get used to each other.

Alongside the model horses and their colours standing proudly in the wind of the living room, sits a silver stirrup entwined with a shining rose. My hands collected it on behalf of Kathryn. She would have been proud beyond measure. The British Horse Society; that most venerable institution steeped in history deemed Kathryn worthy of meritorious work in support of young riders. When the letter came announcing the posthumous award, I cried. It was the first positive letter to drop through the letter box since she died. With records dating back to AD 1160, the Worshipful Company of Saddlers is one of the oldest livery companies in the City of London. It is rare in that it has two mottos; 'Our trust is in God' is one. Yet as I collected Kathryn's award in the Saddler's Hall I stared at the coat of arms. Centre stage is a shield, flanked by two rearing silver horses, then the words; 'Hold fast, sit sure.' I felt her hand holding mine. We held fast together, sitting sure in the thronged stone, in the chivalry of the moment.

That day the kingdom of the horse honoured one of their own. The great and the good of the equestrian world took a step back; they nodded to the grace of the ghost in the room. As they did two silver horses looked down from the pennant on the stone wall. North of the capital in a field that is the true kingdom of the horse; a grey horse ran free and danced on the wind. He knew too, so he ran for her in joy.

CHAPTER TWENTY-SEVEN

Every Road Leads Home to You

The answer lies in our minute,
Our tree of time, not in the quest laid down by history's search.
It lays down in my hand and yours, the grasp,
That will hold, long after any sun has set.

'I'm here!' was her statement of arrival. Whether it be landing into the hall, front door banging, or coming down the stairs with her hair just about dry, she would shout 'I'm here.' If we were out and she went into a shop, she would come out and announce to me, 'I'm here!' I think when she arrived in heaven in a whirl of hay and straw, she'd have shouted 'I'm here' and just like me, God would have smiled.

I think he was smiling on one winter's day too. On the 3 December 2017 Kathryn's family, my mother, friends, plus Harold and I walked down the little track that leads to the bottom of Cross Lane's fields. We walked past the little paddocks on the left as Soul stood and watched. It was a slow walk for it was an important day. Kathryn's dad carried a screwdriver and a box of brass screws, Harold carried a slate sign covered in bubble wrap.

The sign was made at Honister Slate Mine, the place we visited on our honeymoon. A trainee vicar was on the till the day I picked the sign up. The vicar expressed her love for the slate plaque and what it meant. It seemed like a sign that it was meant to be.

Our little group stood by the entrance to the field that we had completed on the Thursday before. It had taken over a year to arrange the funds to buy the field; Kathryn had dreamed of buying it but could never afford it.

On the horizon the ancient hunting grounds glinted off the hedges, fox tracks lay on the last of the early morning dew. Ollie watched from the corner of the field in the hope of getting fed. 'I'm here,' he silently shouted.

Her dad secured the slate sign to the weathered wood that borders the field whilst Harold held it in place. In white writing it simply states, 'Kathryn's Field'. Harold spoke a few words about Kathryn.

'I would just like to say one thing; if you all don't mind,' he began. 'This field was promised to Kathryn, and I'm so proud that it is now hers. For this field will always be Kathryn's, and I'm also glad that Steve is looking after it for her.'

No one else said anything. It was too big, too emotional. She should have been there, to see the moment when the field became hers. I wish with all my heart I could have bought the field when she was here, but that's not how the cards were dealt. My mum had bought a red rose and offered it to me to place on the sign, but I declined. I would offer the rose to her later in private.

Her dad shook my hand, and when he did, I knew the right thing had been done. I had never been sure of what they thought of me taking on their daughter's yard. They keep their thoughts to themselves, and they keep calm and carry on. They do it without the T-shirt or the mug. It's their way, as it has been for generations of people brought up in the old world, a world without social media and the instant sharing of thoughts and problems. As we walked steadily back up the track to the yard I walked beside her dad.

'I don't think I can do any more than that, that's the best I can do; secure the field for her,' I said nervously.

Her dad looked at me. 'I think you're right; she would be proud.'

I don't think I've been happier about something her dad has said to me. We stood in the yard and waited for the kettle to boil, there were cakes to eat which is normal now at Cross Lane when there is a gathering. There was laughter and we talked. Harold spoke of Kathryn and of what she achieved, and that now no one would ever forget what she did here, on this land, for horses and for people. The return of the journey was falling into place now, of finding the peace in our lives. And that is priceless.

There will for ever be a corner of England that is Kathryn's, and those of us that stood there will slowly take our turn and join Kathryn in whatever lies ahead. And when we have all gone, the field will remain.

There are no intentions to carry out an 'Oates'; to leave the tent's comfort and walk off into the snow. Kathryn wouldn't allow that and I agree with her. The demons are there in the darkness, but I don't mind them now. I have the weapons and the tools to deal with them; they enable me to smile back. I have the shield and sword and armour Kathryn gave me. I also know that unlike Scott I'll reach the hut one day, for her smile on our honeymoon is with me in spirit and my pocket every day.

Stephen

I will carry your armour and shield with pride, although at times it can be a heavy burden to bear. And sometimes I may shudder, you can be sure that when you are ready, I will be there.

The horse is strong, the sword is sharp. You will fight with strength and honour, and hope. And you will prevail.

Kathryn x

She wrote those words in the early days, when our world was young. Yet now those words give me strength, she speaks to me across the gulf that lies between us. Her words give comfort when the darkness creeps in, they banish the monsters that lie in the lonely rooms and light the candle of hope, of faith. Of her love. A love that can't ever die, that lights the way on the return journey.

It's strange now, as the depression I suffered for many years is no longer there. I think the shock of her going combined with the sheer will to survive drove out the darkness in my soul. I believe that when we are provided with a stark choice – live or die – the survival instinct wells to the surface. Although some days the sheer act of being alive without her is so hard I need to sleep, just to lie there and remember. The laughter on the yard I find hard to engage with sometimes, so I quietly wander off and sit in the field. Or take Romeo for a long walk through the trees. Sometimes I struggle with horses and people and the tie that binds me to my history. I accept this as part of the process. There are days when I do just rest, for to continue this exploration the rest days are needed. Days in the tent of a duvet recharge the batteries and bring some kind of strength to the mind.

The days, months and years that lie ahead are an expedition. It's a way of dealing with the situation. It's about living for both of us, telling her about my day in the quiet of the night, or down the field when I'm alone. Some friends have mentioned that in time I may meet someone else, yet I keep moving forward because I still love my wife. After landing on the moon, and getting back home, Neil Armstrong never flew into space again. His argument was that he had gone higher, faster and further than any man had ever done before. I feel I've flown with the best swan on the lake. So, I'll be like the swan Kathryn saw on that lake one day: enjoying the moments yet to come, safe in the knowledge of the love I still have.

Before Frodo accepted the ring there was the tale of *Beren and Lúthien* in the epic story by Tolkien. The mortal man Beren marries the immortal elf Lúthien; they ride forth on dangerous and epic quests. And they never leave each other, even in death. Love beats dying; I like that concept, the continuous ring of gold I wear reminds me. Reminds me that words given in truth must stay, must be stood by. For a vow is a vow, and I gave it to Kathryn. Both in church and in the hospital.

Even so, nowadays I struggle with difficult decisions, change and complex situations at times and need to be back at the yard, to be close to the field and our house with Romeo on the sofa. Breaks away are a vital part of the healing process, interludes during life's gladiatorial struggle. They are like depots on the ice, little great life-saving rest points.

I go away to the Lake District to wander the fells for a couple of days now and then. The mountains do not feel; they exist as objects the wind cannot touch; unlike the world in the field that loves and lives. The sense of loss doesn't disappear when I go away, it stays at arm's length, always there like old slippers tucked under the sofa. I visited an old expedition friend Carolyn at her home in Baldersdale, a remote part of County Durham. She was home from the Antarctic and spending time at the houses she has done up with her partner Simon. There where the wind blows fresh off the Pennine Moors, we walked to the sound of skylarks and curlews, tramped the deserted wild places and talked of life. At the end of the valley we came across a house for sale, a large rambling building with nineteen acres. The owner was outside and spoke to us of his wife's death two years ago and his need to sell up and move away. I couldn't help but think what a gorgeous place it would be to move to, to leave the pain of home and the daily struggle filling Kathryn's boots. And what a place to move to, under big skies and large vistas of sweeping land. Ollie could run free in the hay meadows and the dogs would live like kings in the open lands. Yet as we walked back to Carolyn's house on the deserted roads, I thought I heard Kathryn's voice in my head: 'We've already got land and stables.'

The actual last expedition I went on was a trip to the North-West Peninsula of Iceland with just one client, less than two years before Kathryn left. She thought it would be good for me; being in the wilderness, walking to a distant horizon, with nothing but wind and open ranges. I found her letter in my passport:

Dear Steve

I can't tell you how proud I am of you for making this trip to Iceland. I'm sure that it will be an amazing experience, a proper wilderness expedition.

I know that your knowledge and experience will provide you with the tools to deal with anything that nature throws at you.

Have a great trip and don't miss me too much, I'm not going anywhere!

Love Kathryn xxx

That was the last letter she wrote to me, on the eve of my last expedition overseas. For eight days we travelled the wild and remote landscape of the north-west of Iceland. We saw only two other people, carrying all our kit and food in very heavy rucksacks. Climbing onto the Drangajökull icecap we were the idle kings of all we saw. Western isles glimmered in setting suns and we camped in glowing daylight. The ice and fire of Iceland held me in its warmth till the flight home; she was waiting at Luton in *Top Gear* car. Standing on the roof she waved her smile across the concrete; to make sure I found her in the car park. God it was good to see her again.

I don't miss the expeditions, although sometimes they call to me. I hear the mountains whispering in the dark of the night. They still lead me away sometimes; with an old expedition colleague Adele I chased the whispers down; finally completed all the 214 fells listed by Wainwright in his guides to the Lake District.

On a long grey day with the wind chasing our heels and the rain just a dance away; Adele and I fled up the final slopes to the last fell. Adele stood off and let the final steps be mine; no stranger to big days herself having summited Everest twice, she let me imagine Kathryn was walking with me. And as the blue-grey sky lifted above the rocks, I stood side by side in heavens wind with her. It was an Everest day.

In the most part though I'm happy to just listen; to dream of what was, what is and what could be. The Elysium mountains lie quiet in their content whisper. I'm happy with that; if I need them, they are there. And I know now even in the wide-ranging spaces Kathryn is there also. Carl has planted an idea to ski to the South Pole when I'm fifty-five. He says it would give closure to all the expeditions that I have done. Lay down a ghost to rest. It's an idea, maybe a dream to aim for. I don't think Kathryn would object. After all, it would just be a boy in a tent once more; with a girl waiting at home.

In the meantime though, I focus on riding in the winds and under big skies until I can't ride anymore. Like Kathryn I too now volunteer as an Access Officer for the BHS; it seems important to keep it in the family. And Ollie and I compete in the dressage competitions held by the Blidworth riding club. Over the year we have progressed from him riding me to a steady mastery of controlling that demon that lives in my soul. I have my own little collection of rosettes now, yellows, purples and blues, pink and green ones. But no red one, no first place; that waits in the days to come. Somehow that seems important.

I ride still in Harlow Wood, but now I ride remembering the memory of what was, in the sunlight of her love. Chasing down the ghosts of the past; searching for the life of the present. All the paths are the same. The trees sway in the wind as they always did. In summer the grass still flows in the breeze and crops grow at the same time. I try to ride with Kathryn's hands, or effectiveness of leg and seat. Try to summon up that which was lost. The forest's tracks of Sherwood echo to what once happened. The dry country lanes of Lincolnshire are empty of her horse's hooves sounding out the trot that once was.

On a dry early morning, steel trotted out in the present. It was Louise's and my birthday, so we rode. On the way back Ollie showed his moods and temper. Testing me with his size and presence.

'Imagine how Kathryn rode him,' Louise said, 'and close your eyes.'

'I can't, he's too strong today,' I said, feeling rising panic.

'Close your eyes, and put your leg on, find her hands and ride like she wants you to . . .' came her calm voice. Putting your leg on when a horse wants to explode feels counter-intuitive. It's like pressing your foot down on the accelerator when the car is skidding. But it works. I put my legs on and held the weight of Ollie.

So, I rode with the past in my hands and the calves of a memory. Gradually Ollie relaxed and we made it home safely and well. Ollie thought nothing of it as he wandered into his field, into the garden of life. And I thought of all the roads and all the horses that lead home to her. Of the expedition that is never the last one.

CHAPTER TWENTY-EIGHT

Sensing the Hut

Finally the arms of their love will hold,
And hold still with no thought of ending,
So all men will know and be at peace,
Thanking the lone light that shone in the beginning.

On a cold January day in 2018 I rushed round the yard showing Anna the jobs she needed to do, as she was covering for me the next morning. Romeo was picked up by Kathryn's parents and I went home and packed for a night away in Chelmsford. I drove the red Golf to the Terra Nova offices and picked up the paperwork for the launch of an expedition to Uganda that evening. In my pockets, the wooden cross, the little knife and the piece of stone from the field. I wore Kathryn's old riding gilet, and for the first time a pair of her socks, for all of mine were in the wash. In the boot was the little bag with her framed picture that sits by the bed at home and her fleece. They too go away with me now.

I arrived at the Essex pub opposite the school in good time. I'd been cautious on the drive, as 'Careless Whisper' was on the radio as I left the house; it always makes me wary in a lost April kind of way. The pub has a small functional block of chalets out the back. On one window there was a note to the occupant instructing them not to bring guests back or the police would be called. The winds blew cold and lonely. I lay on the bed and finished off the presentation that I was delivering that night to the students of the high school. An old episode of *Top Gear* on the TV kept me company.

We sat in the teachers' staff room and drank tea whilst talking about Uganda and expeditions in general. Time played tricks as the sunset outside the school windows waved farewell to the light, change had happened but the sky knew nothing. I was introduced by the deputy head as a long-standing friend of the school, a school I had first led trips for in 2005. It was the school that catapulted BPE into what it was; our first major contract. The ghosts lay heavy and swam around the assembly hall.

Tennyson's 'Ulysses' came up on the screen, just as they had done at Bohunt. The endless time of strength and honour. The same image of Ollie and Kathryn coming out of the water ditch imprinted itself on those watching. I fiddled with Kathryn's watch as images played out of the past trips that the school had done; from Japan to Greenland and from Canada to Patagonia. All four points of the compass. My compass with its heartfelt words from Amy sat in my bag on the hall floor. Kathryn's rings were in my pocket.

I talked of global risk analysis, of risks involved in travelling overseas. In my mind the risks of fetching a horse out of a green field ran amok, cantering through the hall. I explained threat levels and the impact of shortages of blood plasma in Kampala. Of the benefits of going on an expedition, the empowerment of leadership, building sanitation at an orphanage in a dusty street and the training weekend that would be held at Cross Lane; home to twenty-two horses and three dogs. Questions were answered and application forms were handed out, it was a good night and I think I did OK. It was a past life with a new twist, a homecoming of sorts. Back to the beginning, where our expeditions started.

Nicole, the head teacher, was welcoming and caring. I felt like I belonged, not a stranger in a strange land. The horses in my mind slowed to a walk, the wind in the field grew silent.

In the pub later I needed a beer. With the launch done I was alone with my thoughts; there was still no one to call. So instead I sent a text to Kathryn's mobile, saying I missed her. After a couple of pints, I walked to the fast food shop and walked back eating tea in a bag. Dave, a teacher that used to work at the school, joined me for last orders. His daughter was in hospital, yet was on the mend after a serious scare. Somewhere over the rainbow Kathryn listened. I slept well with her fleece and the photo watching me.

It was a nice change not to have to feed the horses in the morning; yet I couldn't wait to get back. I pointed the Golf north and we headed for home. Hannah called and asked how it had gone; one life from the past embedded in the present. Anna called to say the yard was fine; another life from the present, embedded in the past. Both merging into one as the road welcomed me home with each turn of the wheels. The closer I got to the yard, the better I felt. Her parents were sat at the kitchen table having lunch. Her dad turned down the TV and we chatted briefly. With my dad gone he is now my father figure on the return journey. Declining a drink, I wanted to go home to the place that calls to me all the time, the yard. I was expecting no one to be there, it was a weekday afternoon. The first day of February, yet cars were parked outside the low white stable block. The wind blew from the north, cold and hard into my face. Hands stuffed into the pockets of my new coat, I felt hugged by a warm glow. This was our land and our home, the stones and sand held her feet as they now did mine. Life was coming full circle; I know how the ship runs now, can feel the deck beneath my feet. I know how she handles in heavy seas and big storms. Know the little things that make her what she is.

I stood by the dog kennel and looked out across Kathryn's yard, our yard. The wind was coming in hard now, north with a cold that owned it. People were busy with their horses. It was a homecoming, the first time I felt like I belonged, that I wasn't just a ghost; vying for acceptance of Kathryn's presence. The first time I could see the hut in the distance, sense its presence. And that Kathryn was happy too.

Romeo and I left the yard and its occupants for the family field. Oliver was his usual self, trying to get into the feed room as I prepared tea. Strip shouted when his was ready and waited in his stable. Time for hay and to pick the poo up on the yard, then Romeo was let out of the Land Rover. We walked to the patch of ground that lays home to Kathryn.

There as the wind came in softly, I knelt down and stroked the stone that has her name carved into it with a kiss at the end. For the first time since she left, I felt a glimpse of happiness, a shy contentment maybe. She was with me, I could feel her. We stood there, Romeo and me, and looked out over the horizon. To the line that stretches back, footsteps and hoofprints that extend all the way back to the time we first met; to the prints in the ground that tell the story of our lives, be they human or horse, and be they on English soil or frozen land at the end of the earth.

One day someone will carve my name next to Kathryn's on the little bit of stone that bears her name. They will scatter my ashes with hers, lay me down to her and home. She has priority, that's her honour. I like to think I will have deserved a place below hers. Two names carved in stone with a kiss between them.

Yet before I get there life lives on. I know my place in the story now; it's to carry on what she left and gave me. Her love and smile. For I am still Kathryn's husband; and the colours that fell with Kathryn in the field, I now carry them for her.

As Tennyson so famously said, we are strong in will to strive, to seek, to find, and not to yield. We all have heroic hearts but time and fate wears us down. And our will is not as it always was. But we will find home.

The return journey is that, for despite all the hardships we face, all the setbacks and heartache we must move forward. Keep walking and riding, to the undiscovered country. The last expedition. And for me the return journey is not about getting back to Kathryn as fast as I can although I thought it was in the early days – I really did. But it's actually about a return to life. And the expedition that is Cross Lane and Ollie. A life worth living, holding her smile in mine, seeing with eyes she can longer see with. Touching with hands she can't touch with. For that is life after death, those of us that live on carry the torch of the departed.

It's a whisper and you have to listen hard, but it's here on earth. It's the love we have all felt at some point, and still can if we open our hearts. It's the sun on grass and a wind that never dies. For all its haunting loss, most of all life is about the beauty of a smile, a smile that never fades.

The next morning the sky was blue, it was cold and still a little windy. I overslept for the first time since the day she died. I did my jobs and then shopped, for dog food and treats. The outdoor school was dry from the wind and no rain. So, I put Ollie's hay net up on the yard, grabbed a handful of treats and went to fetch him. He walked up slowly and then settled in to eat his hay. I groomed as usual, a quick pick out of his feet and scrubbed off the major mud marks and dust. As I tacked him up Carl called from Norway. We talked about people crossing Antarctica on their own, without support and assistance. About impossible goals at the end and edge of human endurance. Chatted distances needed to cross a continent in a set number of days. Expeditions that haven't been attempted yet or maybe never will. With my head bent over to cradle the phone I finished tacking Ollie up, walked him through the gate. We said goodbye to each other as I settled down in the saddle.

For half an hour in the deserted school, under a clear blue sky Ollie and I rode. We didn't do a lot; I wanted him engaged, walking with a purpose, trotting forward and cantering with enjoyment. Turning, halting and half-halting we moved in our dance round the sand school; standing by each other. Her old gloves held my hand as I squeezed and felt down the reins, searching for that connection between rider and horse, the connection that Kathryn had with him. And he gave it, in glimpses, in fleeting touches. For the first time Ollie and I connected and he felt like my horse, that a gift had been given from her to me. That in him she had given me a reason to smile and live and carry on. To return to the living. After cooling him off we stood there for a while. Just standing in the sand with no noise in the air. I pushed my heels down and relaxed in the saddle. He relaxed his neck and I patted him with her battered glove. After unsaddling him, he went to drop his head on my shoulder as he always did with Kathryn. Usually I don't let him, but that day I did. Ollie misses her too.

CHAPTER TWENTY-NINE

Elysium

And as the gull cries aloft the stripping rig
Voices sing hoarsely in triumph
For the voyage is seen to the end becoming
The streaming flag of the king is folded now
Its role fulfilled . . .

With no warning a great storm blew in. The hut was in sight, smoke curled dreamily out of the chimney from the fire she had lit; unaware of the thundering hoof wind. The return journey was in touching distance. So sudden in its force was the storm, I was buffeted to the core. All year we had inched forward in the dressage competitions, a fourth place then a third. And one late evening a second place; I rode Ollie well and knew it. Going into the last competition I practised hard, I wanted that red rosette; it was the hut. It was a taking back of the control that was ripped out of my life. I'd just finished reading a book about a fictional pilot who'd lost his daughter, who lost control, fought to get it back. Chased the outer envelope of life and death, I related to it and recognised I'd not truly faced my own darkest fear. For all the months on the yard I'd been in denial; I had pushed away the accident; thought I was brave to take on the yard; that I'd done the right thing. Patted myself on the back for standing by my wife. But the demons of the head collar chased me down and I became terrified of horses, leading them, handling them, riding them. Riding Ollie.

Louise came down for a final practice ahead of the competition. On a slow end of summer wind, as the distant sound of an ice cream van sung on the breeze, Ollie and I finally faced the loss. The little victories we had scored on the way so far were just false summits; teasers of happiness. Now was the time. He was strong and I was not, I made a mistake and we headed to the gate; out of control. I saw Kathryn being dragged, grass blown aside and the horses screaming. I was Kathryn and the head collar. Her death finally died in me. I knew the dead gallop up the field. Saw the field from above and saw Kathryn lying still, no dirt under her nails. Saw Ollie watching. The dirt was under my nails, not hers; the rope was round my neck.

For I had failed; I hadn't saved her. When she needed me most I wasn't there for her, as she had always been for me. At the ending of all things I was not by Kathryn, standing toe to toe, hand in hand. I gave no warning, or shove of heaven sent guidance as the storm came in. Instead I was home, safe and well. I should have been in the field with her, doing what a husband does; protecting his wife, or at the very least, riding the grey with her into the face of the storm.

As Ollie shifted his weight beneath me I saw everything for the first time. Felt her going again; for real, without me there. Felt my guilt bleed openly across the sky and into the field. The valley of Thor opened up in front of me and the dazed light of Ragnarök shone into me, a white pennant with her name on blew in the wind of my mind.

'I can't do it anymore . . .' It was a primeval scream.

People on the yard heard. Ollie breathed his grey weight into me and all the days since the April of her going rose up out of the sand.

'Yes, you can,' replied Louise, quietly. 'You didn't sign up for a one trick event, you made a promise and you both agreed Ollie would be yours one day.'

I looked at her, through her. She continued; 'It's your time now, remember the promise. Remember and ride, ride for you now.'

Deep down from somewhere I hadn't seen, a remembrance drifted in. A power that came from life.

'Just ride,' came Kathryn's voice; silent and smiling; cutting through the welling inside me. 'Ride for me; ride for us.' So, we walked, then trotted and suddenly Ollie was working in an outline. Listening to me, and me alone. He was my horse now, he was the atonement to the fallen girl and the boy who wasn't there with his shield and sword. And he was Kathryn, saving me once more. The control and connection came, then the tears. An outpouring that had been dammed up for two and a half years. Around the moon and through the stars we rode in the school. Through the power of a grey horse Kathryn charged the guilt in my soul away with her smile. The wind that took her in the field whispered in my soul and left a loving embrace. Back home I felt purged, I'd never truly faced it. The yard had hidden the truth, Kathryn was gone. I thought I'd done well but in reality, I'd only fought running skirmishes. The war itself I'd ignored. The war in my mind of a grey horse watching my wife die; and my inability to stop the tragedy.

So just within reach of getting there, we fought the last battle. The war to be my own person again, of being happy without fear. Of not missing her without the gulf of loss. Of facing the field and all that it was, is now and what it represents. Of the unification of our love and the worlds we lived. And ultimately the acceptance of not being able to save her as the hero is supposed to; and that each day from here on in is a penance of my failings. A penance of love and forgiveness.

As a grey horse looked on, with her shield around me and her sword in my hand, I strode into the hut and knew for the first time that Kathryn's love is ongoing. All life is never-ending; death is just a doorway that we all pass through. But it doesn't stay shut; our love keeps the door ajar.

The next evening Ollie and I entered the last dressage competition of the season. In the dusty arena we met the storm head on, rode into Elysium. A peace descended into my heart and the sand under Ollie's hooves stood on restful ghosts. I saw all the truths of our lives laid bare, and I wasn't scared anymore. Banished too was the guilt of an April wind; in its place only everlasting love.

Ollie and I rode as a pair, a partnership for the first time. And for a few brief eternal moments Kathryn and I danced once more; we danced together on a grey horse and smiled. I left before the results, the emotion, physical effort and drama had exhausted me. I was sat in the pub when the phone rang. 'You won!' exclaimed Louise. She talked on, but I was lost in the relief. I hadn't walked to the south pole and back, nor climbed the pinnacles of Everest's North East Ridge, but I felt like I had. And for the first time since Kathryn left, I felt happy without feeling guilty. I finally felt I'd broken the cycle of staying in the strange comfort of cuddling grief. Banished the duvet of death to the pillow of love. And the light shone through the slightly open door and smiled. A beam of heaven's light from Kathryn onto my little red Rosset. We all have our Ollies, the challenge that can consume us. If we let it. We all chase away the mortality that haunts us, instead of embracing the life we have. We all have a Kathryn, someone we call home, someone we love beyond life and death.

One day, but not yet I hope someone is there to tell me when I can go home. They will quietly say, as my mum did to my dad, that I lived a life worth living and a life after the storm. That I returned with my head held high and I didn't give in. Did Kathryn proud. That I smiled once more, and maybe; just maybe

I did it right. I will walk into the field through the door now fully open and stand next to her; for she will be waiting. Won't be lying down. I'll tell her of a tale that she will laugh so loud at, the horses will tremble. A tale of hardihood, endurance and never giving in. They will run and gallop, the earth will shake. I won't be wishing for five seconds to say goodbye anymore. For she and I will have eternity to say hello. And I hope that meeting is a way off yet, for the stories will build and become larger than the gulf of missing.

After the final test I'd led Ollie back down the lane, escaping the busy yard behind us. He snorted and jogged a little. He didn't attempt to show off to Soul as he passed him in his field, just walked by my side. Through the gate and past Kathryn's name we walked along the grass strip to the field. I turned him back to me as I went through the entrance, gave him a treat and patted him. After a quick drink from the trough he turned and looked at me. Then Ollie walked down into the field and a lone swan flew over the trees and I stood by the hut, at the end of my return journey. I could touch its wooden frame, I could be happy without shame or fear. Away in the hidden trees the monsters under the bed watched in shame, for they are still there – they always will be – for that is the nature of loss. They all have names; Grief, Trauma, Guilt, Longing and Nameless. But the weapons to fight them back are to hand now. Yes; sometimes they win a day's blood. When they gang up they are hard to beat. But they can't beat true love. And woe betide them if they cross Kathryn, for she's still my angel.

As the swan drifted away on the compass sky I felt content, sensing that Kathryn was watching and helping in the way only she can. She has given me the greatest gift; the horses, the dogs and the fields. The place where the wind blows hard in winter and in summer the grass grows long and deep.

'Good luck with your watch,' she had sat up and patted the duvet. Then she walked out of our bedroom and I never saw her alive again.

The watch measures time perpetually, measuring off the years for far longer than I will ever live. Its mechanical heart beats in memory to Kathryn's heart. The white grey cross on its side ticks to home. It is Kathryn's watch now, and along with her wedding ring, engagement ring and eternity ring, these are the most treasured and priceless things in the world to me. I wind it up thirty-nine times each night, a wind for each year of her life; and one more for the field of dreams.

T. S. Eliot wrote:

We shall not cease from exploration. And the end of all our exploring will be to arrive where we started and know the place for the first time.

To arrive at the beginning after all our exploring is to come home. I see the field for what it is now, a place where an ending and a beginning happened; the horses run free and there is nothing but love. And the peace lies content over the ground, comforting those who walk its soil.

Kathryn had never seen the play *War Horse*; it was with some trepidation therefore that I left the field for another theatre of dreams. To watch the puppet horses, act out their life without her by my side. Yet, as the guns exploded onstage and the lights shone down, my sense that I wasn't alone was profound and comforting. I watched as the horses danced on the stage, as they became one with my past and Kathryn's, the fiction merged with life; as Ollie and Strip leaped from the stage. Kathryn is in me and all around me, in the fields and the clouds. Watching the play, for the first time I realised that my return journey and the path I now follow is not about the ending. It's about the beginning. My journey and everyone's journeys are just as much about the ride of life itself, in all its glory, not just the ending. That's what keeps us moving forward; for me it happens to be a large rose-eating grey horse and a field that shines in the wind. For despite whatever happens, the darkest hours do pass. Life is glorious and it moves on. We all have a flag of love we hold true to, we are all trying to find our home. The journey is the return in itself.

War Horse ended and the theatrical horses were laid to bed, their play finished for the day. Out of a long darkness I drove her silver Defender home into the light. I'd been gone for only a few hours. The dogs acted like it was for ever. Maybe it was. I shoved my brown gloved hands into my pockets and opened the school gate. Crossing the arena, I took one hand out, reached for hers. And with my hand in hers I went down to the field to feed Ollie. Thinking of a meeting one day with a girl in a white blouse and a smile, but not yet. For the horses don't haunt me anymore; they make me smile. Especially Ollie.

For he's the promise to the ongoing field; it was just a moment ago she had said that one day I would ride Ollie. So now I do, I try to ride her big grey the best I can. I ride for both of us. That's my truth. I carry the colours that fell once upon a time in a field of dreams; they stream in the pure blue light of everyday. For they are Kathryn's colours.

It was a summer evening all those years ago when we walked up Nottingham Road away from The Plough. Turned left onto Windsor Road and walked the length of it till it reached Berry Hill Road and Littleworth. She wore a pair of jeans and a white blouse. I can't remember what I was wearing. Her lipstick stood out subtly, as she never wore make-up most of the time. It was the first date we had, maybe the second. At the junction of the two roads; one leading up to my house, one leading down to hers on Prospect Street, we stood. She asked me if I wanted to come for a coffee. She didn't drink coffee; but I didn't know that at the time. I declined the coffee and said I needed to go home. She didn't seem to mind. I said we would do coffee next time, I think. Then she walked down the hill to her house and I walked uphill to mine.

I've come to realise that grief and the journey of coming to terms with it, is just like that junction all those moments ago. A decision, to accept the light and turn towards it; or refuse the love and head into darkness alone. I choose the light now, I walk readily into it. For when we meet again at that junction and she asks if I want to go to hers for coffee, I'll say yes. I'll walk down the hill with Kathryn; to her house. And there we will stay. In the field of Elysium dreams where a grey horse looks on.

EPILOGUE

Maximus Goes Home

Thunder-strength of Pegasus grey on the horizon,
Armour gleaming, hands through corn in loving winds,
The bugle triumph; everything is just a calendar moment ago
We are one, let's lay to bed, sound the recall,
And take this ride home, colours flying.

I got up early as Kathryn's parents were on holiday and I was doing the family field, feeding and sorting out Oliver, Strip and the other horses. There was a dusting of snow on the ground as I drove along the lane at 7.30 in the morning.

I stepped down from the Defender into a cold eastern crosswind. The air had that Antarctic polar smell, the waft that hits you when you step off the Ilyushin onto the blue ice runway in Antarctica. But this was Blidworth and it was home.

It was to be a quick feed and put out the hay, check waters and sort out any rugs. Oliver always tries to get in the feed room and help himself as I prepare the feeds so I led him to his stable.

In the back of Oliver's stable Strip was lying down, rolling a little and trying to paw the floor. He didn't look great, so I got him up and out of the stable. Covered in muck I led him to his stable, yet he got down again and rolled some more; displaying classic symptoms of colic. As I gave the other three their breakfast,

I called the vets and got through to the on-call vet. She promised to be with me as soon as she could. I already knew what was going to unfold in the next hour and felt sick inside.

I knew that at some point, sooner rather than later Strip would go. Yet he was happy, eating and drinking and warm. I knew he would tell me when the time was right. And in that snowy field in February he did. But Christ it was hard, it brought back the loss of Kathryn in full colour. Strip was her horse, the horse she'd had for over twenty years, her greatest love. He was the last link to the days when we met and rode and first loved. It was always Kathryn's hope that she would find him one morning, peacefully passed in the night. But here he was, and so was I; as Kathryn watched.

I held Strip's head collar and got him back up, leading him out onto the yard and then the snow-covered grass. He would only go a few yards before getting down again; we repeated this process several times. All the time I kept glancing over my shoulder to where Kathryn's stone was, asking her for help and advice. Yet, in my heart of hearts I knew this was Strip's time. As he lay there, I stroked his head and tried to comfort him.

I made two phone calls, to the past and the present: to Zoë, of Bloomsgorse, she was unavailable, and to Louise, who was on the school run. I kept looking across at the stone with her name on though; gained comfort from it. I knew what I had to do. I felt both Strip and Kathryn were telling me. I realised I didn't need to make any more calls; my wife was with me.

My hands got colder and colder, so I made a quick dash to the Defender and grabbed the nearest gloves I could find. They were old brown woollen ones of Kathryn's, with holes in the ends. As Strip lay there, I stroked him with Kathryn's hands and he seemed to relax; he felt the old familiar touch of her hand. Felt her love. Knew he was OK and this was all going to be all right.

The vet arrived and was lovely; young yet cool and competent. She checked Strip's gums and tried to check his heart rate.

'He's thirty-two and an ex-racehorse,' I said. 'My wife's horse.'

'Is she at work today?'

'No, she's over there,' I said, and pointed to Kathryn's stone.

'Oh,' she said, and looked a bit shocked.

Strip closed his eyes a couple of times and sighed, yet seemed to keep fighting. But he couldn't ignore the call from her, from across the great divide. The vet and I agreed we would help him find her. His time was now. The drugs to send him to sleep had been in her cold car overnight, so it took an age to draw them down into the syringe.

'I'm sorry,' she said.

'It's OK. Death doesn't need rushing.'

Strip was on the ground, for the last time I thought. Let this be easy, let it be good, I willed. Yet he stood up one last time and suddenly dragged me to the little enclosure that houses Kathryn's stone, Jack's stone and Bruce's stone. He was racing again; I couldn't hold him, the lead rope burned in my hand. And then he stopped. He stood by Kathryn's stone; just stood there. Looking out for something, his ears were twitching and his eyes were alert. He heard the sound of a feed bucket being rattled in a far-off place; he pawed the ground once and sniffed the grass. He looked fit, willing and ready to race once more. The hairs on my arms stood out despite the cold. Then he turned and walked a few steps and stood for the very last time. A lone robin watched from the fence. I held back the tears; the moment was so intense in its purity. From across the sky she called him, a cry from the field of dreams; a whistle and shake of a feed bucket. He was Maximus in *Gladiator*, and Kathryn was calling him home.

There is a photograph taken by me just outside the gate of Cross Lane, on the lane. Otto is far right, then Jack next to him. Kathryn is holding them both on the leads, and in her right hand she has Strip Cartoon. Now they are all together.

After I buried Strip, I found a stone and chiselled away; wrote his name. It now lies next to Kathryn's with a red rose separating them. I'll plant a mountain ash tree in the summer, just like the one that grows next to Kathryn and Jack. I think that's what she would like. As the late afternoon sky scrolled in, I sat on Kathryn's bench drinking some tea and eating a bit of cake; looked at her brown woollen gloves. She had blue, black and brown ones, always drying on the radiator in winter. For the first time I felt like I could wear them now. Felt proud as I watched the clouds moving forward to the west winds. Just like the clouds, the time rolls on.

So, Maximus went home. He went home to his mum, cantering down the fields of wheat into loving hands. The gate had opened in a sweep of old wood, the lane beckoned and he ran faster than he had ever raced in his life. He ran for love and for home, he ran for Kathryn. All of life smiled and cried in the same instant. Robins danced in the air of all light and they swooped over the house and over the field. I know because I saw them, and so did Kathryn.

Snow flutters against the canvas of my shelter,
The barrier lies off to the horizon on a northern bearing,
All horses and the dogs too are spent, save two, they stay with me,
The big grey is by my side and the black hound curls by me,
I read her note and snuggle into the down of my bag,
Providence has guided me and steers me to the light,
I can sense the presence ahead of me, by me and holding me,
She's waiting at the hut for she knows I'm coming.

PART THREE

Appendix

'I do not regret this journey, which has shown that Englishmen can endure hardships, help one another, and meet death with as great a fortitude as ever in the past.'

Captain Robert Falcon Scott
11 miles from the depot.

March 1912

'The armies of heaven were following him,
Riding on white horses.'

Revelation 19.14

*I really hope that you'll enjoy yourself, although
I'm sure it'll be hard graft, and that you come home
strong and well (and that you miss me!)
That'll do for now, looking forward to seeing you.*

KATHRYN BULL

THE MAP OF GRIEF

Latitude and longitude have merged,
One authentic map left, one contour to a summit home,
My star whispers in solitude, reaches for the hand,
I take bearings on faith.

Understanding and dealing with deep sudden loss is traumatic, complex and bewildering. There are no quick fixes, no easy roads to home. For me, I have held true to a deep-seated belief in a romantic quest, a last expedition. A mythical heroic quest in my mind. The return journey from a distant coast line to a point at the end of the earth, then back again. With Kathryn by my side, this has been my key to dealing with death at its worst. But that's my way; it's not everyone's way though. Each person has to find their own path. For each person's grief is different, everyone's circumstances are unique. The only unifying factor is that death comes to us all, one way or another.

I believe in some way Kathryn left me a map, a map that if I sought hard enough, with all my soul I could find a way back. A way back from grief to a smile in the sunshine once more. And this map she left me is accessible by everyone; if you have the strength of heart and honour of love to believe in.

The key to the map is to accept in the first instance there is such a thing, for if we don't acknowledge that there is no way out. When we are lost, we all need a map to get back home. A compass that guides us in the darkness.

I also think everything in my life, every event and everything I have done and experienced have all prepared me to face down grief. To do this for her. All the tragedy and all the hardships faced have given me the strength to move forward. And Kathryn herself prepared me for this, in fact she is the single reason I can do this. She gave me the power to act and save myself, and therein is the love. But it takes self-belief to acknowledge this and know it for what it is; help. Just because the one you love is physically not here with you, doesn't mean they can't still help you.

At risk of sounding trite, here are the key facts I've learned on my last expedition. Maybe they will help one single person; and if so then these words have been worth writing.

First, all expeditions need planning. Kathryn and I never talked about one of us dying. Who does? Couples plan weddings with great enthusiasm and excitement, births also. But the other great milestone in our lives, the funeral, is left unsaid. So, talk about it, for the one left behind it's the simple but big things you don't know. Cremation or burial? Where do they want their ashes scattered? Details that will help you in the first part of the journey.

In order to help keep you sane it's also good to write down somewhere safe all the passwords and account information for all the basic utility accounts. If like us only one dealt with the bank, the water, gas and electric companies; it's a nightmare to the one left. Plan ahead, for death will come to one of you in the family at some point.

When the worst happens, there are no rights or wrongs in dealing with loss. All rules go out the window. Break them, make your own.

The start of the journey is the easy part, that's not easy to accept. But it's best to understand that at the beginning. Take each minute at a time if you have to. Don't think too far ahead or the size of the task will destroy you. Like a long polar journey, walk each day. Camp. Then repeat each day until you get home. And if you have to split the day into sections; then do that.

In the early days everyone will support you, love you and be your friend. This will pass, so you need to steel your heart for the long haul. Accept every offer of help, but don't rely on it. Some will walk with you all the way, but many won't. The ones that are true, hold on to them.

Take time to grieve, I didn't do this. And it set me back on the journey, so just sit and cry, cry and cry and cry. It helps.

The passage through grief can't be taught, we can only play the game how we see fit. So, don't force the issue. What works for someone else might not work for you. There are many 'models' of grief; but death doesn't follow a formula.

People will tell you to keep busy. It actually doesn't make a difference; do what's right for you. If you need to sleep for a day, do it. Even nearly three years in I still need to lie and rest all day, or sometimes just a couple of hours under the duvet.

Accept the fact that the loss will never go away, and that it's all about finding a peace within.

Grief will highlight your best character traits and your worst; prepare your friends for this.

Your life has changed beyond all recognition, the person you were before you won't be again, that takes some getting used to. Take time to get used to a new you.

Anger and rage will be in danger of consuming you, so find an outlet to dispel them. A friend to talk to, go for a walk; anything that takes your mind off the hell within.

Do something that makes you feel scared, for me that was Ollie. He made me realise I wanted to live. You need something that is bigger than death.

Go to counselling but find the right person for you. Someone who can listen to the dark stuff and help you find yourself again.

Read poems, I found the writing of some poets a great help. I didn't read books on grief because they scared me; so, I found my own path and took inspiration from dusty poetry books.

I also found watching films about people going through traumatic experiences helped me. I could identify with the grief and it didn't make me feel so alone.

In terms of films, watch *Rocky Balboa*, *Stand by Me*, *Gladiator* and *Top Gun*; in that order.

Getting out of the grief is the hardest part; the warmth of the grief starts to take hold. You need to find a way to be happy again.

Understand that anniversaries are tough, and that like going to the dentist to have a tooth out, the second time is worse. For you know what it's like.

There are well-documented articles on the cycles of grief, I never read them. What I did read was a book called *The Last Pilot* by Benjamin Johncock. The closest writing anyone has ever got to loss.

Understand that you are in a fight for your life, and that you must do anything; anything it takes to survive. You owe that to the person you have lost.

Remember the love. Let the person who has gone still love you. Hold on to that love and never let go. Ever. Because they've still got you.

AUTHOR'S ROUGH NOTES

The decision to publish *The Return Journey* has been an exceptionally difficult and heartfelt one. I've tried to think what Kathryn would want me to do. So, I went back to the beginning, asked her parents for permission, just like I asked them for their daughter's hand in marriage. They willingly gave it. The first draft was given to them, complete in all its flaws.

There have been several times when I have thought the story would be best left to the wind in the mountains. Or left to lie in an unopened drawer. Yet Kathryn touched so many lives, in the expedition world and the equestrian world, and I don't want her time here to go unnoticed or forgotten. For as Chris Bonington wrote about the North East Ridge expedition; 'If you don't write it down, a great expedition vanishes; the wonderful times we had together.'

This memoir is also about the essence of our lives; we don't have to go to the ends of the earth or climb Everest to be on an expedition. Each and every day we all live is an exploration. And all expeditions need a map; if the paths aren't clear then it's possible to follow your own. Take a bearing and trust to honour, valour and strength. But above all love.

Whilst writing it several people have asked if the process has been cathartic. In a way it has, it's taken over two years to write, the first chapters in the first weeks. Then I had to stop; it was too painful. But the pen drew me back; to tell what needs to be told. The process of writing has without doubt saved my life; I have written for the right to live, for the right to stay in the present, and for some kind of future. The hardest part has been stopping writing, for creating this memoir has been like living the life Kathryn and I had together all over again. And I don't want that to end. But all things end, even loss. As my mum once said; 'It's not always dark at six o'clock.'

I hope Kathryn would be proud for maybe the tale of our lives will help someone coming to terms with great loss; they may find solace that in the end there is light and daffodils will come again in March. Kathryn will then have helped people in her passing as much as she did in her life.

To quote Scott lying in his tent; 'It seems a pity; but I don't think I can write anymore.' Not because I'm lying frozen at the edge of the world; but because new life is slowly warming my body, warming my limbs with her love and the smile of life. Kathryn's life, a life that I will always be in love with. Our life.

The expedition members of Scott's last expedition, after they had found and read his diaries, erected a cross on Observatory Hill. Looking out over the route of the return journey, to the pole and back, an expedition that lasted just over two years. It now stands with words written by Tennyson on it. The closing lines of 'Ulysses'.

To strive, to seek, to find, and not to yield.

With words written on it by Rossetti, taken from Kathryn's diary, a cross now also stands in the field. On a hot dusty afternoon in June the simple wooden cross was set in the grass, looking out over our return journey. Mel, who had just been riding Soul, asked to say a prayer. So, with just the trees looking on, Mel spoke. 'Remember me when day by day . . .' The two of us stood there in quiet silence for a minute. I think Kathryn watched us with a smile. It felt like an ending, but not in a sad way; it was also a beginning. It had taken over two years of exploring to get to this point, to know that the grass will grow again, that we can smile once more, and move forward with her Kathryn's blessing.

Finally, as the last edits were completed on this book I took Zac, Bruno and Romeo down into the field to say hello to their mum. To get a blessing at the cross; from Kathryn. As the sun faded over the field Romeo ran down to the cross; he stopped. Then raised one paw as a pointer does; sniffed the air and wagged his tail. Then he ran in joy across the field; as if Kathryn had never left.

They say everyone has a book in them, if that is so then this is Kathryn's and mine. For we are a pair and these words tell our tale, for better or worse.

ACKNOWLEDGEMENTS

As on any expedition there are numerous people who have helped to make it happen. The people that reach the pole or summit are just the tip of the iceberg. The return to a smile, to the realisation that because one life finished too early doesn't mean another should end is down to many souls. It is difficult to mention everyone, all the people involved in the journey have given so much.

I am not an easy person to know; Kathryn knew that better than anyone. I am in debt without measure therefore to the following people who have stayed with me throughout the journey. They have given without question and accepted me for who I am and not who I cannot replace. All of them have understood the flowing tide of grief and have learned to sail the waves with me. If I have failed to name someone out there in the mist, my sincerest apologies.

Steve Stout, Michelle Green, Hannah Vasey, Adele Pennington, Carolyn Bailey, Jo Smith, Su Gripton, Phil Avery, David Turrel, Carl Alvey, Helena Malenczuk, Craig Offless, Peter and Anne Fuchs, Deanne Gardner, Sam Betts, Fiona Weston, Amy Trammer, Anna Wheldon, Harold Smith, Charlotte Smith, Fergus Hunter Spokes, Julian Brown, Richard Barrow, David Tait, Ted Grey, Andy Utting, Calum Grant, Ann Leyland, Andrew and Verity Smith, Emma and Stuart Anderson, Christine Dove, Andrew Dove, Richard and Jack Bull.

Acknowledgements

Sarah Oldershaw and Kim Carmichael.

Mel Alvey and Lucy Taylor for being constant.

Alison Smith for being there.

Louise Barras for the grey horses.

Michael Asher for helping with Kathryn's field.

Jane Turnbull.

Sadie Mayne, Clare Christian, Heather Boisseau for making the book a reality. And all those at RedDoor.

Sir Ranulph Fiennes for agreeing to write the foreword.

Benjamin Johncock for his faith and belief.

Those from what was Bloomsgorse Trekking Centre, especially Zoë Grant and Jayne Martin.

To all those that supported Bull Precision Expeditions Ltd.

The staff at Berry's Jewellers, Nottingham.

To those that continually support and help Cross Lane Equestrian; Kathryn's Yard. I am forever grateful.

Everyone that helps and supports Blidworth and District Riding Club.

All those that help and believe in The Kathryn Bull Memorial Trust.

Harlton's Fields of Dreams and Romeo Causeway.

My mum who has been who she is; my mum. Who has never given up on her sometimes wayward son.

Ian and Sheila Dove for giving me the greatest gift; their daughter Kathryn, my wife.

'From the ends of the earth I call to you,
I call as my heart grows faint,
Lead me to the rock
That is higher than I.'

Psalm 61:2

Just snippets, I miss you at odd times. I think of things I'll tell you when I see you

KATHRYN BULL

SELECT BIBLIOGRAPHY

Fragile Edge, Maria Coffey – Arrow Books 2003

Everest: The Unclimbed Ridge, Chris Bonington and Charles Clarke – Hodder and Stoughton 1983

Captain Scott, Sir Ranulph Fiennes – Hodder and Stoughton 2004

The Hunt in the Forest, John Burnside – Jonathan Cape 2009

The Last Expedition, A Year in Poems, Steve Bull – Amazon 2017

The Light Beyond the Forest, Rosemary Sutcliffe – Knight Books 1986

Horse, J. Edward Chamberlin – Signal Books 2006

In the Footsteps of Scott, Roger Mear and Robert Swan – Grafton Books 1989

Captain Oates – Soldier and Explorer, Sue Limb and Patrick Cordingley – Pen and Sword Military 2009

The Last Letters – The Polar Museum 2012

The Company of Swans, Jim Crumley – The Harvill Press 1997

Soul Food, edited by Neil Astley and Pamela Robertson-Pearce – Bloodaxe Books 2007

An Afterclap of Fate: Mallory on Everest, Charles Lind – The Ernest Press 2006

South, Sir Ernest Shackleton – Century 1989

The Faith of Edward Wilson of the Antarctic, George Seaver – John Murray 1948

Four Quartets, T. S. Eliot – Faber and Faber 2001

The Waste Land and other Poems, T. S. Eliot – Faber and Faber 2002

The English Parnassus, An Anthology of Longer Poems, collected authors – Oxford University Press 1961

Black Beauty, Anna Sewell – Hamlyn Classics 1954

To The Ends of the Earth, Sir Ranulph Fiennes – Simon and Schuster 2014

Gone Hunting, Mary Staib – Ragged Bears Publishing 2005

Good News New Testament – Collins 1976

Beren and Lúthien, J R Tolkien – HarperCollins 2017

Scott's Last Expedition, Captain R. F. Scott – The Folio Society 1964

'Like English Gentlemen' to Peter Scott, J. M. Barrie – Hodder and Stoughton 1913

LIST OF PHOTOGRAPHS

Dedication page Kathryn – Strength and Honour (Steve Bull)

I heard my country calling page – Kathryn on honeymoon (Steve Bull)

Page 5 – Harlton's Field of Dreams (Steve Bull)

Part 1 page – Ollie in the field (Steve Bull)

Page 136 – The Polar Plateau, Antarctica (Steve Bull)

Part 2 page – Kathryn on Ollie (Steve Bull)

Page 270 – The last ride (Steve Bull)

Page 274 – Kathryn and Strip Cartoon (Kathryn Bull)

Part 3 page – Steve on Ollie (Anna Leivers)

Page 282 – Kathryn and Steve (Carl Alvey)

Page 285 – Cross Lane (Steve Bull)

Page 287 – Kathryn and Jack (Steve Bull)

Page 288 – Kathryn and Great Gable (Steve Bull)

Author image – taken by Carl Alvey

ABOUT THE AUTHOR

Steve Bull is the husband of Kathryn Bull. Together with Kathryn, he founded an expedition company: BPE. He now looks after Kathryn's yard, Cross Lane Equestrian. And does his best to care for Kathryn's horse, Ollie the big grey, along with the dogs, Bruno, Zak and Romeo, the greyhound. Upholding a promise. When not doing these things, he likes to wander the fells.

Find out more about RedDoor
Press and sign up to our
newsletter to hear about our
latest releases, author events,
exciting **competitions**
and more at

reddoorpress.co.uk

YOU CAN ALSO FOLLOW US:

 @RedDoorBooks

 Facebook.com/RedDoorPress

 @RedDoorBooks